Ian Chaston

Knowledge-based Marketing
The Twenty-First Century Competitive Edge

SAGE Publications

London • Thousand Oaks • New Delhi

First published 2004

SAGE Publications Ltd
1 Oliver's Yard
55 City Road
London EC1Y 1SP

SAGE Publications Inc.
2455 Teller Road
Thousand Oaks, California 91320

SAGE Publications India Pvt Ltd
B-42, Panchsheel Enclave
Post Box 4109
New Delhi 110 017

British Library Cataloguing in Publication data

A catalogue record for this book is available from the British Library

ISBN 0 4129 0002 6
ISBN 0 4129 0003 4 (pbk)

Library of Congress Control Number available

Typeset by C&M Digitals (P) Ltd., Chennai, India
Printed in Great Britain by The Cromwell Press Ltd, Trowbridge

Contents

List of Figures and Tables

Figures

Tables

List of Abbreviations

4Ps	product, price, promotion and place
AI	artificial intelligence
API	applications programme interface
BCG	Boston Consulting Group
B2B	business-to-business
CAD	computer-aided design
CAM	computer-aided manufacturing
CGI	common gateway interface
CRM	customer relationship management
DOS	dual-objective segmentation
EDI	electronic data interchange
EOQ	economic order quantity
ERP	enterprise resource planning
fmcg	fast moving consumer goods
FTP	file transfer protocol
GNP	gross national product
HRM	human resource management
HTML	hypertext markup language
HTTP	hypertext transfer protocol
IP	internet protocol
ISP	internet service provider
IT	information technology
JIT	just in time
LAN	local area network
MBO	management by objectives
ODBC	open database connectivity
OECD	Organisation for Economic Co-operation and Development
OEM	original equipment manufacturers
OLAP	on-line analytical processing
PC	personal computer
PDC	parts distribution centre

PLC	product life cycle
R & D	research and development
ROI	return on investment
SDMI	Secure Digital Music Initiative
SME	small and medium size enterprise
SPSS	statistical programming for social sciences
SQL	structured query language
SWOT	strengths, weaknesses, opportunities, threats
TCP	transmission control protocol
TQM	total quality management
URL	uniform resource locator
VAP	value added partnership
VAR	value added reseller
VAT	value added tax
VEL	value equivalence line
WAN	wide area network

Preface

Traditionally the value of a company's share capital has been based largely upon the net worth of the balance sheet. In recent years the gap between balance sheet and stock market values has widened dramatically. One reason for explaining this difference is that in some cases this represents investors' perceptions of the knowledge and skills that reside within the organisation.

In recent years governments around the world are beginning to understand that knowledge is a critical contributor to stimulating the rapid growth of entire economies. It is argued that in a modern economy, knowledge is the most important resource within companies based within any country. Some academics have even gone as far as proposing that knowledge is now more important than labour, capital or land. This latter assumption is posited on the basis that knowledge is the primary resource that permits organisations to achieve uniqueness within the market place.

Knowledge is frequently an intangible product, tacitly stored in the minds of managers and employees. The advent of the internet and automated e-business systems has provided an important catalyst for firms wishing to exploit the benefits of using knowledge to support their electronic trading activities. In order for these organisations to implement an effective on-line, knowledge-based strategy they have been forced to ensure all organisational data are converted into an explicit form capable of real-time access for utilisation in the provision of goods and services to their cyberspace customers.

The vast majority of texts on knowledge management tend to focus on the information technology (IT) aspects of managing the concept. Although management of technology is critical, there is an equally important need for the provision of materials describing how knowledge can be utilised in the execution of functional management tasks. In view of this situation, the goal of this text is to assist students and practising managers to comprehend how knowledge can be utilised to underpin and enhance the marketing management function within organisations. The concept is presented by drawing upon various published sources and through the use of case materials to illustrate knowledge management in practice.

Chapter 1 provides an introduction to the concept of knowledge and the management of process, and suggests appropriate internal organisational structures for optimising the storage, accessing and exploitation of knowledge. Chapter 2 reviews the evolving pathway of marketing from origins within mass marketing through to more recent theories about mass customisation. The increasingly important role of knowledge in supporting modern marketing practices is discussed. Chapter 3 examines how e-business is radically altering the execution of the marketing task. The issue of knowledge management and the use of appropriate cyberspace platforms are reviewed.

Chapter 4 examines how firms can map the external environment in order to determine how different knowledge sources can impact organisation performance. Chapter 5 reviews the strategic, financial and functional level organisational competencies that determine performance. Knowledge management is presented as having a critical role in the effective development and exploitation of organisational competence. Chapter 6 examines alternative marketing positions available to the firm. The role of knowledge supporting alternative positioning options is covered and the role of networks creating market positions is also discussed.

Chapter 7 reviews alternative planning philosophies in the context of their use of knowledge. The influence of knowledge on the resource-based view of the firm is examined and examples are provided of how a marketing plan can incorporate the exploitation of knowledge. Chapter 8 is concerned with how knowledge can support existing and new product innovation. Product portfolio management and processes for optimising innovation practices are reviewed. Coverage is also provided on the subject of managing knowledge in the context of complex innovation practices. Chapter 9 examines how knowledge can be utilised in the effective execution of a firm's promotional strategy.

Chapter 10 reviews alternative options associated with exploiting knowledge to optimise pricing and distribution decisions. Chapter 11 examines the increasingly important role that knowledge management plays in the execution of service sector marketing strategies. Chapter 12 covers the recognised problems associated with the provision of leadership, employee development and process structures to accelerate the use of knowledge within the marketing process.

Knowledge and the Organisation

CHAPTER SUMMARY

Knowledge is the new asset that impacts the market value of companies. In terms of storage, knowledge can be held by an individual or through formal systems distributed across the entire organisation. Acquisition and exploitation of knowledge involves organisations being prepared to learn. Organisational learning can provide the basis for new forms of competitive advantage. Management of knowledge has been made much easier through the advent of IT systems and more recently by the arrival of web-based technologies such as extranets and intranets. For effective exploitation knowledge must be acquired, codified, stored and re-accessed. To achieve this process organisations have developed knowledge systems and knowledge platforms. Additional knowledge exploitation can occur through the creation of information exchange links with other organisations in a supply chain or market system.

INTRODUCTION

Traditionally the value of a company's share capital has been based largely upon the net worth of the balance sheet. Any difference between net assets and market capitalisation represents the perceived market value of non-tangible assets such as patents, brand names and quality of management. In recent years the gap between balance sheet and stock market values has widened dramatically. One reason for explaining this difference is that this represents investors' perceptions of the knowledge and skills that reside within the organisation (Herbert 2000).

In relation to knowledge it is necessary to recognise there are two component contributors, namely:

1   **Data or information**, which are the facts describing events that occur both within an organisation and between the organisation and the market

environment of which it is a part. Such information has value and in some cases (for example, credit reference agencies such as Dun & Bradstreet) forms the basis of a product which can be sold to customers.

2 **Knowledge**, which resides within the organisation, either located in the minds of the employees or codified and stored in an organisational repository such as a company policy manual. These sources of knowledge can be considered as the application of information to permit understanding that can lead to the execution of tasks such as the resolution of problems or employees fulfilling their assigned job roles.

Information can be considered as a component part, but not the whole, of knowledge (Gore and Gore 1999). It can be proposed, for example, that knowledge is an all-encompassing term that incorporates the concept of employee beliefs and attitudes which are themselves based upon available information. Knowledge, in addition to incorporating information, is also dependent upon the commitment and understanding of the individuals holding such beliefs. Furthermore as beliefs are affected by interaction between people within the organisation, this activity can influence the development of judgement, behaviours and attitudes. Consequently knowledge will usually be associated with a perspective which in turn will influence actions and is usually context-specific.

When considering the issue of knowledge it is necessary to delineate between the knowledge held by an individual and that held by an entire organisation. Polanyi (1996) posits that organisational knowledge is comprised of corporate knowledge and the shared understandings of employees. Organisations can be expected to evolve and change as knowledge moves from the domain of individuals and becomes an understanding shared by others. The sharing process is a social interaction that has the potential to enhance the future performance of the organisation. The knowledge which is contained within the organisation has been described as covering (a) 'know what', (b) 'know how', (c) 'know why' and (d) 'care why' (Quinn et al. 1996).

Possibly one of the significant contributions to the identification of the importance of knowledge was that made by Toffler (1990). He proposed that knowledge is a critical contributor to stimulating the rapid growth of entire economies. At an organisational level in a modern economy knowledge is the most important resource within the company. It is now more important than labour, capital or land, and it is knowledge which is the primary resource that permits an organisation to achieve uniqueness within the market place.

KNOWLEDGE AND LEARNING

Following recognition that the exploitation of knowledge can provide added value to a business operation, not surprisingly over recent years increasing attention has been focused on how organisations can effectively exploit the information that has been acquired over time. One of the conceptual themes which has emerged in relation to exploiting information is *organisational learning* (*www.learning.mit.edu*).

Learning how to build stronger relationships with customers has for some time been recommended as a way of ensuring the survival of firms in the face of turbulent and/or highly competitive market conditions (Webster 1992). In commenting upon this scenario, De Guess (1988) has suggested that in situations where products and processes can be rapidly copied, the only real source of competitive advantage is to stimulate learning by employees. This will assist these individuals to identify innovative ways of working, which in turn permits the organisation to differentiate itself from the competition.

Bell (1973) proposed that the information and knowledge acquired by employees is now more important than the more traditional orientation of assuming the technology contained within the firm's capital assets can provide the basis for delivering product superiority over the competition. Similar views have been expressed by Slater and Narver (1995), who concluded that one of the most effective ways of acquiring competitive advantage is to exploit the skills learned by employees as a route through which to offer superior value and build closer relationships with customers. This perception is echoed by Woodruff (1977), who recommended that firms should focus on acquiring new learning because this activity is central to being able to deliver greater customer value.

The origins and theoretical foundations of organisational learning can be traced back to the work of academics such as Cyert and March (1963), Argyris and Schon (1978) and Senge (1990). Over the last few years the literature on this topic has grown very rapidly, attracting interest from a diverse variety of academic perspectives. Easterby-Smith (1997), in his review of the theoretical roots from which the subject has evolved, suggests contributions have been made from:

1 **Psychology/organisational development**, which focuses on the issues of the hierarchical nature of learning – adjusting individual learning to suit organisational learning needs – and recognition of the importance of cognitive maps underlying the thinking process.
2 **Management science**, where the primary concern is with the creation, utilisation and dissemination of information.
3 **Strategic management**, which is concerned with how the principles of learning can lead to competitive advantage and how the capability of firms to learn can permit new responses to changing market circumstances.
4 **Production management**, where the primary concern is with the use of productivity as a measure of learning and the impact of organisational design on the learning process.
5 **Sociology**, where the interest is directed towards the broader issues of the nature of learning, the processes that underpin it and how organisational realities such as power, politics and conflict impact on process.

3

6 **Cultural anthropology**, where the primary concern is the importance of values and beliefs, especially as these relate to the cultural differences which exist in different societies and the impact these may have on the learning process.

Easterby-Smith also commented, however, that this diversity of sources may have impeded the emergence of sufficiently robust paradigms, which can be utilised to offer clear guidance to managers about how organisational learning can contribute towards enhancing performance. Within the strategic management literature, authors such as Senge (1990) have proposed that a clear relationship should exist between the learning process and the acquisition of competitive advantage. Hamal and Prahalad (1993) have expressed the view that merely being a learning organisation is not sufficient. They perceive the learning process as an activity which should be translated into the acquisition of new knowledge that can be used to upgrade those areas of competence which permit the organisation to be more effective than their competition. As noted by both Sinkula et al. (1997) and Morgan et al. (1998), it would appear that there is also a need to research whether a relationship exists between organisational learning and the acquisition of competencies which influence the successful execution of the managerial functions within organisations. For example, as noted by Slater and Narver (1995), in the case of the marketing function, because it is positioned between the external environment and the internal activities of the firm, it is possibly most able to exploit the benefits that can accrue from organisational learning. Sinkula (1994) has posited that although the conceptual reasoning for such an argument is very apparent, research needs to be conducted in order to elaborate on whether an empirical relationship can be demonstrated between learning and organisational competencies. This view has been echoed by Morgan et al. (1998) who noted that very little empirical evidence exists in the literature about how organisations seek to acquire new knowledge which can improve internal capabilities, thereby providing the basis for evolving new forms of competitive advantage.

Jaworski and Kohli (1993) concluded that the ability of a firm to respond to identified changes in market or customer behaviour is an important feature exhibited by successful firms. Similarly in the organisational learning literature, there have been comments about the importance of organisations being able to respond to changing external environments by exploiting new knowledge to evolve innovative work practices, perspectives and frameworks. Such perspectives have been important catalysts, which have influenced researchers interested in wishing to determine whether an association exists between market performance, learning and knowledge.

The common objective of such studies has been to examine how the effective acquisition of knowledge can benefit organisations in terms of being able to acquire and analyse information relevant to understanding

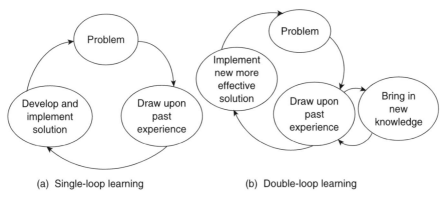

(a) Single-loop learning   (b) Double-loop learning

FIGURE 1.1   ALTERNATIVE LEARNING STYLES

customer needs (e.g. Jaworski and Kohli 1966; Slater and Narver 1995; Morgan et al. 1998). These authors have concluded that market orientated organisations tend to exhibit the behavioural characteristic of seeking to exploit new sources of knowledge. This approach, defined by Argyris and Schon (1978) as *double-loop learning* and by Glyn (1996) as *higher-level learning*, permits organisations to be more versatile, flexible and adaptive. As illustrated in Figure 1.1, this approach can be contrasted with a *single-loop learning* or *lower-level learning* style, which occurs in those organisations where virtually no new learning occurs because of a tendency by management to rely upon utilising existing knowledge in the problem–solution process.

Learning at St Paul Companies

As the St Paul Companies (*www.stpaul.com*) expanded into the global market for life insurance, the company recognised that permitting people to access knowledge and information was critical to success (Owens and Thompson 2001). To achieve this goal the company has placed priority on using organisational learning to transfer best practices and lessons learned across the workforce. To support the initiative the company has launched the St Paul University, which is constituted of 13 colleges that focus on specific knowledge domains. All employees are required to complete at least 40 hours of learning each year. To deliver learning an on-line gateway, the Edge, has been created through which employees can complete on-line courses, search for learning and access external learning opportunities.

The core of the St Paul learning strategy is the use of knowledge communities. These communities are supported via the Knowledge Exchange, which is a web site offering tools and processes to share expertise and resolve problems. Work group communities usually include people from the same department. A virtual project team community typically involves a cross-functional group working on a time-specific project. Where

---

specialist knowledge needs sharing a centre of expertise is formed. This acts as a hub that can be accessed by employees around the world. For example, the centre in London serves as a hub for underwriters and was used by Australian staff to capture $15 million in new business. Where staff need to share learning this is achieved by the formation of a virtual classroom community. The content developed by a classroom community can become a resource which other communities can then exploit. For example, a risk control manager in South Africa learned that a local hospital was having difficulty with a viral infection. She was able to contact other healthcare risk managers worldwide and within 24 hours determined how to manage the infection. By helping an insured hospital contain a disease, the company not only helped a healthcare provider but concurrently reduced the company's exposure to medical malpractice suits.

MANAGING KNOWLEDGE

By the 1990s, many firms realised that processing information using computer technology was a valuable methodology through which to access knowledge sources more rapidly. A key advantage of exploiting advances in IT was that this offered a more effective means to capture, analyse and distribute information. An accompanying disadvantage was that IT can produce such a wealth of information that this can lead to 'information overload'. Hence as IT became the dominant communication channel for many firms, there has been increasing pressure to identify mechanisms through which to extract and exploit the knowledge contained within organisations' databases (Lahti and Beyerlein 2000).

Ikuiro Nonaka (1994), in commenting upon one of the factors influencing the successful emergence of Japanese firms as global players, proposed that knowledge is one sure source of competitive advantage. He divided knowledge into two types, tacit and explicit. *Tacit knowledge* is stored in the minds of individuals and is usually shared with others through dialogue. *Explicit knowledge* is more precisely formulated and articulated by being documented in locations such databases or in company manuals. Zack (1999) noted that explicit knowledge is playing an increasingly important role in organisations and that in a knowledge-based economy it represents the most important factor of production. He further proposed that the following types of knowledge exist:

1 **Declarative knowledge**, which is a shared descriptive understanding of concepts, categories and descriptors that form the basis of effective communication and knowledge sharing within organisations.
2 **Procedural knowledge**, which describes how something occurs or is performed. Shared knowledge of this type lays the foundation for effective co-ordination of activities.
3 **General knowledge**, which is broad in nature and is shared between different communities both inside and outside the organisation.

4 **Specific knowledge**, which is applicable to particular organisations describing issues such as defining customers, order processing and product logistics.

To exploit explicit knowledge effectively requires that knowledge is stored in a form which can be readily accessed by employees. Under these circumstances knowledge will need to be labelled, indexed and stored in a form which permits retrieval and manipulation. Prior to new knowledge being added to a repository it must undergo cleansing, labelling, sorting, abstracting, standardisation, integration and categorisation. In today's firms most data acquisition and storage in an appropriate form is undertaken using automated IT systems. Under these circumstances it is critical that managers in charge of knowledge storage recognise their responsibility to ensure information is stored in a form which is readily accessible to all employees across the entire organisation. Failure to fulfil this requirement will merely render the knowledge system ineffective.

This latter outcome was demonstrated in a PhD project at Plymouth Business School on the creation of a new IT system for South West pathology laboratories in National Health Service hospitals. The system specification was created without any discussions with the system users, the laboratory staff, and upon installation, virtually no training was provided in system usage. The outcome was that the system failed to deliver on the promise of enhancing and upgrading execution of the clinical diagnosis tasks being undertaken by the pathology laboratories.

A firm can classify knowledge processing into two types: integrative and interactive (Zack 1999). *Integrative applications* exhibit a sequential flow of data into and out of a data store. Information providers and users interact with the stored system rather than with each other. Once such example is the storage of product specifications by the company engineers. These data are then accessed by sales staff seeking to deliver responses to customer enquiries. To be effective such systems must be continually updated and rigorous quality standards applied to ensure effective presentation of the stored knowledge. To achieve this goal, large integrated databases will require the services of individuals responsible for managing access, distribution and delivery of the available knowledge.

Interactive applications are primarily designed to permit sharing by individuals who have access to tacit knowledge. Content is dynamic and emergent with data storage being merely a by-product of interaction and collaboration. Examples of interactive systems include chat rooms, e-mail forums and intranets containing categorised (or 'threaded') records of electronic conversations. It may be the case that these interactive applications are researched by assigned employees to extract data-rich knowledge that may be of wider interest to other employees. Thus, for example, a consulting firm which has used an Intranet to manage a project for a specific client may assign an employee the task of extracting 'lessons learned' and placing these into the organisation's integrated database.

GAINS FROM KNOWLEDGE

Long before the phrase 'knowledge management' began to appear in business magazines or academic journals, back in the early 1990s British Petroleum (BP) (*www.bp.com*) was already adding value to existing operations by extracting knowledge from projects and sharing these data with others across the organisation (Wah 1999). In the sharing of knowledge over the construction of European retail garage sites it is estimated construction cost savings were achieved in the region of £50 million.

BP's initial approach to sharing knowledge was based upon an informal programme called 'vir-tual teamwork' and used the simple framework of generating learning by examining projects before, during and after completion. The company now has a corporate intranet containing information on about 10,000 employees. Furthermore some 1,500 staff have video conferencing and application sharing technologies on their desks to accelerate the exchange of knowledge between employees, suppliers and BP customers.

One of the champions of knowledge management at BP was Kent Greene (Stewart 1999). Based upon his observations of how a team used knowledge sharing to bring on-stream the Schiehallen oil field in the North Sea at a cost of £60 million less than estimate, Greene approached unit heads to persuade them of the benefits of exploiting knowledge management to resolve difficult problems. Projects where the approach proved successful have included entering the Japanese retail market, reducing downtime in a polyethylene plant and a major refinery refurbishment. Greene insists that the key to successful knowledge acquisition is to ask four stock questions, namely:

1   What was supposed to happen?
2   What actually happened?
3   Why is there a difference?
4   What can we learn from this?

Another process industry example concerning the value of knowledge is provided by Dow Chemical (*www.dow.com*) (Dzinkowski 1999). Since 1992 the company has focused on productivity improvement through process innovation and cost reduction projects. Their Leadership Development Network initiative has trained over 3,000 middle managers in the utilisation of knowledge to resolve operating problems. The company has also established a sophisticated customer-technical service system. Via a call centre, technical problems are routed to an automated solution database or to a company expert. It is estimated that this system has, in only a few years, contributed a research and development (R & D) cost saving of almost 30 per cent.

The company also undertook a programme to acquire a better understanding of assets by cataloguing what Dow owned. A primary focus of attention was the company's 3,000 patents because these represented the vast proportion of the firm's intellectual assets. The analysis permitted the firm to enter into over $1 billion worth of new licensing agreements with other organisations such as customers and suppliers.

SUCCESS FACTORS

To gain a clearer understanding of the factors impacting the success of knowledge management initiatives, De Long and Beers (1998) undertook an in-depth review of a diverse range of projects across 31 different organisations. These projects ranged from R & D to sales through to production. Some projects were self-funded by charging users a fee for knowledge generated, others relied on corporate funding and others were paid for out of operating overheads. Analysis of the case materials revealed there were four broad types of attributes shared by the various projects, namely:

Creating knowledge repositories.
Improving knowledge access.
Enhancing the knowledge environment.
Managing knowledge as an asset.

Within the context of knowledge repositories, different types were identified. One type was the competitive intelligence system used to filter, synthesise and add context to information about a firm's external environment. A second type involved a structured repository in which information and knowledge are stored. At Hewlett-Packard (*www.hp.com*) for example, Electronics Sales Partner provides technical performance information, sales presentations, customer/account information and other support tools for use by field sales personnel. The other type of repository was that of the tacit data stored in the minds of employees. Many of the firms studied recognise that this is not the most appropriate data storage mechanism and are working to extract this knowledge for redepositing in electronic databases. It is recognised that some data is most effectively communicated in a verbal form and hence firms encourage regular socialisation between staff during which 'popular war stories' can be exchanged.

Many firms are seeking to enhance the effectiveness of knowledge storage systems by the addition of export networks capable of being accessed by others who might benefit from such knowledge. Microsoft (*www. microsoft.com*) has an expert network for matching software teams with others in the firm who might be of assistance. The system uses a database and an electronic interface to store knowledge competency categories and personal profiles. BP Exploration uses a video conferencing system, document scanners, data sharing tools and a telecommunications network to rapidly overcome problems which might be encountered by their engineers while working in the field. This latter system permits suppliers, customers and engineers at other remote sites to interact in a real-time, data exchange environment in order to rapidly implement the most appropriate solutions.

Many of the firms which contributed to the research study recognise that a very necessary antecedent to knowledge management is the requirement to change the social norms and values related to the degree to which employees were prepared to openly share their experiences, both good and bad. One computer firm uses an ongoing seminar series to persuade engineers to appreciate the greater value of minimising time to market instead of seeking to invent a new solution to every encountered problem. Another firm uses customer feedback to assess the degree to which staff are committed to the open and frank exchange of data. A third firm has installed a decision audit programme to assess whether and how employees are applying knowledge to reach key decisions.

There was some variation in the degree to which participant firms have decided to value knowledge. Skandia (*www.skandia.se*), a large Swedish financial services company, internally audits intellectual capital for inclusion in the annual shareholders report. Dow Chemical, as mentioned earlier, uses ownership of patents to value acquired knowledge. Most firms, however, perceive that such formalised processes would demand major changes in accounting philosophy and as yet are not prepared to progress the introduction of such fundamental changes in the way they structure their balance sheets.

Although some of the projects researched by De Long and Beers involved major organisational transformations, most were focused on operational improvements limited to a particular function. These included activities such as new product development, customer support systems, employee education, process redesign and software development. As such the authors admit it was extremely difficult to evaluate how somewhat narrowly defined improvements could be measured in the context of determining their contribution to overall organisational performance. Nevertheless on the basis of case materials acquired it was possible to identify the following factors which are likely to contribute to the success of a knowledge management project:

1 **Link to value.** Projects which overtly lead to money being saved or earned are possibly the easiest to assess and are of greatest appeal to senior managers. Hoffman-LaRoche (*www.roche.com*), for example, has concentrated on projects designed to reduce significantly the time to market for new drugs. The motive for this specification is easy to understand when one realises that one day's delay can represent $1 million in lost revenue.

    The ability to link projects to measurable savings is important because many knowledge management projects are expensive to implement. The consulting firm Ernst & Young (*www.ey.com*) calculates that 6 per cent of their revenues are expended on knowledge management and their competitor McKinsey (*www.mckinsey.com*) estimates an even higher figure of 10 per cent of revenue.

2 **Infrastructure.** Projects are more likely to succeed if an investment has been made in appropriate infrastructure. In many cases this infrastructure is of a technological nature using software tools such as Lotus Notes for the storage and management of acquired information. Another

pervasive technology is desktop computing and communications. This means that at minimum, project participants can access a networked PC (personal computer) system to undertake document exchange and communication.

Although often seen as less critical, successful firms also ensure that staff are equipped with the skills necessary for effective information interchange and that group facilitators have the capability to manage the effective distribution of accumulated knowledge. As such skills are rarely intuitive, many firms now invest in training schemes aimed at enhancing employee team membership and electronic communications skills.

3 **Knowledge structures**. Knowledge is not the easiest thing to define, categorise or store. However, unless an appropriate database exists, once stored knowledge may become inaccessible to others. Hence many firms now utilise database managers to standardise procedures for all phases of knowledge exploitation from initial acquisition through to redistribution. Additionally these systems must exhibit the attribute of flexibility in order to permit easy updating and revision.

4 **Culture fit**. Evidence from the case materials would suggest that similar to other managerial initiatives such as change management, mergers and acquisitions and empowerment, knowledge management systems must be designed to be compatible with the organisation's operational culture. It would seem the most effective cultures are those where employees (a) have a positive orientation towards exploiting knowledge, (b) have no inhibitions about knowledge sharing and (c) are comfortable with the objectives specified for a particular project.

5 **Language**. Evidence emerged that many employees are not comfortable with phrases such as 'organisational learning' or 'knowledge management'. Under these circumstances care needs to be taken to develop an alternative language which describes any proposed project using words and phrases that are compatible with the linguistic culture which exists in a specific organisation. Thus, for example, a project concerned with acquiring more knowledge about variations in customer needs might be perceived as more acceptable to employees if referred to as a 'customer service improvement' programme.

6 **Motivation**. Most knowledge management projects take a long time to reach fruition, involve people working across departmental boundaries and undertaking tasks which require new skills sets. Under these circumstances motivating project participants is no easy task. In some cases firms adopt short-term incentives such as bonuses for well executed activities. Other firms perceive that given the longer-term and often fuzzy nature of knowledge development projects, specific inclusion as an opportunity for positive employee feedback in regularly scheduled staff appraisal schemes is a more effective mechanism through which to sustain a positive motivation.

7 **Channels**. It is rarely the case that one single channel is the most effective mechanism through which to transfer knowledge. Successful projects

tend to use various channels including informal discussions, direct and formal one-to-one contact, meetings, seminars, newsletters and data-bases to ensure that information is shared between participants. Sometimes very simple changes can have an important impact. Chrysler, for example, attributes much of the company's recent success in new car development to the act of locating everyone involved in the project into the same building.

8 **Senior management support**. As with virtually any project which has the potential for impacting future performance, it is usually extremely helpful if senior management are willing to overtly express their support for the initiative. This can be achieved by them widely communicating the message about the importance of exploiting knowledge, providing the necessary financial resources and clarifying which areas of knowledge management are seen as most critical to the company's future performance.

KNOWLEDGE SYSTEMS

To gain further understanding of how organisations orchestrate the acquisition and exploitation of knowledge, DiBella et al. (1996) undertook an in-depth study of four different organisations, Electricité de France, Fiat, Motorola and Mutual Investment Corporation. From collected case materials, they concluded that an effective learning system was constituted of the following seven elements:

1 **Knowledge source** is defined by the extent to which organisations prefer to develop new knowledge internally versus exploiting ideas from external sources.
2 **Product-process** *focus* describes a preference for the accumulation of knowledge related to products and services versus an orientation towards investing in knowledge to improve the processes which support internal organisational activities.
3 **Documentation mode** covers the systems whereby the organisation stores knowledge. At one extreme, knowledge may reside inside the minds of employees and at the other extreme, all knowledge may be carefully documented within detailed company operating manuals.
4 **Dissemination mode** concerns how the organisation manages the transfer of knowledge between employees. One possibility is to create a highly structured, formalised approach whereby insights are shared across the entire organisation. Another approach is to adopt a more informal attitude, leaving employees to decide whether they wish to share knowledge with others who constitute the project team of which they are a part.
5 **Learning focus** describes the learning style utilised within the organisation and can be of a single- or double-loop variety.

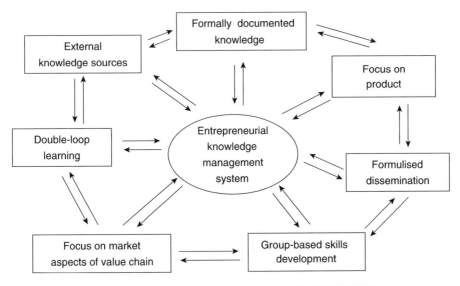

FIGURE 1.2 ENTREPRENEURIAL KNOWLEDGE MANAGEMENT SYSTEM

6 **Value chain focus** indicates in which areas of the value chain (for example, marketing, manufacturing, design, logistics) the firm concentrates the majority of learning activities.
7 **Skills development** covers what approaches the firm adopts in developing employee competencies. This typically means that the firm decides whether the learning approach should be focused on the training of individual employees or is based around some form of team or group learning.

To gain an understanding of the nature of learning systems in conventional and entrepreneurial firms, Chaston et al. (1999) undertook a survey of knowledge management practices within small, UK manufacturing companies. This study revealed there are very distinctive differences between the learning systems used in entrepreneurial firms when compared with their more conventional, traditional thinking competitors. The study provided the basis for proposing that the learning system found in entrepreneurial firms would exhibit the attributes shown in Figure 1.2.

In relation to *knowledge sources*, conventional firms are biased towards drawing upon information from within their organisation. This contrasts with entrepreneurial firms who are biased towards exploiting knowledge sources external to the organisation. Bias in the case of entrepreneurial firms in relation to the issue of *product-process focus* is towards ongoing development of products or customer services, whereas conventional firms usually seek ways of further upgrading internal organisational processes. On the issue of *documentation mode*, the conventional firms adopt a somewhat informal approach to knowledge storage, whereas entrepreneurial firms tend to create a formalised, central record system to act as a repository of key information critical to the effective operation of the organisation's memory system. Accompanying this latter approach to knowledge colla- tion, entrepreneurial firms favour the creation of formal systems for their *dissemination mode* to ensure that information is shared between all employees. In contrast, conventional firms appear to adopt a somewhat informal orientation, apparently assuming individuals will share know- ledge with each other on an 'as needed' basis.

The *learning focus* of the conventional firms is orientated towards single- loop learning. Similar to views expressed by other researchers, the study of UK entrepreneurial manufacturing firms revealed that their learning focus is double-loop, seeking to draw in new knowledge as the basis for enhanc- ing the effectiveness of their problem solving activities. In relation to *value chain focus*, conventional firms focus their attention on activities associated with further improving the efficiencies of internal organisational processes. Entrepreneurial firms appear to be biased towards seeking to add value to those dimensions of the value chain concerned with offering greater value to customers. Management of *skills development* in entrepreneurial firms is centred around improving the competencies of work teams. This is con- trasted with conventional firms where training is directed towards upgrad- ing the capabilities of individuals within the workforce.

KNOWLEDGE PLATFORMS

Once a company decides to embrace e-business as a path through which to exploit new, entrepreneurial opportunities, then an immediate outcome is that the organisation's knowledge platform becomes much more closely linked with other knowledge sources elsewhere within the market system, such as suppliers and customers. The reason why this occurs is that once buyers and sellers become electronically linked with each other, the volume of data inter- change dramatically increases as trading activities begin to occur in real time. The outcome is the emergence of very dynamic, rapid responses by both cus- tomer and supplier to changing circumstances within the market system.

There are a number of new forms of knowledge exchange which can result from the creation of an e-business system. The platform permits a much fuller interchange of information between supplier and customer about the nature of product benefits and attributes which are being offered to the market. Furthermore the data interchange can be interactive and customised to meet the specific knowledge needs of each customer. Hewlett-Packard, for example, has a system which assists the customer to select the best printer option by asking questions about needs (for example, price, need for colour, speed of printing). The answers permit the system to present a customised version of the company catalogue recommending what the company believes is the best solution for the customer.

Where the customer is seeking very significant volumes of additional information that are hard to acquire through more traditional distribution channels, the e-business platform is also able to meet this demand. Virtual Vineyards (*www.wine.com*), for example, is an on-line supplier which provides details on their winery, the type and quality of wine and the best wine for serving with different foods. As far as the supplier is concerned, an additional benefit offered by an e-business platform is that it provides a much more cost effective medium through which to deliver vast quantities of knowledge when compared with more conventional channels such as mailing catalogues or communicating by telephone.

Platforms are also able to deliver instant knowledge. This attribute is especially critical in those situations where rapidly changing conditions require very quick decisions. Thus, for example, on-line stock market trading permits the customer to acquire instantly the data needed to determine how to act in those situations where new, emergent trends in the financial markets indicate a need to reconsider either the immediate purchase or sale of a portfolio of investments.

Additionally knowledge systems, by tracking and storing every aspect of a customer's search activities and purchase decisions, allow the supplier to acquire a profile on the buying behaviour of every individual with whom the firm has had contact. Once this knowledge reaches a certain critical mass, the supplier can begin to customise future responses to meet the specific needs of each customer (for example, Amazon's on-line service selecting and recommending new books to their regular customers). Additionally by linking this knowledge to an organisation's manufacturing systems, the firm may be able to provide an almost instant response to a request for a customised product or service. Motorola (*www.motorola.com*), for example, having obtained a customer's stated specification for a pager, can transmit this to their manufacturing plant, produce the item and, by the next day, deliver it to the customer.

KNOWLEDGE NETWORKS

As organisations come to appreciate the value of acquiring new knowledge as the basis for gaining competitive advantage, new intra- and interorganisational structures are beginning to emerge to provide mechanisms for delivering new, more entrepreneurial business strategies. A common denominator shared by many these initiatives, which are seeking to embed innovative responses to changing market opportunities, is the need to break down boundaries between areas of functional management, to replace an attitude of competing for scarce resources with an orientation directed towards fostering co-operation and ensuring the effective communication of information. The spider's web appearance of such forms of collaboration has caused the emergence of terminology of *knowledge networks* or *learning networks* to describe these new organisational forms (Chaston 1999a).

15

There is growing evidence to suggest that the formation of a knowledge network (*www.tomoye.com; www.psdn.org.ph*) is possibly the most effective way through which a company, facing the need to implement fundamental change, can achieve the aim of enhancing entrepreneurial behaviour within the organisation. Some of the earliest evidence of this concept emerged from studies of simultaneous engineering in the car industry (Clark and Fujimoto 1991). This trend in car manufacturing is based around a shift away from functional, departmental structures towards a more integrated form of working. As is usually the case, the first exemplars are provided by the Japanese car companies such as Mazda, Honda and Toyota, which were seeking both to improve and accelerate new product development processes within their respective organisations. Four factors critical to the success of these knowledge networks are:

1 Co-location to engender social interchange between all parties involved in the development project.
2 Formalisation of co-operation procedures to ensure cross-functional activities are implemented effectively.
3 Basing working practices around a team culture which stresses the importance of shared responsibility.
4 Ensuring that the network remains in close contact with the 'voice of the customer' at all stages in the product development process.

Ford Europe

Attempts to replicate the concept of knowledge networks in Ford Europe (*www.fordeurope. net*) encountered the massive obstacle that a deeply embedded functional, departmentalised structure initially resulted in a failure to establish a genuinely co-operative attitude between various groups within the organisation (Starkey and McKinley 1996). The overall driving force for change was the need for Ford to develop new exciting vehicles in order to demolish the firm's image as a conventional car producer. Under the project banner of Ford 2000, fundamental changes in structure have been implemented involving a move towards establishing a cross-functional, team-based, matrix approach. Paralleling this move, the company has sought to achieve a fundamental shift in organisational values to create a learning environment in which employees pursue co-operation and integration in the place of internal competition and separation. Clearly the scale of actions associated with the move towards a networked approach to embedding knowledge management into the organisational culture will take some years before the company can genuinely claim that simultaneous engineering is the new operational philosophy which drives the organisation. Early signs of success within Ford, however, are demonstrated over recent years by the launch of the highly innovative Ford Ka and Ford Focus products.

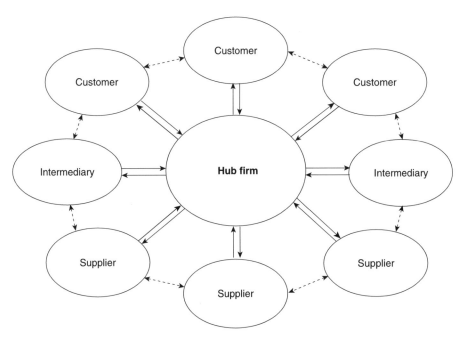

FIGURE 1.3   A HUB KNOWLEDGE NETWORK STRUCTURE

Another approach to building knowledge networks is for an organisation to create a hub structure by becoming the central clearing house for knowledge. As shown in Figure 1.3, with this type of *hub knowledge network*, the role of the central organisation is to bring together knowledge exchange between market system members such as suppliers, intermediaries and customers (*www.intrinix.com*). The creation of hub networks has been greatly assisted by the emergence of e-business technology within market systems as organisations have sought ways of more rapidly processing information as the basis for seeking entrepreneurially to exploit new opportunities. The move by firms to replace conventional, sequential assembly line processes and linear information flows with integrated knowledge interchange systems has been described by Norman and Ramirez (1993) as a 'value constellation' market system. The much strengthened trading position, which can result from becoming a hub organisation, does mean that it seems extremely probable that over the next few years many entrepreneurial firms will seek to exploit their knowledge management capabilities to occupy the central position within their respective market systems.

A problem that faces many large original equipment manufacturers (OEMs) is the need to become a more powerful guiding force in the

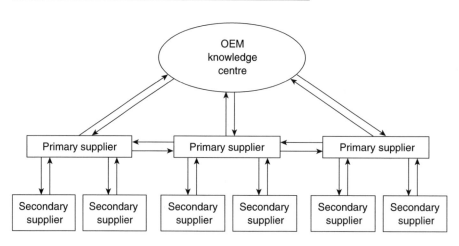

FIGURE 1.4   A CASCADE KNOWLEDGE NETWORK

development of new product forms and services. For manufacturing firms, this can only be achieved if they can find ways of reducing their involvement in component production and subsystem assembly work. Most OEMs are part of a market system which in the past has relied heavily on smaller firms to supply their needs for a diverse range of components and services. The more entrepreneurial OEMs have recognised that if they moved away from adversarial, price-based procurement and instead acted as a knowledge centre, this would permit them to delegate a larger proportion of the design and manufacturing of subassembly systems to their suppliers. This has resulted in *cascade knowledge networks* of the type illustrated in Figure 1.4. Within these networks, the OEM accepts the role of guiding and resourcing the learning process within their market system. This type of network has been created, for example, by the aircraft engine company Pratt & Whitney as a system for upgrading the ability of smaller firms on the eastern seaboard of the United States to act as suppliers of specialist parts to the company.

In the case of service firms, their aim is usually to develop new knowledge among their suppliers so that the latter are able to undertake a greater proportion of the responsibilities for managing additional aspects of the value chain. An example of this type of cascade network is provided by supermarket chains such as Tesco in the UK. These organisations are creating internet sites which can be accessed by suppliers seeking knowledge on a whole range of issues from manuals on store-level delivery policies through to examining stock movement at individual store level. This latter information permits both the supplier and the supermarket to identify sales velocity rates and immediately instigate actions to exploit changing consumer purchasing trends.

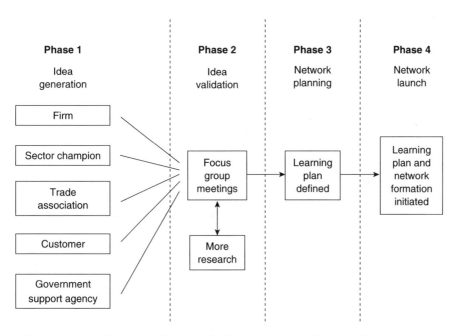

FIGURE 1.5   PROCESS MODEL FOR FORMATION OF A NEW MULTI-FIRM
KNOWLEDGE NETWORK

A common constraint of small firms is that they often lack both key knowledge elements and the resources to execute entrepreneurial actions. One way this obstacle can be overcome is to form a co-operative relationship with other like-minded firms to create a *horizontal learning network*. Examples include software firms coming together to acquire the ability to complete a systems integration project, manufacturing firms seeking to acquire scale in the creation of an e-business trading system and groups of independent retailers wishing to build an 'own brand' operation. The creation of such networks, as illustrated in Figure 1.5, is usually a four-phase process (Chaston 1999a). In phase 1, an idea is generated. The idea can come from a whole range of different sources such as the firm itself, a trade association, a customer or a government agency involved in assisting in the creation of industrial clusters. During phase 2, a series of meetings will occur as participants discuss the idea, refine their thinking and begin to evolve mutual trust and commitment. It is frequently the case during phase 2 that further research is needed to assist the discussions in progress. Once an idea is selected, then, in phase 3, an appropriate learning plan needs to be crafted. Finally in phase 4 of the process, the formation of the network occurs and the agreed learning plan is implemented.

Another form of learning network is that created due to formation of *clusters*, which are a geographic concentration of firms involved in the production of goods and services for a specific industry sector. Clusters take numerous forms, some are concentrated at a single level (for example, a cluster of fish processing plants), whereas others may be constituted of firms from various levels within a market system (for example, the footwear and fashion industry in Italy (www.furnishingsfromitaly.com)). These structures have become of increasing interest to governments because it is now recognised that the creation and expansion of clusters can provide a very effective mechanism through which to implement regional economic regeneration strategies (Porter 1998).

Many of the earlier writings about clusters tended to focus on the economic benefits offered, such as their existence providing rapid, low cost access to specialist inputs from local sources, higher productivity due to the existence of a pool of highly trained workers and the opportunity to reduce operating costs through the sharing of common services such as distribution and marketing. There is now, however, increasing evidence to suggest that one of the most powerful features of clusters is their ability to acquire and share knowledge, thereby assisting participant firms to become global leaders in innovation, able consistently to pre-empt their competitors located elsewhere in the world. Clustered firms are also able to discern buyer trends faster than their more isolated competitors. Furthermore having determined the nature of innovative opportunity, firms within the cluster have easy access to local sources of components, machinery and support services. The combined influence of these factors is the reason why, for example, IT companies based in Silicon Valley, California (www.photonicsclusters.org) and Austin, Texas (www.ctdxcc.org) are able to respond entrepreneurially to new market opportunities at a much faster rate than other firms in their industry.

Attempting to comprehend the antecedents to cluster formation is a task which has been challenging academics for some years. It would appear, however, that there can be a multitude of explanations including access to raw materials, geographic location and well developed distribution infrastructures. Furthermore chance events can influence the formation process. For example, the decision of the US Strategic Air Command to locate in Omaha, Nebraska led to the installation of a fibre-optics communication system. The creation of one of the most efficiently operated telecommunications systems in the world then led to numerous telemarketing firms entering the region to open call centre operations.

In terms of knowledge-based industries, it is apparent that an important catalyst in accelerating the creation of clusters is the emergence of a critical knowledge mass. Typically this will occur either because of commercial opportunities emerging out of research being undertaken in a leading academic institution (for example, the technology strip which has developed around the Massachusetts Institute of Technology (www.masstech.org); the IT industry around the Stanford University in California) or because a very large organisation involved in leading edge technology has established a major manufacturing site (for example, the opening of the Boeing Aircraft Corporation plants on the West Coast of America to build B-29 bombers during the Second World War) or because of the creation of a new firm which is dramatically successful and grows into a major global player (for example, the heart pacemaker pioneer Medtronics (*www.medtronics.com*) in Minneapolis; Microsoft in Seattle).

Some writers have suggested that the advent of the internet and associated communication technologies will permit the emergence of virtual clusters linking together individual entrepreneurs and small entrepreneurial firms based anywhere around the world. In considering such predictions, it is necessary to note that most entrepreneurs are still social animals who find face-to-face interactions are critical in terms of stimulating their thinking and causing the creative juices to flow. Furthermore it is also apparent that across different industrial sectors, entrepreneurs do appear to have lifestyle aspirations that cause them to flock to certain locations (for example, the IT techies' love of California; yacht designers' preference to live in the south west of England; fashion designers attracted to Paris or Milan (*www.globaltechnoscan.com*)). Hence the emergence of virtual reality clusters may take somewhat longer than is predicted by certain experts on the possible form that the 'future world' will take.

What is more certain, however, is that the internet and associated technologies will continue to play a major role in permitting the more effective storage of information and the more rapid interchange of knowledge between interested parties within market systems. Thus in the twenty-first century, it can confidently be predicted that knowledge networks of various forms will become an increasingly dominant operational structure through which to ensure the effective management of entrepreneurial activities in both private and public sector organisations.

2

Marketing and the Application of Knowledge

CHAPTER SUMMARY

Marketing is a managerial philosophy which emerged after the Second World War and is concerned with the use of knowledge to understand and satisfy customer needs. Early successes were achieved by firms such as Lever and Nestlé operating as mass marketers. In the 1960s, many of these firms realised that by acquiring knowledge about different market segments they could develop a broader range of products more suited to meeting need variation within the marketplace. Niche marketing is about focusing upon a very small group of customers and using in-depth understanding to provide specialist products or services. The process is mainly practised by smaller firms. More recently many organisations have recognised the importance of building long-term customer loyalty. Known as relationship marketing, this philosophy is especially popular with service sector firms. Effective execution of a relationship marketing strategy requires in-depth knowledge of customers' behaviour prior to, during and after the purchase process.

INTRODUCTION

The 1950s saw the emergence of the managerial philosophy known as the 'marketing concept'. Essentially the philosophy proposes that achievement of organisational goals is best fulfilled through understanding the needs of customers and acting to deliver satisfaction superior to that available from the competition.

In 1985 the American Marketing Association proposed that the management of the marketing process could be described as 'the activities associated with planning and executing the conception, pricing, promotion and distribution of goods, services and ideas to create exchanges with target groups that satisfy customer and organisational objectives'. Clearly this definition underpins the perspective that marketers have been using knowledge management long before this latter phrase began to be popularised in the management literature.

The foundation stones upon which many of today's marketing management practices are based are those evolved by US corporations in the period following the end of the Second World War. Companies such as Procter & Gamble and Coca-Cola demonstrated that by exploiting the benefits of mass production and then investing heavily in activities to build customer awareness of the benefits offered by their products, it was possible to dominate markets successfully. Their managerial philosophy of achieving a high market share for a standard product became known as 'mass marketing'. A key factor which influenced their success was that media such as television, cinema and radio permitted easy, low cost access to a large proportion of a market's potential customer base.

Richard Tedlow (1990), a business historian at Harvard Business School, has analysed the life history of a number of well known US companies in the automobile, electrical goods, retailing and soft drinks sectors. From his research on company behaviour both before and after the Second World War he has formulated some generic guidelines which can be used to specify the nature of the knowledge required by organisations to implement effective strategies for establishing successful mass market brands. These knowledge requirements include:

1 The knowledge to be able to exploit the economies of scale associated with mass production to generate high absolute profits by selling large volumes of low margin goods.
2 The knowledge of how to reinvest generated profits in high levels of promotional activity as a mechanism through which to shape and mould market demand.
3 The knowledge to create a vertical system in which raw materials are sourced, production operations managed and products delivered to the final consumer. This vertical system usually involves integration within the firm of some steps (for example, the Ford motor company owning both car assembly and component manufacturing plants) accompanied by contractual relationships for other elements within the distribution system (for example, the move by Coca-Cola to reduce costs by supplying concentrate syrups to bottling companies which managed production and distribution in a specified market area).
4 The knowledge, having achieved market dominance through being the first company to exploit a strategy of high volume/low unit prices, to create economies of scale barriers to ward off attacks from competition.

To implement an effective mass marketing strategy the firm will need to draw upon two sources of knowledge, namely knowledge of market conditions (for example, customer needs, behaviour of competitors) and the knowledge to implement the functional managerial processes associated with the procurement, production and distribution of standard goods.

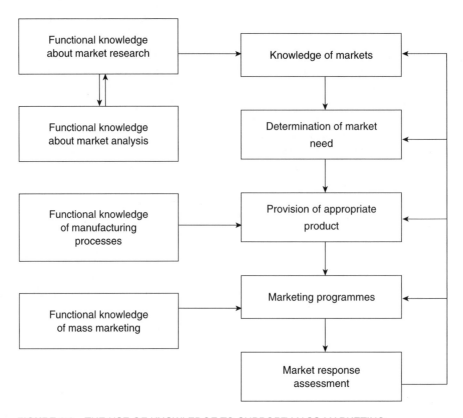

FIGURE 2.1 THE USE OF KNOWLEDGE TO SUPPORT MASS MARKETING

These elements are summarised in Figure 2.1. In the context of the total mass marketing process, the majority of knowledge is vested within the functional tasks of identifying market opportunity and then utilising the capabilities of mass production to manufacture high volume/low cost goods for distribution to the final customer.

Within many fast moving consumer goods (fmcg) companies, traditionally the level of resources allocated to market research in order to generate information about markets and customers has tended to be somewhat limited. Typically expenditure on research will cover activities such as (a) the purchase of store panel audit data, (b) monitoring of competitor activities (prices, promotional spending, sales promotions), (c) studies of consumer awareness of company advertising campaigns and (d) surveys of consumers to assess usage and attitude patterns. A primary reasons for this apparently limited knowledge requirement is that within many mass markets customer needs are perceived as homogenous. Hence the generation of understanding about issues such as buyer trends, attitudes and behaviour is perceived as a relatively simple task.

Staying Ahead with Knowledge

The ongoing problem facing the major mass market brands is surviving in the face of competition from private (or own) label products offered at a lower price by supermarket chains. For national and international brands to sustain their premium price in the face of such competition requires that the companies use their knowledge of customers and technology to make available superior products which can continue to differentiate their brands from private label offerings.

In the US there has been growing concern among consumers about the problem of bacterial contamination in the home (Teng 2000). Published research on the accumulation of germs in washing machines has heightened these worries. Procter & Gamble used this knowledge about an emerging consumer need to reformulate their most popular detergent brand Tide. In 1999 they launched liquid Tide with hydrogen peroxide and this was followed by a reformulated Tide powder with bleach. Both products are specifically designed to kill bacteria when clothes are being washed.

Major brands can also exploit new technology developed for one solution by applying the same knowledge across a range of products. Procter & Gamble's use of cyclodextrins is an example of how to leverage technology (McCoy 2002). Cyclodextrins are ring shaped glucose monomer molecules which have the capability of trapping small compounds. Procter & Gamble, which holds patents on the technology, first applied their knowledge to develop a fragrance delivery vehicle for their Bounce fabric softener brand. In 1998 they used cyclodextrins as an odour-removing vehicle in their Febreze spray. This was followed in 2000 by Febreze Wash, a liquid laundry additive that helps remove unwanted odours. Concurrently the company developed Febreze Antibacterial which is a new spray that can kill 99.9 per cent of bacteria on areas such as kitchen surfaces.

Going International

Many of the world's best known global brands (for example, McDonalds, Pepsi-Cola, Wrigleys) started life in America and then spread around the world as US corporations evolved into multinational operations during the 1950s and 1960s. Although some brands such as Levi Strauss found overseas market acceptance could be achieved with virtually no requirement to acquire new knowledge about different customer needs, in some cases global marketers have found it necessary to modify their product proposition.

One such example of the need to utilise new knowledge to frame a revised strategy is provided by Kentucky Fried Chicken's entry into the Japanese market (*International Journal of Retail and Distribution Management 1993*). When the company first entered Japan in the 1970s, it utilised the proven US strategy of opening drive-in stores in shopping centres, positioning the product proposition as a 'fast food' for the entire family. The strategy in a country where most people still went shopping on a bicycle proved disastrous.

Utilising information generated from in-depth market research of Japanese lifestyle, attitudes and buyer behaviour, the company recognised that their existing mass market strategy was not the best way of seeking to build a successful beach head in Pacific markets. The decision was to reposition the brand by opening fashionable stores in upmarket shopping areas and near railway stations in upper-class residential areas. Promotional activity was primarily directed towards young people and communicated the message that Kentucky Fried Chicken represents a new eating trend.

Some academics such as Kotler (1994) have suggested that mass marketing is now a dying proposition. He argued that even by the 1960s, it was being replaced by firms offering a range of goods to increase customer choice (for example, the diversity of vehicles manufactured by General Motors) and that through techniques such as 'target marketing' based around focusing marketing effort on a specific customer group (for example, beer advertising directed towards heavy users such as 18 to 25 year old males). Undoubtedly there is some truth in this view. Nevertheless it can also be argued that expanding a product line or target marketing, although moving away from the classic 'one product for all' approach, in reality is merely a case of blue chip fmcg companies using brand variety as a way of expanding market coverage for what essentially are still mass market product propositions.

This viewpoint is illustrated in the detergent market by Procter & Gamble and Unilever. Both companies have a range of brands, each offering a slightly different product usage benefit. Essentially, however, the basic benefit proposition is that of a product capable of washing clothes, with this message being communicated by ongoing reliance upon mass marketing media such as television advertising.

Understanding the Customer

One of the reasons that mass marketing still retains popularity with large firms is that although there is wastage of media funds because mass market promotional messages will be seen by both users and non-users, the unit cost per user seeing the television commercial is still relatively low. Furthermore as pointed out by Rapp (1990), it is often very difficult, even using the best available market research, to know exactly when each customer will need to purchase the product. He illustrates this viewpoint by the example of a firm such as Warner-Lambert marketing their allergy remedy Benadryl (*www.allergy-cold.com*). The firm can never exactly predict when a specific consumer will develop a case of the sniffles. Under these circumstances, mass market advertising is still cost effective even though only a small group of people will actually be in the market for allergy relief on a specific day.

This situation, however, does not mean that one should ignore the advent of new technology being used to enhance mass marketing activity. In the case of Benadryl, as well as using television advertising, the company also created a toll-free call centre which people could contact to get information on the pollen count in the area of the country where they live. As well as reinforcing the brand promise message, the system provided Warner-Lambert with the basis for building a customer database of allergy sufferers in the US who could then be the target of a subsequent direct marketing campaign.

KNOWLEDGE-BASED COMPETITION

Once an industry has been established for many years and leading firms have come to dominate the sector, the entry of an outsider is no simple task. An example of a firm which has excelled at converting information into knowledge as the basis for launching a new form of competitive advantage is Nucor Corporation. The entrepreneurial driving force behind the firm's exploitation of knowledge has been the founder Kenneth Iverson. His managerial philosophy is that of using knowledge to challenge sector conventions (Slywotzky 1996).

In the 1950s and 1960s, the sectoral convention which drove the US steel industry was that of producing a broad line of products delivered at a competitive price through investment in high fixed cost, high productivity, steel plants. By the mid-1960s, these massive, highly integrated plants were generating huge revenue flows and nobody in American steel towns such as Pittsburgh was too concerned about the fact that the Japanese were gearing up to challenge the Americans through the simple process of following the same conventions but building even more efficient steel plants. By 1971, Japanese and US output was almost equal. Then to add to the industry's problems, some major customers such as the soft drinks industry switched from steel to aluminium as the raw material for drinks cans.

Kenneth Iverson evolved a completely new vision for the steel making industry. The vision was founded upon using scrap steel as a raw material instead of iron ore, and then building small, low cost, highly flexible factories located near to customers to offer low cost steel using a just in time (JIT) operating philosophy. From this vision emerged a whole new industry know as the 'mini-mills'. By the 1980s, the shareholder value of Nucor at £1 billion was almost equal to one of the largest and oldest steel makers in the world, Bethlehem Steel.

Nucor's success is not explained by factors such as industry structure, access to raw materials or other external factors. Instead success is founded upon the principle of continually seeking to exploit knowledge to evolve proprietary capability across areas such as market identification, plant construction, process technologies and introducing new technology ahead of the competition (Gupta and Govindarajan 2000). Thus having single handedly created the US mini-mill industry, in the 1980s the company began to examine opportunities in the production of flat steel products for the automotive and appliance industries. Up until that time nobody believed mini-mills could succeed in this sector. Nucor proved everybody wrong because in 1987, in Crawfordsville, Indiana, the company built the first mini-mill to use thin slab casting technology to manufacture flat steel.

Inside Nucor the organisational culture revolves around effective exploitation of knowledge to enter new markets and build market share by successfully confronting more traditional thinking steel makers. To encourage the sharing of knowledge, Nucor uses a systematic approach to measuring performance of every work group as the basis for uncovering opportunities for sharing best practice between departments and operating sites. To further stimulate knowledge sharing the firm operates a financial incentives scheme which makes payments based upon individual and group performance. To ensure rapid communication flow the company has a policy of keeping employee numbers at each plant within the region of 250 to 300 individuals. Both plant managers and their employees are encouraged to visit other sites to share views and ideas. Furthermore to ensure knowledge is both retained and recycled, the company builds and renovates its own plants rather than relying on outside contractors.

MARKET SEGMENTATION

By the early 1960s in many Western nation consumer markets, products had moved into maturity on the product life cycle. The outcome was confrontations between brands seeking to sustain growth by persuading customers to switch their purchasing loyalty. In a classic article Smith (1956) articulated the view that to sustain growth in apparently non-growth scenarios, companies should adopt the concept of market segmentation. The essential logic behind the proposition was that by acquiring a deeper understanding of variations in customer needs, companies could develop new products specifically aimed at satisfying different groups of customers. Possible benefits from the approach might be (a) by specialisation, companies could stimulate greater consumption and thereby market expansion and (b) if there are few competitors within a given segment, promotional costs might be reduced (Cahill 1997).

In considering a move to segmentation, it was necessary for marketers to recognise that additional costs would be incurred (Moschis et al. 1997). Probable causes of increased costs are expenditure on product development, the rise in manufacturing costs caused by moving from a single to a multiple product system and higher logistics costs.

Early attempts at market segmentation were strongly influenced by the nature of the market information which could be generated about variations in customer needs. The standard normative approach was that of seeking to aggregate groups of customers into *natural clusters*. The assumption was that within a cluster customers are expected to exhibit similar needs. The restriction facing the marketer wishing to undertake any degree of more sophisticated data analysis was that computer time was expensive and most available statistical tools required that the user had a high degree of programming expertise. As a result many early segmentation techniques relied upon easily accessible data sets such as the geographic location provided by postal addresses or socio-demographics (age, education, income, occupation).

Although today's market researchers with their access to powerful low cost computers and easy-to-use software tools such as Statistical Programming Social Sciences (SPSS) might look with scorn on these earliest attempts at segmentation, at the time such approaches were perceived as adequate for achieving the stated task of evolving more customer-specific market propositions. In addition given the requirement that marketers usually expect market research to be cost effective, in the 1960s many market researchers were expected to rely upon existing low cost syndicated data-bases as their information source when undertaking *cluster analysis*. Additionally it is necessary to admit that academic researchers were not really able to offer significant guidance to the commercial sector about how to undertake effective segmentation exercises. Instead the academic community tended to restrict their advice to generalisations such as 'segments must be measurable, substantial and actionable' (Gibb and Simkin 1997).

Despite the tendency of some academics to be critical of standard normative clustering techniques using syndicated data, even today the approach can still generate meaningful information. This fact is demonstrated by the research undertaken by Giacobbe (1994) on segment identification in the US retail sector. Syndicated geo-demographic data describing variables such as income, occupation and education were extracted from a database containing 10,000 names and addresses from a sample frame covering a geographic area of two million residents. The cluster analysis revealed four natural clusters, namely: established wealthy people, mobile professionals, average middle-class and disadvantaged families. A subsequent analysis of different supermarket chains revealed which supermarkets were the most effective providers of retail services to the identified segments.

Experiental Knowledge Management

The academic literature describes a highly structured normative process whereby information on customers is acquired through research, extensive data analysis is undertaken and the output provides the basis for knowledge management decisions over market segmentation. Danneels (1996) undertook research, however, which raises questions about whether such normative models are always the basis of the market segmentation approach used by all companies.

The researcher interviewed retailers in the Belgian apparel industry. What emerged was that contrary to espoused theory that retailers should use empirical market research to divide the market into customer groups and then determine need by segment, respondents indicated that their approach was more likely to be based upon an intuitive perception of opportunity. Most of these retailers adopt a marketing approach based upon trial and error. When a shop is first opened, there is a tendency to offer a wide range of styles and brands. Product lines are then adjusted on the basis of trading experience in which in-store observation of customer behaviour leads to the generation of knowledge about the nature of different customer segments.

It would appear that in the case of the Belgian apparel market, retailers have rejected a socio-demographic approach to customer group classification. Instead these retailers tended to perceive customers as fitting into different lifestyle groups using their own self-developed customer taxonomies. Additionally, the research also revealed that in large store groups, there is interaction between different departments and levels of management. In some cases, this pooling of knowledge led to a successful outcome but in other cases, political struggles between contributors of different views caused somewhat questionable segmentation decisions to be made.

The advent of low cost, computerised databases has permitted many firms to move beyond syndicated socio-economic databases and to undertake more complex internal analysis using accumulated customer records (*www. dssresearch.com*; *www.marketsegmentation.co.uk*). In the early 1990s most of the leading banks in the Western world began to use their customer files to examine whether usage clusters could be identified. These files contain both personal information provided when a customer first seeks a financial service and also data on their patterns of services purchased. In most cases these clusters can provide information on different purchase patterns and lifestyles. This knowledge can then be utilised to develop both segment-specific services and more highly targeted promotional campaigns.

Pechman (1994) has reviewed the research undertaken by banks and presents a disguised example of how cluster analysis revealed information which permitted the specification of the following customer segments within the credit card market:

1 **The uncommitted** who are new to using cards and tend to make relatively small purchases, usually because they are people who have low incomes.
2 **Convenience users** who use their card to make frequent purchases and normally pay off their outstanding balance at the end of every month.
3 **Starting out** is a group of young adults with lower than average incomes which only permit them to make moderate purchases with outstanding card balances often not paid off at the end of the month.
4 **Channel shoppers** are older people who exhibit low loan delinquency and incur few service charges even though they are quite heavy card users.
5 **Credit addicts** tend to be married with children, have above average incomes and are heavy card users.
6 **Cash driven** are relatively new card holders with moderate credit limits but because they rarely pay their outstanding balance at the end of each month, incur high interest charges.
7 **Borderline** are young people on low incomes who rarely use their cards.

In the face of growing evidence that in many markets demographic data could provide misleading results in segmentation studies (Bone 1991), researchers have suggested a number of alternative approaches for accurately segmenting markets. For example, Sorce et al. (1989) suggested that firms should incorporate lifestyle information into their analysis. This recommendation has been widely adopted by industry and the outcome is that *psychographic segmentation* is now perceived as one of the more accurate ways of extracting knowledge about customers using appropriate statistical techniques. One illustration of this approach is provided by Oates et al. (1996). In their study they combined psychographic variables with retail store attributes to determine whether there are differing market needs in older people's purchase of over-the-counter drugs. Cluster analysis revealed five clusters, namely:

1   Family orientated.
2   Young and secure.
3   Active retirees.
4   Self-reliants.
5   Quiet introverts.

Analysis of each group's views about various store attributes revealed that the five segments do have varying needs concerning the optimal provision of retail services by pharmacies.

Another approach to segmentation which has been made possible by the development of low cost software is *benefit analysis* (Green et al. 2000). The approach assumes that customers have varied needs concerning the bundle of benefits sought from a specific product. Analysis can reveal variation between which benefits are sought and the relative importance of different benefits. This knowledge can contribute to the identification of potential segments. The approach is made feasible through a development in mathematical psychological tools known as conjoint analysis. By the application of various algorithms the researcher can develop cardinal scales for assessing the contribution which each benefit item makes to overall customer satisfaction. Having used conjoint analysis to identify potential clusters, the researcher can utilise discriminant function analysis to model the interaction between identified benefit bundles.

A further approach to segmentation made possible by lower cost software is *dual-objective segmentation* (DOS) (Forsyth et al. 1997). A key advantage of the technique is that unlike some clustering models which define segments that have insufficient commercial potential, DOS is a modelling tool designed to identify financially viable clusters. The start point in the analysis is to ask customers to determine scores for an available range of product benefits and attributes. Data are then modelled using discriminant function analysis. Following visual inspection of the data, which usually reveals a number of non-viable clusters, the analyst reruns the DOS process using a software algorithm which makes tiny changes in the segmentation system by reclassifying customers on the periphery of one segment into another segment. Correlation analysis is utilised to confirm that the revised classification is statistically valid.

Segmentation in Practice

Any successful knowledge management project, whether involving marketing or another functional area of management, depends upon the analysts concerned being able to effectively and accurately interpret available information. In a review of the processes associated with the utilisation of customer data as the basis for informing the marketing process, Jenkins and McDonald (1997) utilised a series of case studies to examine potential differences between conceptual theory and actual outcomes. In the case of British Airways they concluded that internal organisational pressures to fill capacity, plus the strong, delegated decision-making power of territory managers around the world, meant that any attempt by the company's marketers to fulfil the needs of different customer segments was never a feasible aspiration.

In the case of a fertiliser company Brunner Mond Ltd (*www.brunnermond.com*), there was information exchange between product managers and the manufacturing operation. Unfortunately due to both pressures to maximise manufacturing output and the orientation towards the product not the customer among the product teams, again viable market management strategies to improve performance by adopting a more focused, segmentation orientation never emerged.

On the basis of these materials, Jenkins and McDonald concluded that internal organisational structures when linked to the attitudes and beliefs of key employees are often a barrier to the effective utilisation of available information to meet the needs of different customer segments. They posit that in the real world one can expect to encounter four different approaches to segmentation.

Sales-based segmentation occurs when sales areas or sales force structures are the basis of the segmentation decision. In most cases this internal, sales management-based perception bears no resemblance to the real customer needs which exist across clusters within the marketplace. *Structural segmentation* is encountered where the manufacturing priorities and marketing department structure are the key influencers in determining operational decisions. Here again the actual needs of customer groups is subservient to internal organisational values. *Bolt-on segmentation* occurs when the firm has access to external data, but the marketing department ignores the fact that the nature of this information (for example, demographic data) does not provide a realistic basis upon which to base a system for accurately determining differing customer needs.

Jenkins and McDonald conclude that the only effective approach is that which they refer to as *strategic segmentation*. Firms adopting this latter approach are market-driven, utilise effective external data sources and organisational processes are orientated to delivering outstanding value to all of the different segments served by the organisation.

[handwritten margin notes: a popular today's market, e.g. luxury products]

NICHE MARKETING

A *niche* (or *micro-segment*) is a very small group of customers who have very specific product needs. To service a niche the successful firm will usually be required to be able to undertake specialist technical operations in the production of output and execute very focused marketing tasks. Success is often dependent upon the fact that within the niche the firm is the sole supplier of the product or services.

Traditionally niche marketing is the strategy adopted by small firms seeking to avoid confrontations with large, national brands. In some cases these small firms have been able to enter a market niche because it contains a group of customers whose needs are being ignored by larger firms. For example some consumers only want to purchase extremely fresh vegetables and fruit. No supermarket distribution system can really cost effectively satisfy this type of market need, thereby leaving a market gap available to small farms or horticulturists to open a 'farm gate', 'pick your own', retail outlet.

In the case of many small businesses, niche identification is an intuitive decision made by the company founder based upon tacit knowledge acquired by observing a market scenario or having spent many years working for a large firm in a specific industrial sector (Chaston 1999a). A significant proportion of small firm niche players continue to exist for many years servicing the specialist requirements of a specific customer group. In some cases this is because the lifestyle aspirations of the owner/manager are such that he or she is adverse to further expansion of the business operation.

Red Mills Ltd

Exceptions to any marketing theory generalisations can always be found. One is provided by the UK snack maker Red Mills Ltd (*Grocer* 1996). The company's origins were in the provision of low cost snacks for children. Although there are some very large mass marketers operating in the UK snack market (for example, KP and Golden Wonder), these companies have ignored the opportunity to use extrusion technology to generate different shapes, textures and flavours. Red Mills is geared up to make small runs of specialist snacks aimed at specific niches within the children's sector of the snack market. In many cases the firm uses character licences of cartoon characters such as Spiderman to create immediate market identity for a new product. Although a niche player, the contribution made by the diverse range of niche products means that the firm is the fourth largest snack food producer in the UK.

In a few exceptional cases, what started life as a niche player can sometimes subsequently become the world leader specifying the standard for an entire industrial sector. One such example of this outcome is Microsoft. As a small niche player in the software industry, the owner Bill Gates might have had the prophetic vision of a computer on every desk and every home. Nevertheless back in 1975 eventually being a significant contributor to achieving this aim must have seemed a daunting task to Microsoft's founder, even in his most optimistic of moods. What made the difference is the fortuitous piece of luck that IBM was desperately seeking an operating system for its new PC product and contracted with Microsoft, which developed MS-DOS. The revenue flow from this contract provided the foundation stone upon which to build the global empire.

Even though the computer industry now tends to be dominated by some very large companies such as IBM, Microsoft and Oracle, there are still niche opportunities available to smaller specialist developers (Synder 1994). As in the world of fmcg marketing, the specialist computer firm usually has the technical knowledge capability to satisfy an area either ignored or not understood by the larger players. Certainly this has been the case in the world of accounting software where firms such as Intuit and Peachtree not only established successful niches, but have been sufficiently competent to beat off attacks by firms such as Microsoft.

Worrying about possible retaliation from a larger competitor should not always be the basis of fear for the small successful niche player. The alternative solution to responding to such a threat is to sell the business to the competitor so worries about a future decline in revenue are wiped out in an instant. One example of this strategy was the decision by Lotus to permit themselves to be acquired by IBM.

In considering whether to sell the business to the competition instead of trying to carry on alone, the niche player should be aware that their software solution may not survive for too many years. This risk does provide another good reason for selling instead of staying and fighting. An example of this scenario is Da Vinci Systems which sold its WordPerfect word processing package to Novell. This latter company also purchased the spreadsheet product Quattro Pro from Borland. Unfortunately due to Microsoft's ability to dominate these markets, over the long term neither of these acquisitions proved to be a very wise move.

From Knowledge to Niche

During the Chinese Cultural Revolution James Zhou, then aged six, was rescued by Chinese Taoists and taught philosophy including the use of medicinal herbs (Dinar 2001). After the Cultural Revolution he was able to enter university to study for a BSc in agriculture and an MSc in plant genetics. He then moved to America to continue his studies for a PhD in biochemistry followed by work as a Research Fellow at Yale. During his time at Yale he undertook studies on anti-cancer and anti-viral drugs. Then in 1996 he was offered financial support to combine his knowledge of conventional and herbal medicine to create Herbsway Laboratories in Wallingford Connecticut.

The company combines herbal extracts to manufacture concentrated herbal teas for a wide spectrum of health benefits. Zhou is exploiting over 10,000 years of Chinese knowledge which believes that different combinations of herbs can be more effective than a formulation based upon a single plant. In developing new products for the herbal tea niche market in the US, he uses his knowledge of Western technologies to permit accurate testing and assessment of each formulation. The company offers 26 varieties of tea concentrate aimed at treating specific disorders. Products include a liver-enhancer that helps balance the immune system, a tea that provides a high level of polyphenols which can help balance cholesterol levels and a natural sugar substitute which has no aftertaste or calories. All the herbs for Herbsway's products are grown organically in the Chinese village where Zhou was born.

MARKETING STYLE

After the Second World War, as Europe and many areas of the Pacific Rim struggled to rebuild their war devastated economies, the American GI returned home to a nation eagerly ready to adopt the mantle of being the leading economic power for the balance of the twentieth century. The expertise and wealth accumulated through acting as the manufacturing hub for the Allied Powers' military materials during the war was immediately directed towards the creation of what subsequently has become known as the American Dream. The post-war growth of the American economy, fuelled by rapidly rising consumer spending power, provided the platform for the subsequent global expansion of firms such as Coca-Cola (*www.cocacola.com*), McDonalds (*www.mcdonalds.com*) and Levi Strauss (*www.levistrauss.com*).

Some management theorists seeking to understand the success of such firms concluded that performance could be linked to the adoption of a business philosophy which assumes marketing is a process concerned with the management of effective transactions. *Transactional marketing* using an understanding of buyer needs to evolve processes for optimising the transactions that occur between supplier and customer was presented as superior to the more traditional industrial model of constructing a plant to produce products and then seeking sufficient customers to purchase all available output.

The founding fathers of twentieth-century marketing such as McCarthy and Kotler were clearly influenced by the classicist view of management. They proposed that the entry point in the transaction management process is to execute a detailed study of both the internal and external environments confronting the organisation. This knowledge then permits definition of future performance goals, the strategy through which to achieve these goals and the elements of the plan necessary for underpinning adopted strategy. Delivery of the plan to generate market transactions is achieved by utilising the marketing mix, frequently known as the *4Ps* (product, price, promotion and place). The proven durability of the concept is demonstrated by the fact that it is the rationale underpinning the brand management organisational structure which is still in use today within successful organisations such as Nestlé (*www.nestle.com*) and General Foods (*www.kraft.com*).

The basic theories of transactional marketing were initially evolved through studies of the battle for market share between major brands in US consumer, tangible goods markets such as detergents and coffee. Researchers in the 1970s and 1980s seeking to validate the benefits of classical theories of marketing management in other situations such as industrial and/or service markets, however, have often encountered severe difficulties in locating evidence that classical marketing concepts are widely accepted by managers within these latter industrial sectors. Initially the apparent absence of a strategic market orientation was often attributed to this being a reflection of the inadequacies of managers who failed to appreciate the benefits of a structured, formalised approach to marketing centred around the formal acquisition of information that could provide the knowledge needed by the marketing department to orchestrate the customer transaction and satisfaction processes.

In the Nordic countries, however, a 'grounded theory' approach of avoiding preconceived hypotheses of management process, observing actual events and seeking convergence in practice has led to identification of alternative marketing models. Pioneering work by the Industrial Marketing and Procurement (IMP) Group proved that firms in many industrial markets, instead of seeking to build market share through emphasis on using knowledge to enter into intensive head-to-head confrontations with other brands, are often orientated towards the concept of acquiring information that can be used to enter into interfirm co-operation. The aim of such co-operation is to build long term relationships based upon trust and commitment.

Writers such as Nystrom (1990) posit that the classical school of marketing is based upon the economic transactionalist theory of the firm in which well defined products are made available in a market where both supplier and customer are fully informed about the relative merits of competing offerings. He argues that classical marketing is founded on the assumption that access to information permits the customers to make a rational choice based upon a comparison of benefits offered by competing firms. Furthermore he feels that classical marketing incorrectly assumes buyers are passive, reactive users who are not interested in any form of interaction with the supplier.

However, studies of the marketing process in service sectors such as finance and retailing have often revealed situations where customers do not exhibit a strong transactional orientated buying behaviour. This situation has thereby permitted supplier firms to exploit opportunities for using information interchange with customers as the basis for evolving the knowledge required to build long term relationships based on working in close partnership with purchasers. In manufacturing environments, a move towards closer customer–supplier relationships has been assisted by the managerial philosophies of total quality management (TQM) and JIT.

TQM is an organisational commitment to exploit information as the basis for fulfilling the customers' expectations over product and/or service quality. Clearly a large OEM such as IBM or Xerox can only fulfil customer expectations if their suppliers have the knowledge necessary to be able to deliver high quality components. For this to be achieved, both the suppliers and the OEM have to move away from the traditional, information poor, price-based, confrontational negotiation style towards an information rich, relationship orientated style based upon respect for each others' contribution to achieving the mutual goal of optimising product quality.

JIT is a concept based upon exploiting knowledge to find ways of reducing finished goods and work-in-progress by moving away from the traditional concept of long production runs of single items determined by an economic order quantity (EOQ) formula towards a highly responsive, batch-type manufacturing system based on matching production schedules to recently received customer orders. Although as with any concept actual achievement tends to be less than stated aspiration, for firms such as Hewlett Packard, by the application of knowledge management they have used JIT to reduce inventory levels significantly and concurrently enhance the firm's image as being able to offer a rapid, flexible response to changing customer needs. Similar to TQM, however, for JIT to be successful, the OEM must create a close, information-rich, working relationship with suppliers in order to implement concepts such as same day delivery, willingness to come onto the shop floor to manage restocking of component bins and automated invoice generation using electronic data interchange (EDI) systems.

During the 1970s and 1980s there was a massive expansion in companies dedicated to the provision of services in sectors as diverse as finance, fast food and management consultancy. Marketers hired by these organisations encountered significant problems when attempting to apply classical concepts such as influencing customer demand through application of the 4Ps to generate customer transactions. The conclusion of both practitioners and academics was that because of features such as the intangible nature of goods, difficulty in separating production from consumption and the heterogeneous nature of customer needs, effective service marketing would require the evolution of new paradigms.

Similar to the marketer in industrial markets, many service marketing theorists focused on the fact that firms which were placing emphasis on single transactions should in fact be attempting to build long term relationships with customers. A strong impetus to this alternative philosophy was provided by Reichfeld and Sasser (1990) who demonstrated that a transaction orientation could result in focusing excessive resources on attracting new customers when in fact the real benefits of marketing come from programmes directed at using knowledge as the basis for understanding how to retain existing customers (or in their terminology ensuring achievement of 'zero defections').

As a result of studies of the marketing processes employed by both industrial and service firms, a new school of thought has emerged which examines how the firm can orchestrate information, internal resources and processes in a knowledge orientated approach to create and sustain customer loyalty. Collectively this new orientation, which has both American (Berry 1982) and Nordic (Gummesson 1987) roots, is known as *relationship marketing*. Supporters of this new form of marketing argue that in order to survive in markets which have become more competitive and more turbulent, organisations must move away from managing transactions and instead focus on using information as the basis for building long lasting customer relationships (Webster 1992).

Some disciples of the new marketing have suggested that traditional transactionally orientated marketing concepts based around the approach of focusing resources on the 4Ps, which may have been appropriate in North American consumer branded goods markets of the 1950s and 1960s, are no longer relevant in today's world. Gronroos (1994), for example, proposes that 'the usefulness of the 4Ps as a general theory for practical purposes is, to say the least, highly questionable'. A somewhat less extreme position, however, has been proposed by writers such as Chaston (1999a). This alternative view is that firms should adopt a segmentation philosophy ranging from building strong relationships with key customers through to continuing to utilise the traditional 4Ps approach for those customers seeking a standardised, generic product proposition. A similarly balanced view was earlier presented by Anderson and Narus (1991) who recommend that firms weigh both customer orientation towards closer relationships and the cost/benefit implications of acquiring and utilising information to sustain close relationships when selecting the most appropriate strategy to suit prevailing market conditions.

Academics no doubt will continue to debate the relative merits of transactional versus relationship marketing. In fact the advent of the internet and e-business seems to have added more 'petrol to the flames' (Chaston 2000b). Perhaps what should be perceived as more important than the style issue is the way information is utilised by marketers. The reality in both the terrestrial and on-line world is that the vast bulk of acquired information is of a historical nature and is utilised to evolve reactive responses to market opportunities. For the firm which aspires to 'own the future', this reactive approach must be replaced with one where information provides the basis for knowledge management systems which support the firm in the evolution of proactive marketing strategies. Possibly one of the most exciting aspects of e-business is that by coupling incoming, real-time customer data with artificial intelligence (AI) engines, the marketer is now able to aspire to executing a marketing philosophy which proactively identifies opportunities and permits the firm to be a 'first mover' in launching products and services even more capable of satisfying customer demands.

ONE-TO ONE MARKETING

In capital goods industrial markets (for example, office block construction, production line automation) the marketer has always adopted the philosophy that every customer has a unique benefit requirement which demands a unique customisation of the product or service package that will be delivered. For many years, any aspirations of consumer goods firms to adopt a similar philosophy were frustrated by the massive cost implications associated with both acquiring appropriate knowledge about each individual customer and then manufacturing one off products.

In 1993, Pine raised questions about the continuing popularity of mass marketing and proposed that more attention should be given to the idea of product or service customisation. He proposed the following five stage process progression that would permit a firm to shift from producing standardised goods to making available customised products:

1 Customise services around a standard product.
2 Develop unique customer services on products that the customer can self adapt to fulfil their own individual needs.
3 Move production nearer to the customer to permit point-of-delivery customisation.
4 Develop rapid response capability.
5 Modularise components to permit customisation of products and services.

The reason that Pine was able to articulate this apparently revolutionary approach to marketing was that during the 1980s and early 1990s companies had been acquiring the knowledge necessary to execute his recommended actions. The two key areas of acquired knowledge were in manufacturing technology and computer-based information management systems. An early stimulus to changing capabilities in manufacturing was the acceptance of TQM, where knowledge was acquired which permits new techniques capable of supporting zero defect production levels. This innovation was then followed by JIT, which focused on ways of acquiring the knowledge of how to minimise operating costs by reducing raw materials, work-in-progress and finished goods inventory levels.

Once companies began to acquire JIT knowledge they soon realised that it might eventually be feasible to operate the ultimate form of JIT, namely production not being scheduled until an order has been received from the customer. Furthermore by exploiting the flexibility and rapid response times permitted through computer-based automation of production lines these same firms acquired the knowledge of how to use 'lean manufacturing' to produce a wide diversity of product forms during a single factory shift.

One of the first firms to exploit this manufacturing concept was Dell Computing (*The Economist* 2001). The company restricts its basic computer to a limited number of hardware modules. Effective management of the supply chain ensures these are supplied on a flexible, responsive basis by the company's suppliers. These modules can be assembled in 4 minutes and a further 90 minutes are required to load the specific software required to satisfy the operating specification defined by the individual customer. The knowledge which the firm has acquired in developing this customisation concept permits it to support an order-to-delivery cycle of only three days.

Achieving a similar flexible, customised, 'build-to-order' capability in more traditional industries is proving a little more difficult. In Europe, for example, some 40 car companies and their parts suppliers are engaged in the '3DayCar' project. At the outset the order-to-delivery cycle was 60 days. Interestingly the first phase of the project revealed actual production takes two days and then five days for delivery from the factory to the dealer. The balance of the time is taken up by paperwork, scheduling parts deliveries and finding a free space in the manufacturing process. Knowledge management approaches have contributed to reducing these time lags drastically with some car makers now achieving a 14 day order-to-delivery cycle. At the moment one of the biggest hurdles to further time reduction is the bottleneck caused by the paint shop. Changing from one colour to another is so difficult that most manufacturers still tend to make large batches at a time of cars with the same colour.

While engineering knowledge workers were striving to build successful lean manufacturing facilities, people in the IT industry were experimenting with reducing the costs associated with acquiring, storing and accessing information about individual customers. One key stimulus was firms such as Oracle developing extremely powerful, programmable relationship database software. Concurrently the move by consumers to using credit cards and the advent of scanners in retail stores reading universal product codes (or bar codes) gave firms access to information on the buying behaviour of individual customers. Further data sets were generated as more consumers opted to contact telephone call centres to purchase goods or services directly from suppliers such as mail order companies, banks and airlines. By combining data processing capability with a wealth of new data, large companies were placed in a position to develop a very detailed understanding of the needs and behaviour patterns of individual customers.

The final foundation stone in the creation of consumer market customisation (or one-to-one marketing) was laid by the launch of the internet in the mid-1990s. When customers began to log on to order goods they were asked to provide detailed information about themselves. It did not take long before new software systems began to read this information and offer the supplier an ability to make a customised response next time the customer came back on-line. One early example of this form of one-to-one marketing was provided by Amazon.com which used the customer's purchase as the basis for subsequently recommending other books that the customer might also like to read.

Customised Printing

An early example of customisation through new technology is provided by the printing industry (Fultz 1999). Traditionally colour printing used offset presses and due to the economies of scale, small print runs were prohibitively expensive. This situation was dramatically altered following the arrival of variable data, digital colour printing. Companies such as Indigo, IBM, Xeikon, Xerox and Agfa have developed printers that accept digital files, process and produce the final product. The printers do not require film. Hence all of the costly, time-consuming activities associated with generating colour proofs when using offset presses are abolished forever. The result is print-on-demand at low cost. This permits the marketer to producing short runs of customised promotional materials.

Possible opportunities could include a mail catalogue specifically designed to communicate only those products known to be of interest to the customer. One example of this type of creative opportunity is provided by Agfa seeking to invite advertising agency executives to a breakfast meeting. Using variable data digital printing they sent out a colour invitation in which they personalised a bowl of Alph Bits cereal so that the executive's name was floating in the spoon.

Another example is provided by Novartis Seeds based in Minnesota. This company had already built a database of farmers who used their seed. They then developed a direct mailing campaign that linked more than 90 fields of variable information extracted from their customer database. These data were used to create product descriptions using customer purchasing histories plus additional information concerning location and growing conditions. This brochure, along with a totally personalised letter, was sent to the seed distributor located nearest to each of their farm customers.

The Advent of E-commerce

CHAPTER SUMMARY

The advent of the internet has revolutionised knowledge management practices. The economics of e-commerce were initially seen as favouring the reduction in price of goods and services traded on-line. More recently firms have come to realise that knowledge accumulated from on-line sources can be used to build stronger relationships with customers. This knowledge also permits the creation of new forms of competitive advantage which permits organisations to be able to avoid on-line price wars. The largest sector of e-commerce is found in B2B markets. This is because industrial firms are using on-line knowledge to create faster responding, more flexible supply chain operations. The internet uses a diverse range of technologies but the core of the process is the storage and reaccessing of knowledge using relationship databases. More recently on-line systems have become automated which further enhances firms' speed of response to customers' need for knowledge, goods and services.

INTRODUCTION

In 1969, the Pentagon's Advanced Research Projects Agency specified the modest aim of wishing to allow scientists and engineers working on military contracts across America to share their knowledge about computers and software systems. The solution, known as ARPANET, required finding a way of communicating information in the form of small packets which could travel independently of each other along a telephone line. The final version of ARPANET offered the added advantage that since there was no direct link between the participating computers, the calling party only had to pay for the first packet switch. In most cases this was the cost of a local telephone call.

By the end of the Cold War ARPANET was in widespread usage in the US academic community. In 1991, the National Science Foundation was assigned the responsibility for opening up the system, renamed NSFNET, to the general public. The NSFNET system is the main backbone of what most of us now know as the world wide web or internet. At the beginning of the 1990s, few people had ever heard of the web or internet. More significantly, even fewer people realised the potential impact that the technology was likely to have on the way the world would be doing business and managing knowledge by the end of the millennium.

The internet as we know it today consists of small area networks belonging to individual organisations (local area networks or LANs), networks spread across large geographic areas (wide area networks or WANs) and individual computers. To connect to the internet, a computer or network uses the transmission control protocol/internet protocol (TCP/IP) protocol. Within the internet there are more networks. These include backbone networks (for example, the NFSNET system), commercial networks (which are businesses with direct links to the internet), service providers which offer smaller firms an internet connection, non-commercial networks belonging to educational/research organisations and gateway networks which provide their subscribers access to the internet (for example, America Online or Compuserve) (Gielgud 1998).

Most internet sites have an address or 'domain name' that performs a role similar to a telephone number for individuals wishing to reach a site. Transfer of information uses file transfer protocol (FTP). These files can contain images, video clips, sound recordings, text or graphics. When a person reaches a site, they encounter an on-line menu or gopher. The world wide web can best be described as a gopher in disguise: the menu has been made more visually interesting by the addition of graphics, pictures and even sound.

Although in the popular press emphasis tends to be given to the world wide web, it is critical to recognise that exploiting this new technology goes way beyond just putting a brochure on-line. Essentially what is happening on a global scale is that technologies such as telecommunications, satellite broadcast, digital television and computing are on a convergence path. As a result of this convergence, the world is being offered a more flexible, more rapid and extremely low cost way of exchanging information. The advent of such high speed communication clearly has significant implications for assisting the evolution and exploitation of knowledge management systems.

When discussing this new technology, it is safer not to restrict any assessment of opportunity to the role the internet. Instead one should expand the debate to cover all aspects of information interchange as the basis for evolving more effective approaches to managing knowledge. This is increasingly being recognised by commercial organisations which are now moving to exploit the huge diversity of opportunities now offered by e-business. Seybold and Marshak (1998) support the idea that firms should extend their thinking beyond the internet to encompass all of the platforms which permit a firm to do business electronically. They propose that electronic business involves applying a wide range of technologies to streamline information interchange and support knowledge acquisition. Examples of information exchange technologies include the internet, EDI, e-mail, electronic payment systems, advanced telephone systems, handheld digital appliances such as mobile telephones, interactive televisions, self-service kiosks and smart cards.

Once a company decides to embrace e-business as a path through which to exploit new, entrepreneurial opportunities, then an immediate outcome is that the organisation's knowledge platform becomes much more closely linked with other knowledge sources elsewhere within the market system such as suppliers and customers (Seybold and Marshak 1998). The reason why this occurs is that once buyers and sellers become electronically linked, the volume of data interchange dramatically increases as trading activities begin to occur in real time. The outcome is the emergence of very dynamic, rapid responses to changing circumstances by both customers and suppliers within market systems.

The degree to which e-business is likely to change the way organisations operate in the future is effectively illustrated by Arthur Andersen's 1999 research project on e-commerce trends in Europe. From this study the consulting firm has proposed the following 'five basic truths':

1 **New structures**. In the past, firms have sought to be self-reliant by maximising their ownership of all aspects of the knowledge required to implement their role within their supply chain such as procurement, design, selling and distribution. The speed with which information and decisions can now be made using e-commerce means that in many cases, costs can be saved and flexibility of response enhanced by sharing knowledge to support the outsourcing of those activities that can be done more cost effectively by others (for example, handing procurement to a sector buying consortium; marketing their goods by being featured in an electronic shopping mall).

2 **Value within the firm**. In the past firms measured success by the value of their physical assets such as land and buildings. Although the financial markets have always recognised that intangibles such as company reputation and brand names have value, analysts have tended to use the fixed assets in the balance sheet to actually value firms. In a rapidly changing world, however, physical assets can be a barrier to restructuring a firm rapidly and/or adopting a different, more flexible response to emerging new market opportunities. As a result there is growing support for the idea that the real value of the firm in the next millennium will be based on the knowledge resources and technological skills of the employees.

3 **Zero cost expansion**. In traditional manufacturing industries to expand the business usually requires new investment to build additional production capacity. The world of knowledge management follows a very different path. For as demonstrated by the computer software sector,

once the initial investment in product development has been made, ongoing costs to support market expansion are almost zero. All you have to do is take some money out of petty cash and copy some more CD-ROMs from your master disc.

4   **Price**. Economists often talk about their theory of perfect markets in which price equilibrium is rapidly achieved because both customers and suppliers have access to perfect knowledge. Through on-line services that offer price comparisons and on-line auctions the world of perfect knowledge may now have almost arrived. The outcome will be that firms will find it increasingly difficult to retain control over market prices because this power will shift into the hands of the customer.

5   **Instant Delivery**. The ability to link all aspects of business, from ordering materials from suppliers through to shipping goods automatically to customers, means that the e-commerce supply chain is one where actions will not be delayed because employees lack the necessary knowledge to interact effectively with each other. Those firms that fail to create integrated electronic communication channels and undertake some actions off-line (for example, manually checking customer credit before accepting an order) will soon find they are being overtaken by competitors who have invested in electronic technology to store the knowledge required that can permit an instant response to a customer's enquiry.

E-COMMERCE ECONOMICS

In comprehending the potential impact of e-commerce on the world economy, one should recognise that the technology has the ability to cut costs, increase competition and improve the functioning of price mechanisms in many markets (*The Economist* 2000b). As such it may bring the world closer to the textbook definition of perfect competition in which there is abundant information, zero transaction costs and no barriers to entry. Although it is as yet hard to test such theories, certainly some products (for example, books and CDs) seem to support the concept of markets moving towards a perfect competition model with a resultant major decline in market prices.

In business-to-business (B2B) markets the internet is also impacting operating costs. Procurement costs are falling because firms can rapidly acquire the knowledge required to locate the cheapest supplier and concurrently, by moving procurement on-line, dramatically reduce transaction costs (Goss 2001). There is also evidence to suggest that supply chain management is being made more efficient because automated on-line purchasing linked to databases for electronically managing the restocking process is permitting firms to reduce inventory holding costs significantly. Goldman Sachs has estimated, for example, that in the electronics components industry these factors have already contributed to generating procurement savings of up to 40%. British Telecom estimates that on-line procurement has reduced their average cost of processing transactions by 90%.

Litan and Rivlin (2001) concluded that the advent of improved knowledge exchange made possible by the internet is reflected in both cost savings and growth in organisational productivity. They point to the fact that for industries such as the airlines, where speed of information exchange can impact both marketing and distribution costs, e-commerce has possibly reduced operating costs by at least 10%. The impact on supply chain economics is illustrated by Bristol-Myers-Squibb where the company decided that improved knowledge flows between partners could reduce inventories and improve customer service/order cycles. The company estimates that the introduction of a web-based knowledge exchange system has reduced operating costs by approximately $90 million. Greater knowledge of market conditions can also lead to increased competition within supply chains, which can drive down prices. It is estimated, for example, that the advent of on-line travel agencies has caused average commission costs to fall from 10% down to 5%, which represents an annual saving to customers in the region of $20 billion.

MARKET TRENDS

The scale of market opportunity which e-commerce represents is dramatically illustrated by a research project commissioned by the American Corporation Cisco Systems and undertaken by the University of Texas (Internet Indicators 1999). The researchers concluded that within the US economy during 1999, e-commerce generated an annual revenue of $332 billion and supported almost 1,400,000 jobs. These figures are made more dramatic if one realises that these US internet-based revenues cause the sector by itself to be one of the top 20 economies in the world, ranked almost equal to the entire GDP of Switzerland. These data also revealed that although the world wide web was only launched in the late 1990s, in terms of total market size e-commerce already rivals well established sectors such as energy, cars and telecommunications.

The Cambridge, Massachusetts market research company Forrester Research Inc. has now forecasted that by 2004 annual worldwide, on-line retail sales will reach $184 billion (*www.forrester.com*). This figure is dwarfed, however, by their estimates for business-to-business markets where annual revenues have already reached $109.3 billion and by 2004 are projected to hit $1.3 trillion.

Back in the mid-1990s some of the strongest supporters of the internet were entrepreneurs from the small business community. They were attracted by the concept that anybody could enter the world of cyberspace trading through the simple action of making a small investment in the creation of a web site. Entrepreneurs were also enthusiastic about the fact that not only are on-line business start-up costs extremely reasonable, the new company would be in a position to generate sales from any country in the world where potential customers had access to a PC. By the late 1990s a vast array of new e-commerce concepts had been launched around the world. Possibly the most well known example is the American on-line bookstore Amazon.com.

As venture capital companies began to perceive the scale of the commercial potential for the new technology, some e-commerce start-ups went public with the sale of their shares resulting in their business founders becoming millionaires overnight. What many of the new e-entrepreneurs and their investors seemed to have ignored, however, is a trading rule which has been understood by small businesses for hundreds of years, namely if one does not rapidly attract sufficient customers, cash outflows will exceed revenues, the debt burden will mount and eventually bankruptcy will ensue. A dramatic illustration of this scenario has been provided by *www.boo.com*. With offices in Carnaby Street, London, the founder and ex-model Kajsa Leander had the vision of seeking to establish a global on-line sports clothing business. The company's plan was bold, with the intention of implementing a simultaneous launch across seven countries. To create this on-line operation required an initial massive investment in the design and implementation of a computer system able to handle the expected high volume of sales (Management Today 2000). This expenditure then had to be followed by a multi-million pound advertising campaign using traditional media such as television commercials to attract customers to the firm's web site. In May 2000 the company's backers in the financial community decided that there appeared to be little chance that revenues would ever exceed expenditure and the company was put into receivership. Similar failures have occurred in the home of the internet, the United States. The resultant degree of nervousness in the US financial markets was dramatically demonstrated in March 2000. Early in the month, the NASDAQ peaked at a record level 5,000 points and then within two weeks a 25% market drop had wiped millions off the quoted value of e-commerce corporations.

An increasingly important influence on share value trends is the recognition that new e-commerce firms face a very major obstacle when compared to their off-line counterparts, namely when establishing the new on-line venture they lack the trading knowledge which their terrestrial competitors have accumulated over many years. In addition these newcomers have to spend massive amounts of money (a) communicating knowledge of their product proposition and (b) building knowledge of their web site address. Although there is little solid evidence on the costs of building market awareness for a new e-commerce venture, a good indicator of the scale of the problem was provided by the Boston Consulting Group (1999). They concluded that in the year 2000, revenues to US retailers marketing goods on-line would exceed $36 billion, which represented a growth rate of 145 per cent for this sector of retailing. However, their study revealed that it is not the pure internet outlets like *www.Amazon.com* which are enjoying the real benefits of the internet because 62% of all on-line revenues are flowing to traditional retailers which have added a web site to their existing

47

shop-based operations. The reason for this trend is that a multi-channel retailer can attract new web customers at a much lower unit cost than their on-line only counterparts. It is estimated that the former are spending about \$22 per customer to attract visitors to their web site, whereas the latter are expending \$42 per site visitor.

The ability of long established firms to exploit their accumulated trading knowledge to enter and then succeed in on-line markets provides further evidence that ownership of cyberspace is rapidly shifting away from the e-commerce start-ups. In terms of both absolute turnover and profit the largest on-line trading successes are being enjoyed by firms such as Dell Computing, IBM, Oracle, Cisco, Intel and Microsoft. The same is true in most areas of the financial services sector, where the long established banks are now overtaking the new, upstart, purely on-line operations.

Less data are available on the small business market and currently it does seem that in this sector new e-commerce start-ups are still proliferating at a extremely rapid rate. Given, however, the investment they also will require to build an adequate customer base, it can be predicted confidently that here again over the next few years the more likely source of long term success will be those small firms which accumulated operational knowledge when linked to an established customer base, which will permit them successfully to add an on-line operation to compliment their existing terrestrial market activities.

The Benefits of Market Knowledge

In the case of internet banking, as in other sectors, it is apparent that e-commerce can lower operating costs and thereby enhance profitability (Goldfinger 2002). Furthermore evidence from another financial service sector, the securities brokerage industry, demonstrates that if reduced operational costs are reflected in lower prices, trading activity by existing and new clients will increase. The logic of lower prices offering a market expansion opportunity persuaded entrepreneurs in both the United States and Europe with knowledge of e-commerce technology to launch new on-line banks.

The apparently slow reaction of many existing terrestrial banks to respond immediately to the threat of these new market entrants caused some industry observers to conclude that major banks were either being extremely myopic or these organisations lacked the knowledge necessary to move into e-commerce. Subsequent events have shown, however, that the terrestrial banks had a greater understanding of their market than these new competitors who were only offering on-line services. The critical market knowledge held by the existing banks, acquired from years of trading terrestrially, is that unlike securities trading, demand elasticity for banking services is extremely low. Thus they understood that for many of their customers a minor reduction in bank charges or a slight increase in the interest paid on deposit accounts being offered by the on-line banks would not be considered significant enough to compensate for the perceived costs and risks associated with switching to a new bank. This scenario means that the real cost of launching an on-line banking operation is not the cost of technology, but the marketing costs associated with attracting customers. Thus the market incumbent with a large existing customer base has a major competitive advantage over any new entrant in the banking sector.

The outcome of having greater knowledge of customer behaviour meant that most terrestrial banks decided to let the new on-line operations expend the promotional funds necessary to introduce consumers to the idea of on-line banking. Only once an adequate level of market interest began to emerge did the terrestrial banks begin to offer service delivery via the internet as an alternative option to using their traditional physical branch networks to service customer needs. Furthermore the terrestrial banks also knew that given the low interest customers exhibit in switching allegiances to a new supplier, the major incremental revenue source is the successful cross-selling of new services. Hence unlike the new on-line banks which were forced to focus on customer attraction, the existing banks were able use the internet as a new medium for expanding their cross-selling activities.

THE BENEFITS OF THE INTERNET AND E-COMMERCE

The importance of existing firms to evolve an e-commerce strategy has been stressed by Eckman (1996). In his article he proposes that all organisations should pose the following questions: (a) does the internet change the target or scope of the market, (b) does the internet help satisfy customer needs and (c) will customers use the internet over the long term? One way of examining these issues is for each firm to examine which of the following benefits can be offered to customers through involvement in e-business:

1 **Convenience** in terms of being able to provide access 24 hours a day, 365 days a year. Furthermore in the case of consumer goods, the customer can avoid driving to a store, having to acquire knowledge by undertaking an in-store search and queuing at the checkout.
2 **Information** as the on-line user is assisted in the process of knowledge acquisition because the technology permits them to rapidly access detailed information about products, pricing and availability without leaving the home or the office.
3 **Less hassle** because customers can avoid having to negotiate and debate with sales staff when buying the product.
4 **Multimedia** which, through exploitation of the latest technology, enables customers to develop detailed knowledge about how their needs can be satisfied (for example, examining 3-D displays when selecting the best fabric design for a piece of furniture).
5 **New products and services** such as being offered knowledge management software tools when accessing on-line financial service providers (for example, in the stock brokering and banking sectors).

The internet also offers the following benefits to firms, namely:

1 **Lower costs** through actions such as replacing a terrestrial outlet with an electronic database which the customer can visit when seeking knowledge about products or services.
2 **Improved distribution** because once information-based products such as magazines or software are made available on-line, the company can achieve global knowledge distribution without having to invest in obtaining placements in terrestrial distribution channels.
3 **Reduced personal selling costs** because the role of the sales person as a provider of one-to-one knowledge can be replaced with an interactive web site.
4 **Relationship building** because via a web site the firm can acquire data on customers' purchase behaviour that can be used to establish a knowledge management system for guiding the development of new ways of delivering higher levels of customer service.
5 **Customised promotion** because unlike traditional media such as television or print advertising, the firm can develop communications materials on the web site designed to meet the specific knowledge requirements for small, select groups of customers.
6 **Rapid market response** because having recognised the need to respond to changing market situations at virtually the click of a button, the company can rapidly distribute knowledge about new products or terms and conditions of purchase to customers via the internet.
7 **New market opportunities** because e-commerce permits firms, at virtually no cost, to add new knowledge components to their product offering and thereby increase the perceived value of their products or services offering.

Some firms now recognise that the internet is a technological tool, the use of which in terms of being utilised for enhancing knowledge management practices will evolve and change as organisations gain more experience of trading in cyberspace. McGovern (1998) illustrated this evolutionary process in terms of 'e-commerce life cycles' in his analysis of how logistics and transportation services providers have implemented their e-commerce strategies. Initially many firms used the technology to provide general information about their firm on a web site as a mechanism for assisting customers to acquire new knowledge about available products and services. This was followed by using on-line marketing as a vehicle to provide customers with the knowledge necessary for evaluating the progress of their goods throughout each phase of the shipment process. The next evolutionary stage is typically that of offering on-line customised rate quotes. More recently this has been followed by the leading firms permitting customers to use an on-line knowledge-based marketing platform to manage more effectively every phase of the shipment process from order placement through to post-delivery resolution of service delivery problems.

Accelerating Supply Chain Knowledge Exchange

For almost 20 years firms have been focusing on how to optimise costs through the restructuring of the supply chains of which they are a member (Sharman 2002). A critical element in this process is to ensure the rapid and effective interchange of knowledge between companies within the supply chain. The advent of e-commerce has greatly simplified the sharing of knowledge such that firms can instantly acquire the information needed for planning and control of production capacity, scheduling, inventory control and distribution. Additionally in comparison with earlier technology such as EDI the costs of internet-based knowledge exchange are an order of magnitude lower.

An emerging trend in internet-based supply chain integration is the creation of multilateral knowledge exchange between networks of suppliers, manufacturers, distributors and end user customers. An example of this scenario is provided by the data networking division at Ericsson. This division outsources manufacturing to firms such as Solectron and Clestica and purchases high-demand components with variable lead times from numerous suppliers. End user customer satisfaction is critically dependent on partner synchronisation. Initially, however, partners were loath to share sufficient knowledge to help each other fulfil their respective commitments. To resolve the problem, Ericsson mandated the use of a common software platform that formed the basis of an electronic knowledge interchange system which enables partners to behave as if they were all members of a single organisation.

The internet can also be used to feed back customer demand information rapidly to members of a supply chain, thereby creating a more market driven system. In the United States a new company USBuild Inc has been created to assist the building industry. Large homebuilders know their material requirements some three to six months before they start a new construction project. USBuild's web-based knowledge exchange hub feeds this market data on future demand to materials suppliers. The company then orchestrates collection of materials, consolidates these materials into 'house kits' for specific projects at their cross-docking facility and undertakes JIT delivery to their customers' building sites.

PUTTING E-COMMERCE INTO CONTEXT

When managers first seek to understand how to exploit e-commerce, it is not unusual that both the apparent complexity of the technology and the diversity of alternative pathways through which their firm can enter the e-business world can overwhelm them. It seems useful, therefore, to attempt to synthesise exactly what is on offer from e-commerce. As illustrated in Figure 3.1, there are two dimensions of application available to an organisation. One is the role of e-commerce in assisting customers to acquire knowledge about issues such as price, product availability and delivery terms. The other dimension is the role of e-commerce in the provision of knowledge to support management of the purchase transaction.

As proposed in Figure 3.1, the degree to which a firm uses e-commerce to provide knowledge to assist the customer and/or support transactions

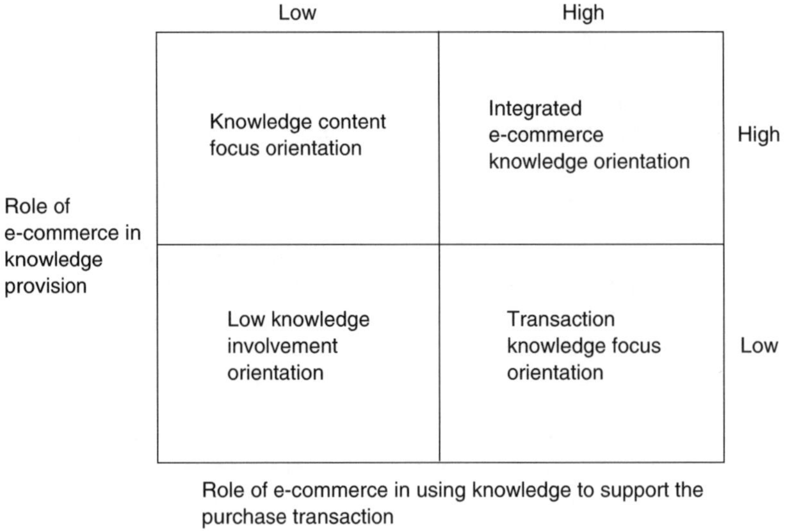

	Low	High	
	Knowledge content focus orientation	Integrated e-commerce knowledge orientation	High
Role of e-commerce in knowledge provision			
	Low knowledge involvement orientation	Transaction knowledge focus orientation	Low

Role of e-commerce in using knowledge to support the purchase transaction

FIGURE 3.1 AN E-COMMERCE ALTERNATIVE ORIENTATION MATRIX

can be classified as high or low. This taxonomy then yields four alternative choices. The organisation can opt to have low involvement in provision of support for both customers and transaction processes. For example many of the fmcg companies have created somewhat static web sites to communicate a limited degree of additional knowledge that can provide added promotional support for their products. Alternatively some organisations avoid using e-commerce to support any transactional activities and merely exploit the technology as a major element in the process of assisting customers more easily to acquire new knowledge. This approach has been taken by a number of firms in the publishing industry which have created free on-line versions of their newspapers and magazines.

A third alternative is to use e-commerce to assist transactions, but concurrently only offer a limited amount of new knowledge to the on-line customer. Typically this scenario will be found in industries where the knowledge sought by customers is extremely complex, but the product or service is simple to distribute electronically. A number of computer software houses have taken this approach in those cases where the primary customer contact point is dialogue with the supplier's technical sales force. Having determined the appropriateness of the software, the customer then orders on-line and in some cases also takes delivery via an electronic channel.

The last option in Figure 3.1 is high involvement in both provision of knowledge to assist the customer and to permit more effective tracking of the order–delivery cycle. UK on-line operations such as *www.thetrainline.com* and *www.lastminute.com* provide examples of this latter scenario. These firms only exist in cyberspace because they have no physical retail outlets that can be visited by their customers.

For the firm only just beginning to evolve an e-commerce marketing strategy, visiting sites such as Dell (*www.dell.com*) or American Airlines (*www.americanair.com*) can be somewhat depressing because clearly a massive investment will need to be made before one can ever aspire to match these 'e-commerce excellent' organisations. The first and possibly most critical point to make, however, is that the organisation should not throw away all the experience and knowledge which it has acquired from its terrestrial business operations over the years. The good news is that as we begin to observe e-commerce in operation, virtually all of the established guidelines about good marketing practice apparently still apply. Cross and Smith (1995) eloquently spelled out this concept in their 'Interactive Rules of the Road', namely:

1 Technology is merely a facilitator for a marketing strategy that focuses upon customer benefits.
2 The marketer must strive to balance the company's marketing objectives against the customers' needs and preferences.
3 Each technology-based programme should provide multiple benefits to the customer.

E-COMMERCE TECHNOLOGY

The original intention of the internet was to create a system to support e-mail and discussion groups. The first generation architecture permitted the distribution of words and pictures to remote locations over the internet. The two components required to support this system are a browser and a server (Harpin 2000). Communication between the browser and the server occurs when the user enters a web address (or URL). This request is sent in hypertext transfer protocol (HTTP) that tells the server where to locate a specific page within its directory structure. This page is written in the format of hypertext markup language (HTML) and allows the author to specify formats as well as links to other web pages on the internet. The server responds to the user's browser by returning the requested HTML page. This first generation internet system permitted the publication of static electronic documents and in terms of potential application merely allowed firms to passively make additional product or service information available to the customer. In 1995 the development of the common gateway interface (CGI) permitted the internet to support dynamic applications. The CGI standard allows browsers to submit a uniform resource locator (URL) request that instead of opening static pages launches an application located on a server. This development created the opportunity for the internet to return dynamic data, search databases, send e-mails and launch a whole range of applications. At this juncture the internet entered the age of being able to offer firms new opportunities to exploit knowledge management to support the marketing process.

Nevertheless CGI did have a significant limitation, namely the application had no memory of previous activity. This meant that the web site was left with no information about the user. The solution to this problem was the creation of 'cookies'. Launched by Netscape, the cookie is a small file created by the user's browser at the request of a CGI application. It allows a server to tell the browser to store information on the user's hard drive and to open up this information when the user again contacts the server. By creating 'memory of prior use', the cookie permits (a) the ability to maintain information across a multiple number of web pages, (b) recognition of the user identity which permits automatic site log-in and (c) the capability to store information about the user on the user's machine.

The advent of cookies caused concerns to be raised about internet security and web operators began to offer the facility for the user to disable the cookie mechanism. Additionally CGI applications were perceived as too slow to support high speed internet applications. To overcome these problems, third generation architecture was introduced known as the applications programme interface (API). This approach enables the server to store the profile and session information without having to resort to sending a cookie to the user's browser. Even more importantly, however, an API permits the use of object orientated frameworks and the ability to handle large numbers of users.

As the world of marketing attempted to learn the lessons needed to satisfy the needs of the on-line customers, an early issue which arose was the potential differences that might exist between a firm's terrestrial and cyberspace target customer group. In attempting to define on-line target audiences it was necessary for marketers to recognise that internet usage is continually changing as potential new customers experiment with what the internet has to offer (Lord 1999). For example early users tended to be highly educated males working in the computer industry. This has now changed with a much larger proportion of the general public moving on-line. Although there is still a bias towards higher income, higher social groups using the internet, within a short time it is likely that on-line demographics will converge with the general demographics of terrestrial buying populations. Nevertheless it must be recognised that for the foreseeable future the total on-line population size will remain much smaller than the terrestrial equivalent.

As the size of on-line populations rises and demographics begin to converge with that of terrestrial populations, the marketer can begin to pose the question: where is my target audience? Lord proposed one interesting segmentation model for the UK composed of the following groups:

1 The **Cybermum** is middle aged, with three teenage children and works in a caring profession. She enjoys using e-mail to communicate but still prefers reading magazines to obtain information.

2 The **Gameboy** is a teenager living at home who accesses the internet from home, at school and at cybercafés. He is deeply into playing on-line games.

3 The **Cyberlad** is in his twenties and uses the internet both at work and at home. He is single and his interests include girls and sport.

4 The **Hit 'n' Runner** is middle aged and has a successful career. Being career orientated these people access the internet at work but do not see the technology as a source of entertainment. They bank on-line and use the internet for purchases such as holidays.

5 The **Cybersec** works in a firm as a senior secretary. She is computer literate and originally accessed the internet as part of her job. She now uses the technology at home for sending e-mails and making on-line purchases.

6 The **Infojunky** is middle aged, married with children and is a middle level manager. They use the internet at work and at home, spending probably an excessive amount of time searching out new sources of information.

7 The **Net Sophisticate** is in his late twenties. He is verging upon being a 'techie' and probably still lives at home. Using the technology is a major component of his lifestyle.

In considering target market definitions, it may be worth noting the views of Baker and Baker (2000). They feel demographic specifications of on-line audiences are less effective in determining customer profiles than their proposed alternative, which they describe as 'vertical markets'. The vertical market is one which is highly definable and industry-specific. Examples might include healthcare, gardening, machine tools and computer software. The claimed advantage of the vertical market approach is that the web site can contain knowledge content specifically directed at helping individual customers solve specific problems. This means that the web site can then be customised to ensure information, merchandising, special offers and prices are of immediate appeal to each individual.

Vertical customers need fast response to their placement of orders and receipt of goods. Also they want access to detailed product information and customer support services. It is necessary to recognise that not all customers will want to purchase on-line, preferring merely to use the technology to obtain information. For these latter groups, the firm will need to (a) leave terrestrial selling systems in place and (b) consider how, by using the technology, customers can still immediately be put in contact with the firm's customer service staff. In many cases to achieve this goal the on-line system will need fast links to other intermediaries and end user outlets which work with the firm in the provision of products and services to customers.

From Knowledge to New Sales

In 1922, the United States Automobile Association began offering insurance polices to the US military community. In the late 1980s, USAA recognised that integrated IT systems would contribute to the more rapid generation of knowledge, which could be used to gain competitive advantage (Straub and Klein 2001). The advent of the internet was seen as offering the opportunity to acquire knowledge more rapidly about customers, which would further strengthen their core business. The company uses customer profile data to develop new products across its range of business operations. The banking division, for example, used knowledge obtained about boat insurance policies to develop a financial package for boat purchasers. The merchandise and buyer services group can access a customer's property loss data and can generate new revenues by suggesting that the company may be able to assist the client in the replacement of lost items.

It is also the case that if firms are willing to act as knowledge sources that can be used by customers this can strengthen customer loyalty, which eventually will lead to more sales revenue. This concept is recognised in the web site operated by MetLife Insurance Company. Visitors have the option of accessing pages about Metlife products and also a range of more general pages providing guidance on issues such as family welfare, health, money, business and insurance. People interested in family welfare can access a whole range of knowledge sources across subjects such as becoming a grandparent, becoming a parent, care for aged loved ones, choosing a summer camp or selecting child care sources.

WE STILL NEED PEOPLE

The appeal of the internet is that in theory if customers can be persuaded to order on-line this will dramatically lower a company's operating costs. Unfortunately there is growing evidence that where the customer requires detailed information in the formulation of their purchase decision, a machine-based response is perceived as inadequate. The solution to this problem is to seek ways of integrating computer-based and human interaction by offering access to both a web site and a call centre (Booth 1999). Clerical Medical, for example, has a web site for independent financial advisors who act as the intermediary in the selling of products. The advisor can click on a screen button that triggers an e-mail message to the firm's call centre.

Recognition of the ongoing importance of human intervention in e-commerce is causing some firms to relabel their call centres as 'customer contact centres'. These centres are evolving to provide the knowledge requested by customers by exploiting a whole range of electronic media such as the telephone, fax and the internet. Further opportunities to enhance knowledge provision will be achieved by utilising 'voice over IP' technology to create interactive television and video conferencing links with customers.

SERVING THE INTERNAL CUSTOMER

In many B2B service sector markets, the role of the supplier is to act as a source of professional knowledge. This role is performed by consultants, lawyers, accountants and bankers. The knowledge which they provide is very complex and for the moment, in most cases, unsuited for delivery to customers via an e-commerce channel (Chait 1999). This situation does not mean, however, that such organisations should not be active exploiting e-commerce technology. The reason for this situation is that their operations are based upon an individual specialist developing a client solution. Major revenue flows can only be generated if the knowledge solution is then utilised by others within the organisation.

The consulting sector recognised this business reality a long time ago. Unfortunately the obstacle confronting any attempt to operationalise knowledge sharing was frustrated by (a) the natural tendency of individuals to retain knowledge in a tacit form and (b) an inability to codify and store explicit knowledge in a form that was readily accessible by others such as staff based in other offices around the world. The latter problem has now been resolved because these organisations are using intranets, web systems and relational databases to store and distribute knowledge to wherever it is required.

An example of this philosophy is provided by the consulting firm Arthur D. Little which uses a web-enabled system to link together their 3,000 staff. To resolve the problems associated with converting tacit to explicit knowledge they implemented staff development programmes to convince everybody of the benefits which could accrue in using knowledge sharing to enhance the provision of services to their external clients. To support this activity two new managerial roles were created: the knowledge advocates, who are staff assigned the task of championing the benefits of knowledge management within the firm and the knowledge stewards, who are individuals with operational responsibility to ensure knowledge is codified, classified, stored and made accessible to others. Contained within the on-line system are data on clients, information on the skills of individual staff members, specification of consulting methodologies and problem solving tools.

AUTOMATING ON-LINE SYSTEMS

Managers seeking information on the design and operation of automated, knowledge management, e-commerce systems will soon find that the same large company examples such as Dell and Cisco seem to be featured in virtually every business magazine article and book. Repeated mention of the same company examples is no coincidence. It is a reflection of the fact that to-date, even in the large firm sector very few organisations have been successful in creating effective, totally integrated, automated knowledge management systems. One of the reasons underlying this situation is that even before considering a move into e-business firms need to exhibit all of the following attributes:

1 **Customer driven.** When using an automated information provision and purchasing system, frustrated customers can move to an alternative supplier at the 'click of a button'. Hence creating a customer friendly interface between the market and the organisation can only be achieved if the company has already developed a total commitment to delivering customer satisfaction. For it is only by being highly market orientated

that an organisation can acquire the in-depth understanding of customer needs that provides the template around which the e-commerce knowledge management system can be constructed.

2 **Long established commitment to JIT and TQM.** In both off-line and on-line markets the primary focus of marketing effort should be that of seeking to retain the loyalty of existing customers. The pragmatic reason for this philosophy is that the marketing costs of acquiring a new customer are at least ten times higher than generating additional sales from an existing customer. Loyal customers introduced to the idea of using e-commerce to communicate with their suppliers have an expectation that events will happen more rapidly on-line when compared to buying the same product in an off-line world. Fulfilment of this requirement can only occur if the supplier is already committed to using JIT to minimise order-to-delivery cycle times.

3 **Expertise in IT-based supply chain management.** E-commerce systems can only deliver their promise of an interactive, rapid response to customer demands if every element of the supply chain has been integrated and there is a seamless flow of data interchange within the organisation and between all members of the market system. Achievement of this objective can only occur where participants have extensive prior experience of developing effective IT-based data interchange and decision support systems. Hence it is no coincidence that an attribute shared by firms quoted as e-commerce exemplars is that these organisations have always led their respective market sectors in incorporating the latest advances in computing and telecommunications technology into all aspects of their operations.

In 1998 Seybold and Marshak undertook the demanding task of drawing upon their firm's extensive consulting experience as the basis for formulating a set of guiding principles that must be considered in seeking to establish an effective on-line business operation. The starting point in system design is the requirement that the entire process is driven by the knowledge which the company has acquired about the needs of the customer. These can include the pre-purchase information they require, the range of products they wish to purchase, the provision of design support for customers who wish to order customised products, the ability to place orders on-line, to make electronic payments and to enquire about the status of their order at any time from point of purchase through to the final delivery of the product to their home or business.

What has to be recognised is that in most markets, customer needs are rarely homogeneous. The advice of Seybold and Marshak is that early focus should be on those customers who represent the most important source of profitable sales revenue. Only after having fulfilled the on-line requirements of this customer group should the firm examine how to exploit the technology to provide coverage of other less profitable market sectors. For many firms, having gained some basic experience of e-commerce it is very probable that their next move will be to examine ways of using knowledge management capabilities to enhance service delivery (Schwarz 2000). This can be achieved by the firm moving to create closer collaborative links based upon knowledge sharing with other members of their supply chain. This move will permit the evolution of new service offerings and the ability to extend their services further downstream in the supply chain.

Service Extension

An example of the philosophy of service extension through e-commerce is apparent in a new e-business hub called NonstopRx.com. Two solution providers, Nonstop Solutions and Supply Chain Solutions have created this for the US pharmaceutical industry. The industry is highly fragmented with suppliers attempting to service numerous end user sites across the country. The new web site seeks enhance supply chain operations by addressing the inefficiencies caused by knowledge, in turn gaps caused by:

1 Large volumes of product and price change information being faxed to wholesalers from numerous suppliers.
2 Highly complex pricing and distribution contracts which currently involve the time of numerous administrative staff and finance personnel.
3 Poor management of product flows resulting in excess inventories and poor on-time deliveries.
4 Rebates and charge-backs creating another massive administrative burden for wholesalers.

The objective of the new hub service is to develop and operate a knowledge-based, e-commerce supply chain model which uses client data to develop logistics systems that can optimise deliveries by determining how best to manage transportation, product handling, administrative activities and inventory carrying costs. Nonstop Solutions has already utilised a knowledge management system to reduce the inventory of the retail chain Longs Drugstores by 44% and freed up $60 million in capital without reducing delivery service levels.

Implementation of the operational model of the type described for Nonstop Solutions would not be feasible within a firm unless steps had been taken to automate the data management systems being used within the operation. This is because customers will want the knowledge provision facility to be able to interrogate the supplier's internal information systems in real time in order to optimise all aspects of the process between on-line search through to product delivery. To achieve this goal, the firm will need to invest in a system of the type shown in Figure 3.2 (Rob and Coronel 2000).

The customer browser, web server and API interface shown in Figure 3.2 are the basic components needed to service on-line customer needs. The

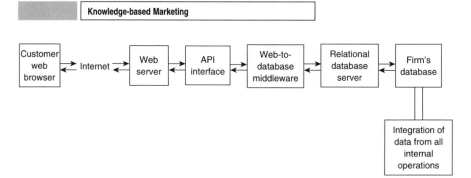

FIGURE 3.2 AN AUTOMATED E-BUSINESS DATABASE SYSTEM

additional components added to the system are the middleware, the relational database system and a database containing information about the firm's trading activities. The reason for the middleware is that a web server is unable to respond to a request for data because it is not capable of connecting to or reading a database. The middleware, which is a 'server-side extension', has the ability to retrieve information from the firm's database and pass this information back to the web server. This is achieved because the middleware is able to read the scripting language communicated by the server, validates the legitimacy of the request, queries the database and then generates an HTML-formatted page of data that can be forwarded back to the server. To fulfil this role the middleware must be able to connect with the firm's database. This is usually achieved by using structured query language (SQL) or an open database connectivity (ODBC) system. The approach used is usually determined by the operating language which drives the firm's database installation.

Once the firm has created an automated database system, then internally the information acquired by the system can provide the basis for creating a *data warehouse*, which can be used to undertake detailed analysis of both customer and internal operational records generated during the operation of the firm's on-line trading activities. To utilise data in this way the warehouse must exhibit the following key features (Inmon and Kelley 1994):

1 All data from across the organisation must be integrated and consolidated into one single location.
2 Data must be organised by topic (for example, sales, marketing, finance) such that functional questions can be answered in any analysis.
3 The database must be accurately representative of changes occurring in circumstances over time. Thus when new data are added to the system, there must be automatic updating of the time horizon that applies to data recorded previously by the system.

4 The data must be non-volatile. This means that once data have been added to the system, because it represents the firm's entire trading history, it must never be deleted.

To extract the invaluable information contained within the firm's data warehouse a whole series of new analytical tools known as on-line analytical processing (OLAP) have been developed. These OLAP systems permit multi-dimensional data analysis which can be accessed by employees through easy-to-use computer terminal interfaces. The power of the data analysis system is further enhanced by linking them to data presentation graphical packages, statistical analysis software and modelling systems which permit the posing of 'what if' scenario questions. Most e-commerce data warehouses are configured as relational databases. This permits the user to undertake relational modelling of available information. The data exist as 'facts' which are numeric measurements or values. A given fact can be given 'dimension' by relating the fact to other data. Thus, for example, a sales figure can be related to the dimensions of location (or geographic source of sale), product type and time of sale. Each dimension contains 'attributes' which are characteristics about the fact. Thus a location dimension could contain attributes concerning country, city, street and street number. These attributes permit analysis at any level ranging from a macro- to a microlevel. Analysing data at different levels is usually known as 'drilling down through the data'. Once the firm has gained expertise in data warehouse operations, which is essentially a reactive activity instigated by interested employees, the next stage in the process is to become proactive by automating the data analysis process.

Automated, proactive data analysis is usually known as *data mining*. The philosophy behind mining is that by instigating automatic data analysis, new anomalies and hence possible new relationships between data will be identified. As such the activity permits the classification of information into groupings that may possibly generate new knowledge which might prove useful in determining new ways of building effective on-line trading operations. Some of the common algorithms used in data mining are neural networks, decision trees, regression trees and memory-based reasoning. Possible outputs from a mining exercise might be that (a) purchase of a specific product by customers will mean that a specified percentage of these individuals will purchase another specific item within 90 days, (b) customers in certain specified geographic locations are more likely to become loyal repeat customers and (c) customers in location x are more likely to place an order if offered free product delivery. It must be recognised, however, that data mining is still a science in infancy. As a result, output can be generated which contains relationships that have no relevance to the marketing planning process. Nevertheless it is obvious that the technique has extremely important implications for the future operation of e-commerce operations.

Knowledge Used or Abused?

Once a firm's relational database begins to fill with information collected from the on-line customers, the firm is in a position to use technology such as neural networks to analyse, categorise and classify buyer behaviour. The knowledge provides the basis for determining the most appropriate response when the organisation's web site is again contacted by a specific customer or group of customers (*Business Week* 2001b).

Levi Strauss claims it has sold 33% more jeans and increased repeat customer web site traffic by 225% since it began to utilise software capable of generating a personalised response. Weyerhauser's Wisconsin door factory uses software to evaluate the revenue flows from different distributors. The system determines which distributors should receive priority and which it would be preferable to lose. Since implementation the company has reduced its customer base by 50% and concurrently doubled annual sales. Hollywood studios are using box-office data-tracking technology to speed up decisions about which cinemas should show which films across the country.

On-line response systems designed to analyse customers in terms of the sales potential they represent use software of the type supplied by the data broker Acxiom. This company offers a service called Infobase Ethnicity System, which matches names against a database containing 95 million records about the housing, income, education and other demographic data which permits the system to determine customer ethnicity. The company offers this system as a net-enabled service using their own proprietary software integrated in standard platforms such as E.piphany.

It is expected that many firms, especially those involved in the provision of financial services, will build knowledge management systems capable of automatically determining when a customer comes on-line and the nature of service, if any, the firm should be prepared to offer. Already some observers are expressing concern about whether these systems can make accurate decisions. Comparisons are being made with an earlier terrestrial event which occurred in America when banks used post codes to decide automatically whether to offer a mortgage to consumers an approach which became known as 'red lining'. The basis of these new concerns are that these automated, on-line customer assessment systems are based upon taxonomic stereotypes and hence may not provide an accurate picture of real world people. If this is the case, on-line customers may be mistreated by their supplier and this outcome is now being referred to as 'weblining'.

Mapping Knowledge Systems

CHAPTER SUMMARY

Success is dependant upon having a detailed understanding of the supply chains and market systems of which the firm is a member. E-commerce has often altered both the nature of knowledge and the nature of knowledge flows within market systems. Determining knowledge contained within systems can be achieved by systems mapping. The core system contains end users, end user outlets, intermediaries, competition and suppliers. End user markets generate knowledge about customer behaviour. The firm needs knowledge of intermediaries' logistics and distribution activities to reach the end user market. Competition must be understood because it can represent a threat. Suppliers are a source of both resources and knowledge that can be used to improve a firm's operations. Surrounding the core system are the generic sources of knowledge influence. These influences include variables such as economic conditions, politics, legislation, financial conditions, technology and societal culture.

INTRODUCTION

Long before Adam Smith wrote *The Wealth of Nations* proposing the economic benefits of task specialisation, *Homo sapiens* had already recognised the commercial advantages of individuals and organisations fulfilling different roles in the production and distribution of goods within society. Thus from very early times, nations' economies have contained components such as primary industries producing raw materials, artisans producing goods, trading companies serving overseas markets and bankers lending money to support cash flows.

Economists have subsequently evolved a range of paradigms to explain the benefits associated with task specialisation. The nature of the principles proposed by economists can be illustrated by the theories associated with the alternative distribution mechanisms which may exist within markets for the same goods. In any market sector a producer has the option of selling directly to the final customer or using middlemen for managing the transaction (Fingleton 1997). The economic historians posit that middlemen tend to emerge because they identify a market niche and develop the capability to service this niche in the most cost effective manner. Economic theory presents the middleman as an organisation which profits because the bid price for a product is lower than the subsequent selling price. The middleman also offers certainty of delivery. This process is known as *intermediation*. If the middleman sets a bid price at a level which is too low to be acceptable to the producer, then the latter may opt to market goods directly to the final market. This latter outcome is known as *disintermediation*. Economists are able, through the application of supply and demand theory, to define which of the two alternatives is most likely to be the probable outcome.

Although economists' models are based upon relationships which exist between supply and demand curves, an underlying factor influencing the way markets are served is that certain organisations have a greater level of knowledge about fulfilling a task role within a market sector than other members of the same sector. An example to demonstrate the theory of how knowledge creates roles is provided by the emergence of banks (Myers and Rajan 1998). The precursors of banks are thought to be the money changers based in medieval Bruges. Their original activity was confined to trading in bullion and the exchange of coins. Unfortunately coins in the Middle Ages were not uniform and hence their value was hard to assess. It therefore made sense to minimise the amount of transactions done using coins. Money changers started taking in demand deposits to create a payment system. They facilitated trade by making transfers and used their knowledge of the monetary system to make simple accounting adjustments, thereby avoiding the process of transferring suspect coins.

There is an old adage that 'knowledge is power'. In the context of the business world, to this statement can be added an additional comment namely 'knowledge is a source of value'. Any organisation that has knowledge which others wish to access can usually exploit this demand as a revenue opportunity. The more unique the knowledge, typically the greater is the price which can be commanded. Understandably the natural inclination in many organisations is to seek to achieve a proprietary knowledge 'lock' in order to maximise the level of financial return achievable upon owned assets. The appeal of this proposition is demonstrated by firms such as Ford, which in the 1930s sought to build a totally vertically integrated company from source of raw materials through to the final point of sale for vehicles. Similarly IBM in the 1950s, through careful design of unique software and hardware systems, attempted to achieve a monopoly supplier position with key customers.

In today's world, however, as technology has become more complex, organisations face increasing difficulties in acquiring sufficient knowledge to optimise ongoing performance across all areas of their operations. The outcome of this situation is that in many sectors firms are deciding to concentrate on those areas of knowledge most capable of generating maximum value. Concurrently firms are outsourcing other areas of activity to external organisations. An example of this scenario is the way that most internet firms have outsourced their logistics operations to companies such as FedEx and UPS.

Possibly one of the most important stimuli prompting a reconsideration of task roles by firms over recent years has been the impact of information technology. This is because in a pre-IT age, paper-based and verbal information flows were both slow and inaccurate. These types of problem have to a large degree been removed once data storage and transmission have been moved onto electronic platforms. As use of electronic communication began to emerge on a significant scale, organisations have become increasingly interested about where within an industrial sector the most accurate information sources are located and, by definition, who are the most knowledgeable organisations in relation to undertaking specific tasks. This search objective has resulted in firms undertaking sectoral knowledge mapping exercises to determine where within a market system knowledge sources are located.

The advent of e-business has caused the marketer to extend the mapping exercise to identify where in the market knowledge is owned which can support the actions of:

1 Reducing the cost of information provision.
2 Increasing the speed of information provision.
3 Making information accessible on a 24 hour, 365 day basis.
4 Providing significantly more detailed information than is typically feasible using traditional channels such as television or magazine advertising.
5 Exploiting the ability to analyse customer behaviour as the basis for providing customised information.

Once the firm has identified these knowledge sources, whether they exist inside or outside the organisation, the marketer is in a better position to implement the actions associated with:

1 Reducing prices and/or increasing the speed of product delivery.
2 Enhancing purchase convenience and/or quality of service.
3 Expanding market coverage.
4 Offering greater product choice.

CORE SYSTEM MAPPING

The Complete System

Most e-business marketing strategies will need to be integrated into an existing market operation. Hence if the marketer is to be successful, he or

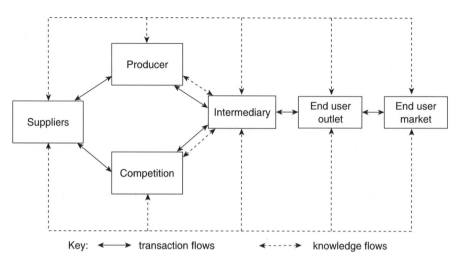

Key: ◀——▶ transaction flows   ◀- - - -▶ knowledge flows

FIGURE 4.1   A CORE SYSTEM

she will need a very clear understanding of how sources of knowledge influence performance within existing terrestrial market systems. One way this can be achieved is to build a map of the market system, which identifies the key sources of knowledge ownership. This then permits the marketer to comprehend how knowledge can be managed in order to implement successfully both terrestrial and e-business marketing plans.

As illustrated in Figure 4.1, a core market knowledge system is constituted of the organisations and customers who are participants in the market sector supply chain. To understand the tasks undertaken by the components which constitute the core system, the marketer will need to map knowledge flows within the system. The reason for this is that the evolution of any subsequent marketing plan will usually involve seeking to optimise the knowledge interchange that supports customer–supplier interactions and purchase transaction processes. To provide an illustration of how the conceptual model in Figure 4.1 can be translated into a real world situation, Figure 4.2 describes the core system for the consumer car market.

The End User Market

The end user market is the point of ultimate consumption within the core system. As shown in Figure 4.1, it contains two elements: the generic and the core market. Within the core market are those customers who are actively purchasing the product or service. Consequently the knowledge provided by suppliers on issues such as product performance, price and promotional message can influence buyer behaviour within this population.

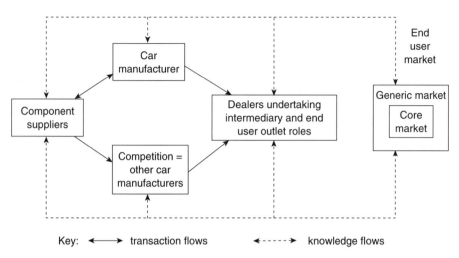

Key: ⟷ transaction flows   ◄----► knowledge flows

FIGURE 4.2 A TERRESTRIAL SYSTEM FOR THE CONSUMER MARKET FOR CARS

Surrounding the core market is the generic market. Actual users are those individuals who have already migrated into the core market. Hence the generic market is a critical influencer of product demand because as this market grows or declines in size, this will impact the number of customers entering the core market. Thus in the consumer car market, dealers might define the size of the generic market in terms of the number of individuals who can both afford and desire to run a car. Thus any change in this generic market (for example, a decline in the number of inner city individuals who wish to own a car) will have a direct impact on the size of the core market for car sales.

USING CUSTOMER KNOWLEDGE EFFECTIVELY

The advent of computer-based systems that offer the technology which can identify the most profitable customers to then permit targeting them with campaigns to increase purchases and loyalty is why customer relationship management (CRM) software vendors have been so successful over recent years. Evidence would suggest, however, that more than half of all CRM projects fail to pay back an adequate return on investment. Upon analysing this situation Gillies et al. (2002) have concluded that many failures are because firms adopting CRM technology were incapable of using the knowledge generated to execute a viable marketing strategy.

One firm which for many years has understood how to exploit knowledge about customers is US credit card giant MBNA. When the company expanded into Europe in 1993 it was meticulous about using its knowledge of customer behaviour to select only the right type of customer. Very detailed credit analysis is undertaken on every application and more than half are rejected. Around 65% of their customers hold affinity cards such as the World Wild Life Fund or Manchester United football club. This is because such customers are attracted by the card's affiliation with their organisation rather than a need for personal credit. As a result this type of customer tends to have a better risk profile.

Another firm which exploits detailed knowledge about the behaviour of different customer segments is the UK-based direct home and motor insurer Direct Line. By removing brokers from its supply chain, as well as saving commission costs, this action provided the company with the ability to analyse customer applications itself. Using this knowledge the company rejects certain categories of business such as young drivers and exotic cars. Once a customer is recruited the company continues to analyse behaviour in order to adjust premiums based upon the overall level of actuarial risk. Its CRM system enables the firm to hold information on 18 million customers and this database is updated by drawing upon the firm's 60,000 daily transactions.

Gillies et al. posit that before moving towards a knowledge-based approach to managing customer relationships, the firm must have already moved from a buyer-orientation towards being a customer-focused operation. They illustrate this view by providing case materials on the UK supermarket leader Tesco. In the 1980s the company had a poor image among customers. Tesco embarked upon a major investment programme to move upmarket, which involved building new superstores and closing unprofitable outlets. Product quality of the goods in-store was dramatically upgraded and staff reorientated towards focusing upon meeting customer expectations. Once all these changes were in place the firm moved towards a computer-based CRM operation through the launch of the loyalty card scheme in 1995. Their Club Card allows Tesco to develop an extensive knowledge of its customer base and to segment customers according to purchases, location and life style. Using this knowledge Tesco offers carefully tailored special offers designed to increase purchase activity and build stronger customer loyalty.

Intermediaries

The primary role of intermediaries is to act as a link in the transaction chain between the supplier and the end user. In many business-to-business markets, where the value of the product is high, the number of customers is relatively low and/or the product is customised to meet variations in product requirement (for example, civilian passenger jets), the supplier deals directly with the customer and no intermediaries are required. This contrasts with most consumer markets where the intermediaries have a critical role in managing the knowledge and supplier/final transaction processes.

In Figure 4.1, there are two tasks specified for the intermediary, namely distribution and provision of end user outlets. In the case of some consumer goods these responsibilities are fulfilled by different organisations (for example, a clothing wholesaler who supplies traditional high street fashion goods shops). Since the early 1990s, however, the trend in many market sectors has been for the distribution and end user outlet role to become the responsibility of a single organisation. For example, in the terrestrial car industry, the main dealers act as centralised buying and distribution systems managing the maintenance of stocks, which they then distribute to their own local garage outlets.

As intermediaries have moved to integrate the distribution and end user outlet role, they and their suppliers have tended to take a more integrated approach to the provision of knowledge to the final customer. Thus instead of the supplier being the sole provider of knowledge through, for example, promotional campaigns, the intermediary and the supplier will form alliances to jointly fund the knowledge provision process. Thus in the car industry during the launch of a new model of car both the manufacturer and main dealers will co-ordinate their promotional activities to maximise the provision of knowledge to potential customers.

RETAINING SYSTEM RESPONSIBILITIES

Rebecca Matthias could not find maternity clothes suitable for being worn at work. So in the early 1980s she started her own business. By 1993 Mothers Work had achieved almost a 50% share of all the maternity clothes sold in the United States. This achievement in part can be explained by the firm's total understanding of knowledge management responsibilities within their core system and using a vertical integration philosophy to ensure an effective co-ordination of activities within the maternity market system (Siekman 2000).

The core component of the operation is to have all of the firm's designers located on the same floor and within the same building as the warehouse co-ordination operation which links the company to its 726 company-owned retail outlets. Each store has a point-of-sale cash register which, by a direct link with head office, means any goods sold are automatically scheduled for replenishment within 24 hours. The critsical need to retain ownership of knowledge within the core system reflects the company's understanding of its customers. These customers are fashion conscious, pregnant females. These individuals cannot wait for items to be backordered, they want to take ownership of their short shelf-life clothing on the day they are in the store. The view of Mothers Work is that in their sector of the clothing market, the time lags associated with employing intermediaries and end user outlets would mean an inability to service the needs of their target customers effectively.

The company's operations are further complicated by the fact that it operates four different types of retail outlet: Motherhood Maternity which sells a middle-market line, Mimi Maternity which serves the needs of younger people, Pea in the Pod which is a high fashion chain and finally, to handle inventory problems, a chain of discount shops has been opened in factory-outlet malls. The starting point of all knowledge capture within the core system is the point-of-sale retail terminals. These capture information about individual customers and generate the daily sales movements reports. The central warehouse operation initiates the stock renewal process in the evening once stores begin to close for the day. A computer issues internal orders to picking stations, providing staff with the knowledge of which items from which area of inventory are to be moved to the thousands of shipping bins in which shipments are dispatched to individual stores. By early the next morning the computer has double-checked the number of items in the bins. Shipment lists defining stock to be distributed are then generated.

Once a week the computer data is reviewed to identify where specific item movements are undergoing change. This knowledge is then distributed by e-mail to store managers both to guide their merchandising activities and where appropriate to return slow moving goods to the central warehouse for redistribution.

New Knowledge for a New Situation

Caterpillar is the world's largest manufacturer of heavy earth moving equipment. Managing the core system for these products is relatively simple because most customers know at least a year in advance when they will need more machines to service new construction contracts. Unfortunately all of this accumulated knowledge was of little use to Caterpillar when it decided to enter the market for small compact machines aimed at the small building contractor market. Suddenly the company found itself moving into a market requiring the ability to distribute high volumes of standardised, price competitive products to a new group of customers who tend to postpone their purchase decision until the very last minute. To further complicate matters, Caterpillar decided also to offer the compacts to the market by opening a chain of construction equipment rental outlets (Siekman 2000).

The initial idea was to distribute the compacts through the firm's existing parts distribution centres (PDCs). Prior to reaching a final decision, Caterpillar admitted to a lack of knowledge about the new core system and turned to Carnegie-Mellon University to determine whether computer modelling could reveal an optimal solution. The outcome was an analysis which confirmed that utilisation of the PDCs was an inappropriate solution. The firm would be better advised to ship the compacts straight from the factory to dealer outlets. The shipping system, however, is based upon not one decision rule, but two. One rule is based upon cost minimisation, the other on maximum speed. Unless inventories have fallen below a specified minimum, the lowest cost shipping route is used. When, however, inventories fall below the specified minimum, then the decision rule is to select the fastest distribution response solution (for example, air freight) and to ignore the cost implications.

Competition

A vital responsibility assigned to the marketer is that of recognising the nature of competition, the potential threat it may represent and the development of appropriate response strategies. Possibly the most widely known source of theories on the effective management of competitors is Michael Porter, the Harvard Business School Professor, whose first major text (Porter 1980) has subsequently been followed by a whole series of writings on this critically important issue. He has proposed that competitive threats can be classified into five major types, namely:

1 The threat of other producer firms already operating within the market sector using their knowledge to seek to increase market share.
2 The threat of customers using knowledge of their purchasing power to dominate terms and conditions of purchase.
3 The threat of a supplier acquiring new knowledge and moving downstream using its control over critical resources to dominate terms and conditions of sale.
4 The threat of a new competitor using its knowledge of substitute goods to enter the market.
5 The threat of a new entrant with knowledge acquired in another market deciding to become a major player in a new market.

Kleindl (1999), in his analysis of competitive dynamics in the virtual market place, has proposed that Porter's contending forces model can be utilised by firms seeking to determine the potential source of threat in e-commerce market systems. Thus the marketer undertaking an e-commerce competitive threat assessment should review the potential impact of each of the following sources of future competition:

1 **Competitive rivalry** between firms at the same market level within the market system (e.g. the battle for market share which is beginning to develop between Dell and other PC manufacturers which have begun marketing their product on the internet).
2 **Downstream system threats** from groups that have sufficient buying power to alter the marketing practices of suppliers. One aspect of e-business is the ability of consumers to acquire information rapidly on prices being offered by different suppliers, not just in one country but also from overseas. If price variations exist in a market sector and this fact becomes widely known to consumers, then eventually the supplier can expect these customers to begin to exert pressure to force prices downwards. This situation, for example, is already

71

occurring in the electrical goods, videos and compact disc consumer markets.

3 **Upstream system threats** posed by a supplier firm which has become the sole source of products or services critical to e-commerce operations exploiting its position of power to force its downstream customers to accept adverse purchase terms and conditions. This is the situation, for example, which prevailed during the late 1990s in the UK where small firms contracted with a software house to construct their e-commerce operating systems. Subsequent to the initial installation, these suppliers then demanded excessively high fees for fixing faults and ongoing updating of web site front-ends.

4 **Substitute goods** entering the market. The fact that e-business provides a very low cost pathway for firms to enter new overseas markets is likely to mean that in those markets where price, not brand image, is important, companies, especially in Western nations, can expect to face increasing price-based competition from overseas producers based in the developing nations (for example, the furniture and clothing markets).

5 **New market entrants** gaining a foothold in markets previously not accessible to them. Prior to e-business, for example, it was usually not commercially feasible for large firms to attempt to gain distribution in niche markets that were primarily served by smaller firms. The low costs associated with (a) offering a wide variety of customised products and services via e-commerce and (b) constructing web sites customised to fulfil the needs of specialist customer groups, does mean that in future many smaller firms can expect to face increased competition from larger organisations in many market sectors (for example, the supply of customised, sector-specific software systems).

Knowing and Taking Action

Charles Schwab & Co. (*www.schwab.com*) is a US company which has been at the forefront of using knowledge about both customers and probable behaviour by competition to achieve and retain leadership in the American stock brokerage industry (Schwartz 2000). In the mid-1990s the company recognised that the internet could be an opportunity if exploited and a threat if ignored. The company established a dial-up on-line trading unit called e.Schwab unit which offered discounted trades. Initially this on-line operation was only a minor part of total revenue. Then in 1998 the company moved its core brokerage business on-line and cut its transaction fee from $80 to $29.95.

The reaction of the stock market was to perceive Schwab had made a major error and the company's stock price plunged. Schwab, however, clearly had greater knowledge of the likely behaviour of customers because within weeks they had a huge number of new accounts and the company revenues grew dramatically.

The company fully understood that their move would eventually be followed by other brokerage firms and have, therefore, continually sought to stay ahead of the competition by adding new services to their on-line operation. One advantage full-service brokers had over Schwab was their advisory services. To counter this problem the company acquired US Trust Corporation which can offer personalised investment services to on-line customers. To gain entry into the day-trading market the company then purchased CyBergCorp Inc. This acquisition provided the firm with the knowledge required to offer fault-tolerant systems and high-speed connectivity to the world's equity markets.

Exploiting Knowledge First

Analysis of case materials of firms which failed to respond to a competitive threat often reveals that the new market entrant has exploited knowledge which was available but ignored by the market incumbents (Geroski 1999). In some cases these new entrants are already part of the existing supply chain and, therefore, enjoy equal access to knowledge about customer behaviour. Starbucks was originally a coffee buyer and roaster which recognised that US consumers were seeking higher quality coffee. Their strategy was to open a chain of coffee bars and in the process severely damaged the business of major incumbents such as Maxwell House, Folgers and Nescafé.

Having market knowledge may not always be sufficient, it will also require an ability to fulfil customer needs. The telephone companies had long understood that their customers wanted greater product portability. Cellular technology provided a cost effective solution upon which to launch mobile phones. Racal and Ericsson were both companies which had knowledge of cellular technology as a result of their work in the defence industry and hence were able enter and challenge the established telephone companies in their national markets around the world.

New entrants often have the advantage that they do not have any preconceptions or mental models of what customers might want in the future or of the business rules which define the existing conventions within a market. Existing firms on the other hand may be locked into following well established business rules and are unable to use available knowledge to develop new innovative solutions. For example, IBM dominated the market for mainframe computers and for many years missed out on the growing opportunities in the minicomputer market. This latter market was dominated by firms such as DEC and Data General. They in turn were blind to opportunities for PCs leaving this opportunity to be exploited by new entrants such as Apple, Commodore and Tandy.

Suppliers

OPEC's restriction of supplies, and their concurrent demand for higher crude oil prices in the 1970s, triggered a global recession. This event caused marketers, possibly for the first time, to assess carefully the impact of scarce resources on the future positioning of products in their respective markets. For example, the need for US automobile manufacturers to begin to offer their customers smaller cars or the requirement of construction firms to improve insulation levels in new houses in order to reduce occupants' energy bills.

More recently, however, firms have begun to realise that suppliers, as well as possibly being able to constrain input resources, can also be a major source of new knowledge upon which to base the development of new marketing opportunities. For example, most of the recent advances in the modern computer's data processing capability have not come from the knowledge acquired by laboratories of the computer manufacturer. Instead the knowledge source has been the entrepreneurial behaviour of their suppliers (for example, Intel Corporation's ongoing efforts to create a new computer chip even more powerful than their world beating Pentium product; the diverse range of Windows products developed by Microsoft Corporation).

Over the last few years, the growing recognition of the importance of working closely with key suppliers has caused many OEMs to move away from the traditional, conflict-based negotiation style of using purchasing power to drive down input prices. They have began to move towards scenarios based on achieving mutual benefits from entering into knowledge exchange relationships with their suppliers. This change in management practice is often described as 'building stronger supplier–customer chains'. It usually involves firms mutually determining how to identify the location within the supply chain of key areas of knowledge. Once identified, the best source of expertise can be exploited as a route through which to allocate responsibilities for the various stages of the value-added processes associated with the production and delivery of goods to end user markets (Storey 1994).

In commenting upon the role of backward integration between OEMs and suppliers Knill (1998) has concluded that knowledge sharing has conferrered the following benefits:

1 Reducing inventory costs.
2 Improving customer service throughout the entire core system.
3 Improving end user customer satisfaction.
4 Decreasing total overall costs throughout the core system.

He notes, however, that such effective knowledge exchange could not have been possible without the advent of automated systems through which to acquire, store and share knowledge. This is because these electronic systems have increased the accuracy of information, made information delivery more timely and provided rapid response to emerging adverse cost trends within the core system.

Beasley (1996) has noted that knowledge exchange between suppliers and OEMs can be of crucial benefit in the development and launch of new products. He notes that 'time-to-market' is a critical aspect of successful new product development. By creating knowledge links between the supplier and OEM, it is possible to achieve 'time compression' within product development cycles. One reason for time compression is the use of knowledge exchange to reduce complexity in product design. Focusing on how to exploit knowledge to reduce complexity provides opportunities to reduce defects and on-hand inventory levels. The other aspect of knowledge exchange to reduce complexity is the benefit this confers on enhancing product manufacturability.

E-COMMERCE AND CORE CHANGES

Although on-line business in revenue terms is still dwarfed by the level of transactions which continue within terrestrial systems, academics and practising managers are already beginning to recognise that e-commerce has the potential to alter dramatically knowledge management responsibilities within many industrial sectors. Jallar and Capek (2001) posit that the move into e-commerce means knowledge has become an even more important component in terms of influencing a firm's scale of value-added activities. The implication of this observation is that new forms of intermediary functions will emerge that have strategic implications for the future marketing processes utilised by organisations.

On-line firms can now better organise and control their logistics, thereby enhancing customer service levels. Federal Express has achieved a first-mover advantage by creating a massive database for tracking clients, packages, trucks, planes and to integrate this knowledge into a form which can be interrogated by both employees and customers. Moving on-line also offers many firms the opportunity to have direct access to customers without going through intermediaries. Thus a company can use its web site to track trends in customer behaviour and use this knowledge to make immediate revisions in its marketing activities. This virtually instant response to changing customer needs also can provide the basis for building stronger, customised relationships, thereby enhancing customer loyalty and maximising customer retention levels.

The potential for gaining new knowledge by directly linking the firm to the final customer has caused some organisations to consider whether now is the time to remove intermediaries from their core system. This move, known as disintermediation, clearly has implications for both the producer and those who in the past have served as a vital link between suppliers and the end user. DePrince and Ford (1999) have proposed that there are two forms of disintermediation. One which they have termed *amazonic distribution* is characterised by the end user purchasing on-line from a distributor with the consequence that terrestrial retailers are removed from the transaction cycle. The other proposed form is that of *dellphic distribution* where the producer of goods or services has mounted a massive effort to migrate customers from traditional purchase methods to purchasing products directly from them. One example is provided by the airlines, which have sought to attract customers away from travel agents. Another example is firms such as Charles Schwab, which were early movers in persuading consumers to start buying shares on-line.

The degree to which existing terrestrial intermediaries might be impacted by changes in links between producers and end user customers in on-line markets is a matter of some debate. Cort (1999), for example, has pointed out that in many B2B markets there will remain a need for distributors located near to customers to provide immediate knowledge and rapid response for immediate delivery of goods. Within the US market, for example, Cort notes there are over 250,000 smaller firms fulfilling this role of distributing knowledge to a large number of customers located in the same area of the country. Similarly Jallar and Capek note that various divisions in functional roles exist between producers and intermediaries which, although they may be changed by e-business, will still require the operation of close links between these two parties within core systems. One function is that of aggregation where the intermediary acts to combine products from a number of sources to offer customers wider choice. A second function is that of the intermediary providing a local source of guarantee in order to protect the end user from purchasing goods from inadequate producer sources. A third function is the cost effective transmission of knowledge in a decentralised market. In some cases an intermediary can fulfil this service at a lower cost than a large OEM located a significant distance away from the end user market. The fourth function is market matching. The intermediary, through a more detailed understanding of local conditions, is usually much better informed about customer characteristics in terms of variation in the need for products and services.

Understanding the Middle

One firm which very early recognised the implications of EDI influencing the future role of intermediaries was Boise Cascade Office Products (Aaragon 1997). This firm distributes offices supplies from 1,200 producers to over 17,000 customers. The company first began to acquire its understanding of electronic data interchange from having created an EDI system to communicate with key suppliers. Hence as the internet began to appear in B2B markets, the firm already had some appreciation that unless changes were made to future operations the company could face the risk of disintermediation.

The firm realised that customers would begin to make direct electronic links with suppliers unless Boise Cascade could add value to existing services. Its solution was to perceive the internet as a way of both simplifying the purchase transaction process and where possible reducing customer purchasing costs. The company internet site was opened in 1997 offering customers the ability to place orders on-line. These customers enter the Boise Cascade web site at *www.bcop.com*, provide a user ID plus password and, if regular customers, can call up an 'easy order form'. Payments for on-line purchases were initially by credit card but subsequently the company has introduced a digital cash system.

The company saved over a $1 million in year 1 by reducing the time customer service representatives spent on the telephone taking orders. On the supply side savings have also been made by cutting out the need for paper-based administrative systems and improving inventory management practices. These savings, plus the improved customer service levels provided from moving on-line, have permitted Boise Cascade to be very confident that as a middleman the firm has a secure future.

Sustaining Knowledge Flows

Especially in B2B markets, most firms have spent years developing relationships with customers within the channels through which they distribute their goods and services. These relationships are critical because having developed trust and expectations channel members are willing to share knowledge over issues such as sales forecasts, customer data and logistics. Jap and Mohr (2002) posit that such firms should take great care not to disrupt such relationships when considering the use of the internet as a mechanism to make direct contact with final customers within a market system.

The authors illustrate their view with the example of the office furniture company Herman Miller in America, which saw the internet as a channel through which to reach customers in the small business sector. Before implementing this strategy it mounted a communications and educational campaign to convince its existing terrestrial distributors that the use of the internet would not erode their existing customer base. These distributors recognised that the handling and selling costs in the small business sector did not justify them becoming involved in the customer transaction. This scenario can be contrasted with Compaq Computers which attempted to execute a similar strategy. The company created the Prosignia computer brand to be marketed to the small business sector via the internet. Terrestrial distributors viewed this action as Compaq indicating indifference to existing relationships and ultimately began to withdraw from dealing with the computer firm.

Firms which have been successful on-line typically have sought to demonstrate continued reliance upon knowledge exchange with existing partners within the market system. Hewlett-Packard, for example, accepts customer orders on its web site and then forwards these to its resellers. These resellers complete the order, ship the product and receive commission. Similarly Estée Lauder believes ongoing collaboration with channel partners is strategically critical to the firm. When a customer orders the Bobbi Brown brand on-line the orders received are transferred to the retailer Neiman Marcus.

Reintermediation

In some markets, the advent of the internet has caused the emergence of new knowledge providers. Their role is to provide a new knowledge point within a core system and thereby enhance integration of an existing supply chain. Known as *reintermediation*, a very successful example is provided in the US car market by the emergence of Auto-by-Tel. Founded in 1995 by Peter Ellis, the company uses the internet to assist individuals in America to locate the best deal on the car they wish to purchase. By linking with a network of 2,700 car dealers, Auto-by-Tel matches the potential buyer with the nearest car dealer able to meet their purchase criteria. When clients put in an order for a specific model, the request is sent to a server which contacts all qualified dealers geographically close to the client. Within 48 hours a product proposal is sent to the client.

The company has approximately 200 staff and in 1999 achieved a 1% share of total new cars sales in America. The core of the operation is the firm's database that requires ongoing, continuous updating. The search service is provided free to clients. Car dealers who want to be an Auto-by-Tel franchisee make a joining payment and a monthly subscription fee.

MACROENVIRONMENTAL KNOWLEDGE

Surrounding every core system is a macroenvironment that contains generic knowledge variables which, if understood by marketers, can be used to further optimise performance within core systems. The common problem of such knowledge variables is that it is often extremely difficult (a) to measure how the additional knowledge can best be utilised to achieve a positive impact on marketing practices within the core market or (b) to accurately forecast how the impact may change over time. This is a critical issue because the prime objective of mapping a system is to evolve an understanding of how any source of knowledge in both the macroenvironment and the core system can be utilised to exploit new opportunities or combat emerging threats.

Economics

All market systems are impacted by prevailing economic conditions because these determine whether customer demand will grow, remain static or decline. Thus the marketer, by drawing upon the knowledge generated by macroeconomic forecasting models, can gain a better understanding of potential future revenue stream trends within an industrial sector. Currently, for example, the downturn in the US economy is having an effect on the electronics, telecommunications and computing sectors around the world. Those firms which appreciated the early warning signs contained

78

within data issued by organisations such as the US Federal Reserve Bank and the Federal Trade Commission have been significantly more successful in taking appropriate steps to recraft their future marketing plans.

Unfortunately many firms appear to ignore these types of data sources and incorrectly remain optimistic about their future. This inappropriate behaviour was demonstrated by many Pacific Rim firms during the late 1990s downturn. They appeared to ignore the economic implications that would occur if the forecasted 'melt down' in financial institutions across the region actually occurred. As a result, some large conglomerates in countries such as Korea and Japan were slow to adjust their market forecasts and did not instigate the type of downsizing which could have possibly permitted them to avoid subsequent closure of their business operations.

Politics

The economic policies of most countries are heavily influenced by the policies being implemented by their respective governments. By understanding these policies the marketer can gain valuable insights into how impending government actions may affect core markets. One issue of interest to on-line companies, for example, is the commitment of governments to take action over telephone access costs (OECD 2000). These access costs typically comprise two components: fixed charges and usage charges. Across OECD (Organisation for Economic Co-operation and Development) countries these costs vary dramatically and are clearly influenced by the attitude of politicians to support liberalisation of their respective country's telecommunications industry. The Czech Republic, Hungary and Poland are, for example, extremely expensive, reflecting very high local call tariff charges. In addition to being prepared to abolish existing telecoms monopolies, the other issue is the degree to which governments are prepared to authorise public sector expenditure to improve telecommunications infrastructures by actions such as the installation of broadband technology and high speed transmission lines using fibre optic technology. Available evidence would tend to suggest that higher levels of public sector expenditure on telecommunications infrastructure are associated with a subsequent more rapid growth in the on-line economy within a country.

Another issue of interest to e-business is the ultimate attitude of governments towards the collection of taxes associated with on-line transactions. In the United States, the consultants Ernst and Young estimate that in 1999, at individual state level, the tax exemptions associated with internet trading caused the states across America to lose $170 million in tax revenues. Some states lobbied Congress to take action over this issue. They were supported by some 'bricks and mortar' retailers who felt it was unfair competition to permit their on-line rivals to escape payment of taxes.

In the European Union there is a similar problem over value added tax (VAT). Customs and Excise departments in Europe are currently trying to find a way of collecting tax on products which consumers buy electronically from suppliers outside of Europe. Following the 1998 Ottawa Ministerial Conference, the OECD is examining many of these issues with the aim of reaching agreement about common legislation by 2005. Even if all the complexities of these issues can be resolved, however, there still remains the problem of whether the customer or the supplier will be responsible for remitting the collected taxes to the appropriate authorities. How this thorny issue is to be resolved is extremely unclear. What is certain, however, is that the final decisions by governments will have a dramatic impact on where on-line firms ultimately decide to base their transaction sites.

Legislation

Legislation is the basis through which governments create statutes and guidelines that provide a framework for regulating the behaviour of both consumers and businesses. A problem facing the e-marketer is that a business activity in one country may be deemed illegal in another. For example in the UK, the Financial Services Act strongly limits the nature of the promotional content permitted in the advertising of shares and other financial products. The question that then arises is how this regulation applies to offshore advertisers who in theory are able to act differently from UK-based financial service firms. Similar problems exist in relation to major differences that exist between consumer protection laws around the world. For example, in the European Union there are potentially 15 different sets of consumer, health and safety and other requirements associated with the sale of goods, all of which in theory would have to be taken into consideration by the e-commerce exporter. Thus until these various legislative matters are resolved, the potential exists for both consumers and businesses to find themselves involved in complex cross-border contractual disputes.

Recent court rulings in Europe have not helped build the confidence of on-line traders (*Business Week* 2000). Compuserve (now absorbed by AOL) temporarily had to close its German operation after a Bavarian court found the company liable for racist material which had been placed on its site by a third party. Lands End, the direct mail company, was deemed to be breaching German consumer law by offering their normal 100% replacement guarantee for clothing that wore out.

On the other hand it must be recognised that governments do attempt to protect consumers by enacting legislation to protect people from risks during purchase or consumption. Such objectives become infinitely more difficult, however, if these consumers go to overseas web sites to purchase products. In the United States, for example, people are purchasing medical drugs from Mexico which have not been approved for use in America by the Food and Drug Administration.

Some on-line legislative issues are simpler to resolve. One example relates to the laws that apply in different states across America. By offering a product via a server based in one state to a customer living in another state, the issue arises that individuals can seek legal redress in either or both locations (Beck 1998). In one case a Californian corporation operated a subscription service across America. In Pennsylvania the firm entered into agreements with seven internet service providers (ISPs). One Pennsylvania company determined that the California operation was using a particular word which violated the Pennsylvania company's registered trademark. The court in Pennsylvania reached the decision that the scale of the California operation by employing seven ISPs across the state did mean trademark infringement had occurred. This is contrasted with a Florida company that operated a brochureware web site. In this case when an Arizona company attempted to sue for trademark infringement the court ruled that the passive, non-transactional nature of the Florida site meant that no infringement had occurred.

Technology

To operate in any industrial sector, the marketer will usually already have an understanding of the technologies that operate within their core system. It is also necessary, however, to be aware of the knowledge implications emerging from the introduction of new technologies which may have an impact on the future performance of the core system. This is no easy task. Hence in terms of monitoring technology without being overwhelmed with new knowledge, the marketer should probably give priority to tracking developments that offer new ways of improving product performance or reducing process costs.

Possibly the fastest changing area of technology is innovation in e-business. Alsop (1999) proposed some key areas of technology that require careful monitoring such as content management, customer acquisition and customer service provision. In the area of content management, new approaches are becoming available to support high speed voice and visual transmission. Under customer acquisition, software firms such as Media Matrix are providing new tools for assessing on-line content effectiveness. Under customer service, new systems are permitting the cost effective convergence of alternative communications media such as e-mail, fax, telephone and web sites.

In the field of on-line purchasing, various software systems are enhancing the on-line search for suppliers (McCright 2001). Thinkstream Corporation has launched *www.Tadaa.com*. which is an information portal and shopping community that allows consumers to search for exact product information. The system goes beyond locating of URLs and generates detailed knowledge about product features, comparisons with alternative offerings, prices and availability status. Tadaa uses a search engine which in real time seeks data from web sites, file servers, databases, desktop PCs and video image sources.

Growing concerns about on-line security also represent a rich area for new technologies (Chen 2000). Companies such as Drug Emporium are examining opportunities to use fingerprint scans to verify user identities when prescribing drugs. Biometric technology, which digitally encodes physical attributes such as voice, eyes or faces, is being actively examined by a number of software development companies. Proton World Technology has recently demonstrated a smart card that can verify the owner through fingerprint identification or iris recognition. Charles Schwab, the on-line share trading company, is using a voice recognition system to authenticate users of their telephone banking operation. Some data management and call centre operations are adopting biometric palm readers to authenticate the identities of individuals seeking access to their operations centres.

As well as on-line customers being worried about security, providers of knowledge products are increasingly becoming concerned about how to retain ownership and control of their own data (*Fortune* 1999). Ownership of knowledge is in theory protected by intellectual property laws. Unfortunately as knowledge has become digitalised, enforcing intellectual property rights has become increasingly difficult. The Secure Digital Music Initiative (SDMI), for example, is an attempt by 110 firms to specify standards for data protection of on-line music files. They are supporting research to find ways of blocking or limiting access to on-line data sources. Their focus is on attempting to build control devices into software systems which are capable of blocking illegal attempts at duplicating materials. Such approaches have been used by other sectors of the software industry to defeat individuals bootlegging their systems. Most of these systems require the user to identify themselves when first installing the software. Some experts feel a more effective approach to protecting knowledge is to use both software and hardware controls. Machine readable 'tags' are placed on the software and the hardware then interrogates the tag to determine if a user instruction (for example, copy or print) is permitted under the terms and conditions of purchase.

Culture

Since marketers first began to acquire knowledge to provide them with greater understanding of market opportunities it has been apparent that both different social groups within countries and populations in different countries will exhibit variations in buying behaviour. One of the key variables contributing to this situation is the cultural background of individuals because this will determine their wants, values, attitudes and beliefs. These behaviour traits will, however, change over time. Hence the marketer needs continually to seek out new knowledge about how culture may be impacting customer behaviour. One recent example is provided by attitudes in the Arab world concerning what materials are considered acceptable for being made accessible via a web site. The net filtering company Net Shepherd Inc., in recognition of this potential market culture opportunity, has formed a partnership with the on-line publisher Arabia.On.Line. Together these two organisations are reconfiguring web sites so that content is acceptable to Arabic customers (*PC Week* 1997).

In the world of knowledge-based marketing, possibly the most important cultural issue is the degree to which customers will permit suppliers to acquire knowledge about them and whether they perceive such data acquisition practices as an invasion of privacy. This issue has become of greater importance because new technologies are permitting suppliers to acquire and store data about the behaviour of their customers more easily. Two recent examples of adverse customer reactions are provided by Intel and GeoCities Corporation (Kelly and Rowland 2000). In the case of Intel, its Pentium III chip had the facility to provide electronic identification of the chip user. Following adverse publicity about this technology, Intel agreed to switch off this user identification feature. In the case of GeoCities, this firm was eventually forced by the Federal Trade Commission to change the way the firm collected and distributed information about its customers, especially children under the age of 13.

E-commerce operations have adopted a number of approaches to acquiring knowledge about their customers. One is to ask the customer to self-divulge information such as their name, credit card number, address and telephone number. Additionally the on-line business can extract other information such as the type of browser a visitor is using, their operating system and country of origin. Another approach is to utilise cookies to store information on the hard drives of their site visitors. Somewhat more surreptitious methods include collecting e-mail addresses and IDs by visiting newsgroup postings and chat rooms. E-mail addresses and customer preference information can also be purchased from direct marketing list brokers.

In America the government's apparent approach to consumer privacy is to favour self-regulation by the e-commerce industry. In one case, however, concern about the rights of children did lead to legislation requiring web sites to obtain verifiable parental consent before collecting personal information from children under the age of 13. Some American corporations have responded to the demand for self-regulation (Vaas 2000). The on-line travel site *www.expedia.com* has posted their policy of no longer being willing to share or sell customer data to others and vowing only to do business with third parties who have adopted similar practices. Another firm, Supergo, has sought to introduce filtering software that permits customised responses without relying upon data deemed by the customer as private.

This type of software analyses customer behaviour anonymously in real time and seeks to identify commonalties with the total pool of on-line visitors. Amazon, on the other hand, feels that using customer data is good business practice. Hence the firm uses customer data to let business partners send e-mail promotional messages to consumers.

Just how long self-regulation remains acceptable across the world is questionable. In 1995, the European Parliament enacted guidelines on privacy under the European Directive on Data Protection. Under these guidelines member states were required to adopt national legislation to protect personal information. The EU directive prohibits the sharing of data with other companies unless permission has been previously obtained from the customer. The growing concern about consumer protection has recently resulted in the EU threatening to halt the flow of data from member states to the United States.

Internal Competence

5

CHAPTER SUMMARY

Supporters of the resource-based theory of the firm consider that internal capability (or competence) can provide the basis for optimising marketplace performance. One model of internal capability looks at the competencies of strategic leadership, strategic planning, financial planning, innovation, productivity, employee practices, quality and information systems. The crucial issue appears to be the ability of leaders to create and implement a vision that is accepted across the entire organisation. The growing importance of knowledge management as a competence requires that information management is given priority in competence development. These systems must be regularly audited to assess factors such as how knowledge is generated, stored and disseminated. The audit should also cover organisational responsiveness to available knowledge.

INTRODUCTION

A number of researchers examining the issue of what makes certain firms successful have concluded that many have an outstanding ability to manage internal organisational processes. Tom Peters (1992) has popularised this concept in his various writings where he presents examples of firms that have clearly discovered the importance of orchestrating internal activities to deliver superior customer satisfaction. Hamal and Prahalad (1993) have conceptualised the importance of managing internal processes better than the competition in their model of firms succeeding through having developed superior *core competencies*.

Goddard (1997) has proposed, that in successful firms, core competencies are:

1 Imbued with experiential and tacit knowledge that competitors would find impossible to replicate.

2 Define what the company does better than, or differently from, other companies.
3 Embedded in the organisation's modus operandi.
4 Limited to only two or three key activities within the value chain.
5 The source of the company's ability to deliver unique value to customers.
6 Flexible enough to straddle a variety of business functions.
7 The basis for defining market opportunities that the firm is uniquely equipped to exploit.

The Wal-Mart Story

Goddard (1997) used the example of the US corporation Wal-Mart Stores (*www. wal-mart.com*) to demonstrate how the competency to acquire and apply new knowledge can lead to market success. The company's ability to exploit knowledge has been heavily reliant upon using advances in IT to build a more efficient retail operation. In 1980 Wal-Mart was a small niche retailer based in the southern states of the United States, yet within ten years the company became the largest and most profitable retailer in the world. Goddard posits that the fundamental ability driving this success was the knowledge used to evolve their 'cross-docking' technique of inventory management. This is a JIT system which keeps inventory on the move throughout the value chain. Goods delivered to their warehouses are almost instantaneously picked for reshipment, repacked and forwarded on to stores. The result is that Wal-Mart can run 85% of goods through its own warehouse system and purchase full truckloads from suppliers to the extent that it achieves a 3% inventory handling cost advantage that supports the funding of everyday low prices.

   The system took years to evolve and is based around investing in the latest available technology to store and transfer knowledge. The company, for example, developed a satellite-based EDI system using a private satcom system that sends daily point-of-sale data to 4,000 suppliers. The firm also worked with Procter & Gamble to develop their 'Efficient Consumer Response', an integrated, computer-based system, which provides the benchmark against the firm's entire supply chain operations. Finally in order to ensure employees have access to critical knowledge, store and aisle managers are provided with detailed information of customer buying patterns and video links which permit stores to share success stories.

DETERMINING COMPETENCE

Success in any market will be influenced by the degree to which a firm can develop unique capabilities in the area of exploiting superior technical knowledge and internal organisational routines as the basis for supporting competitive advantage. This perspective leads to the conclusion that knowledge management provides an important example of how the resource-based view of the firm will provide the basis for determining whether a firm will achieve market success (Hitt and Ireland 1985; Mahoney and Pandian 1992).

The internal functional competencies influencing market performance have been understood for many years. In view of this situation it seems that one should not attempt to create an entirely new resource-based paradigm to incorporate the application of knowledge management as a process for enhancing organisational performance. Instead one should seek to modify an existing organisational performance competence model.

One potentially applicable competence model is that developed by Chaston and Mangles (1997). The attraction of their model is that it was developed through a careful review of the performance literature of the source types shown in Table 5.1. This was followed by extensive quantitative validation across a diverse range of market sectors including manufacturing, production of hi-tec goods and the provision of services (Chaston 1999b). By drawing upon the data in Table 5.1, it is possible to evolve a resource-based model (Figure 5.1) of the strategic, financial and operational strategic competencies which can have critical influence on the goal of successfully managing an e-commerce business operation.

STRATEGIC COMPETENCE

Complacency is a dangerous attribute in a world where competitors sit like vultures waiting to exploit any mistakes that might be made by others operating in the same market sector. Under these circumstances, the long term survival of all organisations is critically dependent upon the ability to identify new knowledge to support the identification of new market trends and to determine how the internal capabilities of the organisation can be utilised to exploit emerging opportunities.

In some cases opportunity exploitation responsibility may be vested in the entrepreneurial skills of one individual (for example, Richard Branson's influence within his diversified Virgin empire; Anita Roddick the founder of the Body Shop). In other situations, although there is an identified leader to whom success is often attributed, this individual typically seeks to build a strong senior management team to sustain performance well beyond the point at which they have retired from corporate life (for example, Jack Welch, the CEO at GE Corporation; Lord King during his tenure as chairman of British Airways).

Tom Cannon (1996) has proposed that an organisation's strategic competence can be evaluated by testing articulated competitive position against the five criteria of being distinctive, sustainable, appropriable, usable and measurable. Achieving a positive rating against all of these criteria is probably unlikely unless the organisation has created effective knowledge management systems for carefully monitoring the external environment and ensuring the ongoing development of appropriate internal competencies.

TABLE 5.1   SOURCE EVIDENCE CONCERNING THE CHARACTERISTICS
EXHIBITED BY FIRMS WHICH ACHIEVE MARKET SUCCESS

A   Coopers & Lybrand (1994) study of UK 'super growth' firms

- Perceive their markets as intensively competitive.
- Are flexible decision-makers.
- Seek leadership through offering superior quality in a niche market.
- Deliver superior pre- post-sales service.
- Use technology-driven solutions to achieve a superiority position.
- Emphasise fast, frequent launch of new/improved products and draw upon external sources of knowledge to assist these activities.
- Emphasise application of technology and techniques such as cross-functional teams and process re-engineering to optimise productivity.
- Recognise the need to invest in continual development of their employees.
- Rely mainly on internal profits to fund future investments.

B   Cranfield Pan-European Study (Burns 1994)

- Seek niches and exploit superior performance to differentiate themselves from competition.
- Operate in markets where there is only average-to-low intensity competition.
- Utilise clearly defined strategies and business plans to guide future activities.
- Rely upon mainly internally generated funds to finance future investment.

C   Comparative Study of German and UK Food Processing Firms (Brickau 1994)

- German firms emphasise acquisition of detailed knowledge of external factors capable of influencing performance.
- German firms can clearly specify their competitive advantages.
- German firms seek niches exploited through a superiority positioning.
- German firms use strategies and plans to guide future performance.
- German firms concurrently seek to improve products through innovation and enhance productivity through adoption of new process technologies.
- German firms fund investment mainly from internal fund generation.

D   Study of New Zealand Exporting Firms (Lindsay 1990)

- Emphasise on R & D to achieve continuous innovation and gain control of unique technologies.
- Orientation towards achieving 'world class' superiority is specialist niches.
- Use structured plans based upon extensive information search to guide future performance.
- Exhibit a very entrepreneurial management style and encourage employee-based decision-making.
- Strong commitment to using superior quality coupled with high productivity as a path to achieving competitive advantage.

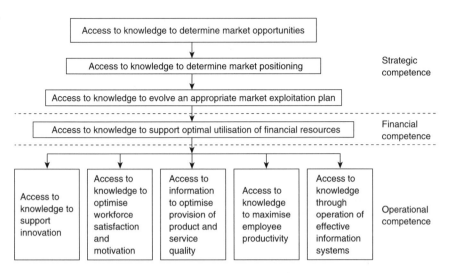

FIGURE 5.1   A KNOWLEDGE ACCESS MODEL FOR SUPPORTING
BUSINESS GROWTH

In the case of e-business markets Ghosh (1998) has proposed that firms may wish to acquire knowledge that permits them to assess which of the following four distinct strategic opportunities provide the basis for real competitive advantage:

1   Establishing a direct link with customers (or others with whom the firm has an important relationship) to complete transactions or exchange trade information more easily (for example, Staples (*www.staples.com*), the office superstore chain, selling supplies on-line to large corporate customers).
2   Utilising the technology to bypass others within a value chain (for example, on-line retailers such as the bookstore Amazon).
3   Developing and delivering new products and services (for example, the on-line share trading system developed by Charles Schwab in America).
4   Becoming a dominant player in the electronic channel of a specific industry by creating and setting new business rules (for example, Dell Computers' dominance in the electronic direct selling of computers to large corporate customers).

Although the concept of using strategy to define future business activities has been accepted for many years, establishing knowledge as a core component of strategy development is still a relatively new managerial philosophy.

Hence persuading managers to identify knowledge overtly within a revised definition of strategy can prove to be a difficult process (*The McKinsey Quarterly* 1998). This is due to a number of factors. Firstly, knowledge is difficult to both value and estimate in terms of how an application will return a certain revenue. Secondly, a significant proportion of knowledge exists in a tacit form, hence codifying and converting knowledge into a form suitable for sharing often proves difficult. Thirdly, knowledge is often perceived as intangible, which means when people meet to discuss strategy it is rarely the case that they place the same interpretation upon the knowledge which is available.

Despite these difficulties some firms have developed the competence to incorporate knowledge into their specification of future strategy. One example is provided by McDonalds, which has recognised that its highly dispersed operation mandates that to sustain customer service quality can be achieved only by using knowledge as the foundation stone for defining the work tasks of every employee. To support the implementation of a knowledge-based strategy the company gets comparable outlets to work together, benchmarking performance and evaluating alternative service propositions.

Other firms evolve their strategy by identifying opportunities which have been overlooked by the competition. Enron Corporation used to be a gas pipeline transmission company. The management realised that the firm owned valuable knowledge about product flow, supply and demand. To exploit this knowledge it launched Enron Capital and Trade Resources which offers a range of innovative risk management services.

As knowledge is perceived as offering the greatest source of added value activities, some firms have decided to withdraw from commodity-type operations and concentrate on knowledge-based businesses. Monsanto, for example, has decided to spin off the firm's very large chemical group and to concentrate on developing new life sciences businesses.

FINANCIAL RESOURCE COMPETENCE

Accountants can possibly be considered as having been involved in knowledge management from the first day that their profession was established. Unfortunately it is also the case that such knowledge often is not widely exploited across organisations. This is due to (a) some weaknesses in the ability of accountants to communicate with other functional areas of management and (b) the poor financial literacy skills often exhibited by managers who are not based within a firm's finance department.

For example, most marketers are attracted by any proposition that offers revenue growth. Too few, however, are able to interpret information concerning how a sales growth strategy might impact a firm's profitability and/or fund flow position. If then at a later date a new, potentially very exciting, proposition requiring further investment comes along, they may fail to use available knowledge to understand that overall financial viability can result in the firm being unable to borrow from shareholders and/or the financial community. Thus it proves impossible to raise the moneys required to implement the new marketing initiative.

Funding A New Opportunity

The capability to resource a new project is illustrated by the disguised case example in Table 5.2 of two firms in the clothing industry, both of whom operate manufacturing operations and have their own retail outlets (Chaston 1999b). Ten years ago, the two companies embarked on market expansion programmes; Company A by acquiring a competitor and Company B through carefully controlled internal growth.

TABLE 5.2 COMPARATIVE FINANCIAL PERFORMANCE (£ MILLIONS)

	Company A		Company B	
	10 yrs ago	2001	10 yrs ago	2001
Profit & loss account				
Sales	100	200	100	150
Gross profit	57	80	57	90
Other expense	44	76	44	67.5
Net profit	13	8	13	22.5
Profit as % of sales	13.0	4.0	13.0	15.0
Balance sheet				
Current assets	50	120	50	75
Current liabilities	20	90	20	30
Net current assets	30	30	30	45
Fixed assets	30	60	30	45
Long term loans	20	45	30	45
Capital employed	30	45	30	45

Industry research has generated new knowledge that although overall sales for up-market fashion goods clothing are beginning to flatten, major growth is forecasted for the sports/leisure wear clothing market. Furthermore an opportunity exists to acquire a successful, international, vertically integrated company in this latter sector. The probable cost of the acquisition is £25 million.

Company A's marketers soon discover that access to new funds through further borrowing and/or issuance of additional equity is impossible because recent performance has already caused the financial community to label the firm as a poor credit risk. This is in contrast to Company B, which encountered no problems raising new capital through a mixture of shares and long term debt. Consequently it is able to execute an acquisition which offers the opportunity of doubling the size of its business over the next ten years.

This lack of financial orientation among many marketers is probably caused by the fact that many start their careers working in large national or multinational firms. Many of these organisations tend to have adequate cash reserves and/or a financial track record which allows them to borrow from external sources such as banks or the stock market. In addition, the tendency in these organisations is for knowledge contained within the balance sheet and fund flow management to be seen as the sole preserve of the accounting department. Consequently few marketers are able to gain appropriate experience in using financial knowledge when developing marketing plans which are compatible with optimisation of an organisation's working capital, asset balances and/or external fund raising position.

To be successful it is clearly critical that the organisation has the financial resources required to fund the level of investment which is needed to support any new marketing strategy. In the case of e-business, to those lacking in on-line trading experience, new knowledge generated from a preliminary examination of market scenarios would tend to indicate that creation of a web site is an extremely low cost proposition. All that seems to be needed is to register a domain name and to then use 'off the shelf' software from suppliers such as Microsoft to construct the organisation's web pages.

This interpretation of available knowledge is correct if the marketer merely wants to use the internet to launch a static brochure into cyberspace. Unfortunately if the web site is also required to attract visitors and generate sales, a much larger scale investment will be required. This investment will be used to (a) establish the hardware/software systems that can provide instant response to the diversity of demands which will be placed on the site by potential customers, (b) create the capability to update the site on almost a daily basis in order to sustain customer interest and (c) ensure integration of the firm's internal information management systems such that customers receive a seamless service from the point of initial enquiry through to final delivery of purchased products (Seybold and Marshak 1998).

Even once the firm has made the initial investment to establish an effective internet operation, there still remains the problem of sustaining visits to the site by both new and existing customers over the longer term. Merely being able to appear high on the list of sites identified by a customer using a search engine such as Yahoo or Alta Vista is not sufficient. For most marketing propositions, the only way to generate a high level of site visitors is to invest continually in building customer awareness through expending funds on traditional promotional vehicles such as advertising, public relations and sales promotions (Chaston 1999a).

INNOVATION

To prosper and grow all organisations need to engage continually in finding new sources of knowledge that can be exploited in the improvement of their products and process technologies. In the case of conservative-transactional or conservative-relationship firms, primary application of knowledge should probably be biased towards optimising the efficiency of their procurement, production and logistics operations.

Innovation Pathways

An example of innovation is provided by Finland's most successful forest products company, United Paper Mills (UPM). Despite an overall world decline in demand for paper in the late 1980s, UPM continued to make investments in new paper-processing equipment. Profits have increased and, additionally, the company has acquired new knowledge that has permitted entry into the lucrative markets of manufacturing high value-added products such as magazine paper and newsprint.

In contrast within the mobile telephone market, although manufacturing process capability is important, long term survival is currently more dependent upon using knowledge to support new product development. The Nordic firm Ericsson has been able build a dominant position in world markets by exploiting research expertise in the fields of digital radio and digital signal processing to support the rapid development of new models offering improved performance in areas such as weight, size and operating life.

Exploting Existing Knowledge

In some cases innovation can result by finding news ways of exploiting existing knowledge. Buckman Laboratories, a $300 million international chemical company, provides an example of this approach to new product development (Zack 1999). The basis of the firm's new strategy is to cease to merely sell products and move into solving chemical-treatment problems. The knowledge to fulfil this redefined role already tacitly exists within the field sales force. To capture this knowledge the company established an on-line knowledge management system. Initially explicit knowledge about customers, products and technologies was entered into a on-line system. These data can be interrogated from any where in the world. To expand and develop the system, field sales staff can use a platform called Tech Forum to exchange applied knowledge and experiences with other employees. The Tech Forum is continually monitored by the knowledge transfer department both to guide discussions and to thread together common solutions.

Opportunity Maximisation

Innovative solutions are at their most productive when knowledge of both technology and market segments permits maximisation of the opportunities which are available (Murphy and Lanfranconi 2001). An example of this approach is provided by PixStream

Inc. The company has expertise in the development of hardware and software that can aggregate multiple audio and video inputs from sources such as direct broadcast satellites, local channel feeds and video servers. Their system permits real-time video processing and the output signal can be adapted for distribution through any type of network. The multiple application opportunities which the firm has identified include:

1   Broadband interactive video services for video conferencing, interactive distance learning and telemedicine.
2   Video courier services such as in-store video advertising, monitoring and video networking between broadcast sites, post-production houses and organisers of live events.
3   Television programme content redistribution where television signals are sent across various types of network.
4   Telephone companies wishing to compete with cable television companies by permitting the telecoms firms to use existing telephone lines to offer traditional telephone services, high speed internet connections and video on demand.

Knowledge Sources

Cisco Systems Inc. is a world leader in the supply of switches and routers to support internet infrastructures. At the heart of the business paradigm is the desire to harness knowledge as a route through which to develop innovative solutions that can be utilised by its customers (Lawson and Sampson 2001). The company makes a clear distinction between new knowledge to support new product development and mainstream knowledge for use in existing operations.

Although the company maintains a small R & D operation, the strategy for sourcing new knowledge is based upon a mix of acquisitions of smaller companies and through the formation of strategic partnerships. The company recognises that manufacturing is not a core competence. Since the early 1990s it has assumed that suppliers are the most important source of knowledge about implementing improvements to manufacturing activities. The company outsources approximately 75% of everything it sells and has ensured that suppliers collaborate over knowledge exchange through the creation of shared intranets and extranets.

WORKFORCE

In most markets, because all firms understand the nature of customer need and utilise very similar production technologies, it is often extremely difficult to achieve a long term sustainable advantage over the competition. Consequently in some cases the only way to reverse a declining market share is to invest heavily in the creation of a motivated and appropriately structured workforce. Clearly, therefore, no marketer can ignore the human resource management (HRM) practices within their organisation when considering future marketing strategies.

Regretfully over recent years, however, the field of people management seems to have attracted numerous gurus who claim, sometimes with almost a religious fervour, that their solution is the only way to proceed. Examples of these 'new faiths' include concepts such management by objectives (MBO), employee empowerment and the creation of organic organisations.

There is no question that employers who create appropriate working environments for the effective distribution of knowledge can expect higher levels of performance from their workforce. It is vital to understand, however, that employee motivation and job satisfaction are influenced by complex interactions between socio-demographic, economic and cultural factors. Hence the marketer would be well advised to ignore some of the 'mine is the only way' advice offered by the management consultancy fraternity. Instead they should seek to understand what causes certain employees to achieve consistently high performance standards within the organisation and then determine how effective management of these factors can contribute to building a market lead over the competition.

E-business provides an example of how difficult it is to sustain a long term advantage over the competition. Two variables which clearly have a critical influence over customer satisfaction are (a) the speed and accuracy of service delivery and (b) sustaining the technical reliability of all on-line systems (Seybold and Marshak 1998). The importance of these variables means that the e-marketer will need to ensure that the HRM practices within their organisation are focused on continually investing in exploiting knowledge to upgrade employee skills. This is necessary because of the critical importance of ensuring all staff are capable of fulfilling their job roles to a standard that exceeds that which is achieved by the competition.

Appropriate HRM practices for achieving optimal workforce performance of staff will usually be based around the same generic principles that are to be found in any type of organisation. At the moment, possibly the greatest HRM problem facing firms wishing expand their knowledge management operations is the recruitment, retention and ongoing skills development of the technical staff responsible for the development and operation of complex e-business systems. Even in Silicon Valley in California, where the downturn in the dot.com industry has generated massive redundancies, the greatest constraint facing firms wishing to gain competitive advantage through knowledge management is the availability of technical staff with an understanding of the advances in network systems operations, database management, telecommunications and programming.

The software development industry has now begun to take greater interest in assisting in the effective execution of HRM policies and practices (McCune 1997). Optimal HRM practices are critically dependent upon the storage, access and utilisation of detailed information about large numbers of employees. Quite clearly knowledge management philosophies can assist in the execution of such tasks. For example, Austin-Hayne Corporation has developed a software system for supporting employee performance reviews and staff appraisal activities. The software guides the line manager through the employee evaluation process. The system can be tailored to suit the specific appraisal needs of different staff such as sales representatives, clerical assistants and customer service representatives.

The move towards the formation of collaborative partnerships and out-sourcing of certain tasks is beginning to blur the boundary of where the firm finishes and the external environment begins. These 'relational' organisational forms will need to function effectively in order to ensure knowledge capture and exploitation is not impaired (*The McKinsey Quarterly* 1998). Additionally the firm is increasingly reliant upon individuals who are not employees having a significant influence over the delivery of customer goods and services. The implication for the HRM function is that knowledge distribution systems are needed to ensure the job satisfaction and motivation achievements are similar across all of the firms who are participants in these new organisational forms.

PRODUCTIVITY

Productivity is usually measured in terms of the level of value-added activities per employee and/or per number of hours worked. By increasing productivity in terms of value-added per employee or per hour of labour input, the firm can expect to enjoy an increase in profitability. This effect can occur in a number of ways. Firstly, if productivity rises, the company can more efficiently utilise available capacity to manufacture more goods or services. Secondly, if productivity is increased by employees being furnished with better equipment, or when human labour is replaced by a machine, costs per unit of output may fall. Thirdly, if improved productivity is reflected in higher quality, this may permit the firm's output to command higher prices in the market. Fourthly, the firm may direct attention towards seeking ways to improve productivity within supplier firms which in turn is reflected by a fall in the cost of input goods (Hornell 1992).

In the 1980s, the Western world lost market share to Pacific Rim firms which recognised the importance of productivity as a strategic weapon through which to increase sales. Studies of Japanese industry revealed that the application of new knowledge to evolve concepts such as lean production, concurrent engineering and JIT manufacturing have all contributed to Japan's manufacturing firms becoming able to offer their customers higher quality goods at lower prices.

In view of this situation, all marketers would be well advised to ensure that their organisations have in place a knowledge management system to contribute towards continually improving productivity. One approach is to establish a benchmarking scheme for carefully monitoring competitor productivity. Data from this activity are utilised in ongoing reassessments of how new knowledge is being applied to enhance employee productivity through actions such as revising process procedures, increasing employee training and investment in new technologies. Without such actions, the marketer should not be surprised to discover that selected strategic positions have been eroded because their competitors are more effective at optimising organisational productivity.

In relation to e-business operations, possibly the two most important elements of the productivity equation are customer interface productivity and logistics productivity (Chaston 2000a). In the case of customer interface productivity, this can usually be maximised by ensuring investment in the latest computer technologies. This is because by utilising automated knowledge management systems, virtually every aspect of servicing customer needs from product enquiry through to ordering can occur without any human intervention by supplier employees. Additionally, however, where human support is needed, this must be delivered by highly trained support staff aided by access to the latest database systems and on-line customer assistance tools in order to sustain interface productivity.

Currently it appears that the introduction of automated systems is creating some of the greatest productivity gains in e-business service industries (DePrince and Ford 1999). Examples include the on-line provision of financial services such as insurance, banking and trading shares. The same approach is apparent in the airline industry as more and more passengers are migrating on-line to both research their trip and purchase tickets.

QUALITY

In the late 1970s, Western nation firms began to realise that Pacific Rim competitors were using superior quality to establish new beachheads in global markets. Possibly the real irony in this situation was the fact that it had been American experts such as Deeming and Crosby who, ignored in their own country, had taught the tiger nations how to use quality as a very effective weapon through which to build customer satisfaction. Perhaps not unsurprisingly, the 1980s were a period when quality became a strategic priority for firms such as IBM, Xerox, Ford and Rolls Royce.

Schonberger (1990) has described the development of effective quality management practices as a journey through the phases of correction, prevention, cost-based quality and ultimately seeking to serve the customer. Correction-based quality was founded on what is now considered to be an outmoded concept, namely waiting until something goes wrong and then initiating remedial work to correct the fault. By moving to prevention-based quality, the organisation exploits new and existing knowledge sources to develop processes that minimise the occurrence of the mistakes which have been causing the defects to occur.

Studies by researchers such as Schoeffler et al. (1974) have clearly demonstrated that companies whose products are perceived to be of a higher quality will enjoy higher profits and a larger market share. Recognition of this fact has permitted quality to move from an operational, process management issue concerned with cost minimisation to a board-level topic of fundamental relevance in the planning of future corporate strategies. Having gained acceptance for the idea that quality should under-pin strategy, it has been a relatively small conceptual step for organisations to understand how quality can provide the basis for sustaining long term customer loyalty. Within only a very short space of time, Western nation case examples have emerged of how good practice provides the foundation stone for market success (for example, Milliken Corporation in the US textile industry; Avis Corporation in the international car rental market).

One outcome of the efforts by the large multinational firms to improve service quality is that customers now have much higher expectations of their suppliers and, furthermore, are willing proactively to seek out alternative suppliers. In relation to the management of quality, e-business can be treated as a service industry. As with any service industry, customer loyalty is critically dependent upon the actions of the supplier being able totally to fulfil the expectations of the customer. As shown by Parasuraman et al. (1985) the critical variables influencing whether the customer perceives that expectations are being met include reliability, tangibles, responsiveness, assurance and empathy. In many service encounters, the customer is forced to accept some degree of supplier failing and continues to patronise the same service source because the supplier is the most convenient source of the service. It is important, however, that the e-marketer recognises the 'loyalty due to convenience' scenario will rarely apply to customers purchasing in cyberspace. For example, if the web site visited fails to fulfil expectations, then at the click of a button the potential customer can instantaneously travel to a new location offering a higher level of service quality (Shapiro and Varian 1999).

All of the same issues of using knowledge to maximise the perceived quality of services within terrestrial companies also apply to on-line operations, namely order fulfilment, customer questions, shipment errors, product returns and guarantees. The only problem is that the lack of knowledge of many on-line customers is such that they are likely to make more mistakes and therefore need even more help resolving problems which their errors originally caused (Bartholomew 2000). For example, Ernst & Young estimate that about two-thirds of people abandon their on-line 'shopping carts' because they become confused or concerned about their purchase decisions. The other cause of service problems is that some on-line operations have failed to link their website effectively to their back-office order fulfilment activities.

Outsourcing to Acquire Knowledge

In response to these problems a number of service companies have decided to utilise the knowledge accumulated by other, more experienced, organisations and have out-sourced the provision to one-to-one live customer representative services. LivePerson in New York (*www.liveperson.com*) is once such organisation which operates a team of customer support people. The company provides a text-based talk back service for their clients. The company has 450 clients, charges a $1,000 start fee and a monthly fee of $250 per operator. A single operator can handle up to four on-line conversations simultaneously. Such services are also used in the business-to-business market. For example the San Diego firm Equipp.com, which markets metal cutting equipment and forming machines, contracts with eAssist.com to provide an on-line customer support service.

Other firms have sufficient knowledge to be able to operate their own customer support systems. For example Consolidated Freightways in California uses technology developed by New Channel Inc. which connects visitors to *www.cf.com* with Freightway service representatives. The system is based around a dialogue box which permits staff to converse on a one-to-one basis with customers, providing assistance, information and sales help.

INFORMATION SYSTEMS

By subscribing to a philosophy of seeking to respond to identified customer needs, perhaps not unsurprisingly, most marketers are critically aware of the importance of creating information systems that can generate knowledge about market environments. As a consequence, standard marketing texts usually recommend the creation of marketing information systems (MIS) of the type shown in Figure 5.2. As illustrated in Figure 5.2, the four critical subsystems are an internal data system, a market intelligence system, a market research system and a customer data system.

To provide inputs to the market research system, marketers use both published sources, panel data (for example, Nielsen store panels) and a variety of research techniques (usage and attitude studies, focus groups, customer satisfaction survey) to track and respond to changing customer behaviour. A common failing of many of these approaches is that limited marketing budgets often means that studies are only undertaken on an infrequent basis (for example, many major firms who execute usage and attitude surveys on an annual or bi-annual basis). Another factor which further weakens the effectiveness of an MIS is that some or all of the firm's key data sources are not linked to other information being acquired by the firm. For example, an accounting department's standard costing system which is not compatible with the manufacturing operation's computer therefore cannot be used to optimise costs during the development of production schedules.

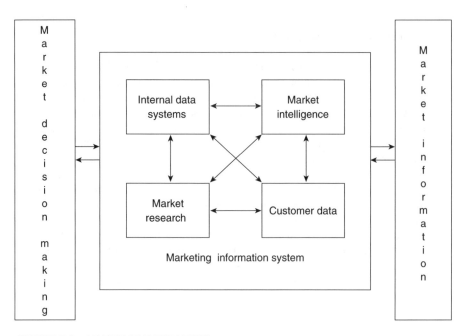

FIGURE 5.2 AN EXAMPLE MIS MODEL

The advent of low cost, extremely powerful computers clearly offers a mechanism through which to develop more integrated MIS operations. Furthermore the move to computerised on-line order entry systems now permits the creation of databases through which to monitor customer behaviour on a daily or even hourly basis. One only has to observe the example provided by the impact on market performance provided to American Airlines through their development of the SABRE seat reservation system to realise that computer technology can, by providing access to new sources of knowledge, deliver significant strategic advantage to an organisation. Unfortunately even today in many firms information management is still seen as the preserve of a centralised computer services department. Data processing managers are often more interested in ensuring that they retain control of all decisions related to the use of computers and approved software systems than providing effective knowledge management support systems to line managers across the organisation. Hence the marketer will need to assess carefully an organisation's data management capabilities. This is necessary in order to ensure these are able to support delivery of the knowledge required to manage activities effectively such as the delivery of customer service and to permit rapid diagnosis of problems likely to impact the firm's reputation in the marketplace.

Merely ensuring that the marketing department is utilising available information will not guarantee knowledge is being exploited effectively by

TABLE 5.3 A KNOWLEDGE UTILISATION AUDIT TOOL

Knowledge generation

1 In this company, we meet with customers at least once a year to acquire knowledge about what products or services they will need in the future.

 1   2   3   4   5   6   7
I disagree strongly   I agree strongly

2 In this organisation, to acquire additional knowledge we do a lot of in-house market research.

 1   2   3   4   5   6   7
I disagree strongly   I agree strongly

3 Our knowledge acquisition activities permit the company to detect changes rapidly in our customers' product preference.

 1   2   3   4   5   6   7
I disagree strongly   I agree strongly

4 We survey end users at least once a year to acquire knowledge concerning the quality of our products and services.

 1   2   3   4   5   6   7
I disagree strongly   I agree strongly

5 Acquired knowledge means we are quick to detect fundamental shifts in our industry (e.g., competition, technology, regulation).

 1   2   3   4   5   6   7
I disagree strongly   I agree strongly

6 We periodically seek new knowledge on the likely effect of changes in our business environment (e.g., regulation) on customers.

 1   2   3   4   5   6   7
I disagree strongly   I agree strongly

Knowledge dissemination

7 We have interdepartmental meetings at least once a quarter to exchange knowledge on market trends and developments.

 1   2   3   4   5   6   7
I disagree strongly   I agree strongly

8 Marketing personnel in our company spend time exchanging knowledge on our customers' future needs with other *functional* departments.

 1   2   3   4   5   6   7
I disagree strongly   I agree strongly

9 When something important happens to a major customer or market, the whole company knows about it in a short period.

 1   2   3   4   5   6   7
I disagree strongly   I agree strongly

10 Knowledge relating to customer satisfaction is disseminated at all levels in this business unit on a regular basis.

 1   2   3   4   5   6   7
I disagree strongly   I agree strongly

11 When one department finds out something important about competitors, it is quick to alert other departments.

 1   2   3   4   5   6   7
I disagree strongly   I agree strongly

(Continued)

TABLE 5.3 CONTINUED

Knowledge responsiveness

12	It only takes us a short time to decide how to respond to our competitors' price changes.	1 2 3 4 I disagree strongly	5 6 7 I agree strongly
13	We never ignore changes in our customers' product or service needs.	1 2 3 4 I disagree strongly	5 6 7 I agree strongly
14	We periodically review our product development efforts to ensure that they are in line with what customers want.	1 2 3 4 I disagree strongly	5 6 7 I agree strongly
15	Several departments get together periodically to plan a response to changes taking place in our business environment.	1 2 3 4 I disagree strongly	5 6 7 I agree strongly
16	If a major competitor were to launch an intensive campaign targeted at our customers, we would implement a response immediately.	1 2 3 4 I disagree strongly	5 6 7 I agree strongly
17	The activities of the different departments in this company are well co-ordinated.	1 2 3 4 I disagree strongly	5 6 7 I agree strongly
18	Customer complaints never fall on deaf ears in this company.	1 2 3 4 I disagree strongly	5 6 7 I agree strongly
19	If we came up with a great new marketing plan, we probably would be able to implement it immediately.	1 2 3 4 I disagree strongly	5 6 7 I agree strongly
20	When we find that customers would like us to modify a service the departments involved make concerted efforts to do so.	1 2 3 4 I disagree strongly	5 6 7 I agree strongly
21	Overall, our organisation is orienated to exploiting all available knowledge to serve the needs of the market.	1 2 3 4 I disagree strongly	5 6 7 I agree strongly

an organisation. For this aim to be met, knowledge must be acquired from all available sources, disseminated across the entire organisation and most importantly put to good use (Jaworski et al. 2000). In order to ensure that the firm has the competence necessary to achieve these goals for the exploitation of knowledge, one approach is to undertake an audit using an assessment tool of the type shown in Table 5.3.

For those firms which decide that e-business offers a new channel through which to attract new customers and retain the loyalty of existing customers, poorly integrated knowledge systems are not an acceptable option. Success can only occur if all data flows are integrated and utilised to achieve the objective of staying ahead of the competition. Thus continuous investment is demanded to achieve the goal of further upgrading and enhancing the company information systems. Such investment is critical if the firm is seeking to execute a brand differentiation strategy based around an integrated system for delivering information which is superior to that being electronically communicated by the competition (Young et al. 1997).

MARSHALL INDUSTRIES

Marshall Industries is the fourth largest distributor of electronic components and production supplies in the United States. The company distributes 125,000 products manufactured by over 100 suppliers through 38 distribution branches in North America and in Europe, through an equity share in SEI. Over 75% of the company's sales are semiconductor products. For many years the distribution of electronic components has been a highly competitive business with firms seeking to exploit competencies in areas such as product availability, prices, customer service, technical expertise and market coverage as attributes upon which to build customer loyalty. In the 1990s, the distribution business needed to respond to a new trend, namely large customers acting to globalise their business and demanding that their suppliers acquire a global sourcing capability. Concurrently distributors were expected to take greater responsibility for managing the inventories of their large customers as these latter organisations moved towards optimising their JIT manufacturing philosophies.

In reviewing the implications of all of these trends, Marshall Industries recognised that it had become a dysfunctional organisation relying on outdated assumptions and knowledge mind-sets upon which to base internal processes. This situation was exacerbated by a tendency for their distribution branches to operate independently of the firm's overall umbrella strategy. The conclusion of the management was that the organisation had become fixated with maximising product sales to the detriment of the more critical goal of responding to the real needs of the customer. Their revised vision, enshrined in the phrase 'Free, Perfect, Now', is based upon the reality that customers, if given the choice, want everything: namely products and services at the lowest cost, highest possible quality, maximum customisation and fastest possible delivery times. To fulfil its revised vision, the company recognised that (a) new knowledge would have to be embedded into the company in order to challenge every sectoral and internal operating convention and (b) there was a need totally to embrace a philosophy of integrating all aspects of internal knowledge management with the systems being operated by its customers.

Some of the changes that were implemented were based upon conventional wisdom (for example, flattening the organisation to improve response times; replacing the reward systems based upon individual merit with a system whereby employee bonuses are linked to overall company performance).

Concurrently, however, the company examined how entrepreneurial approaches to the use of IT to support knowledge management could result in acquiring market leadership in an e-commerce world. To achieve this goal, the company decided against huge investments in totally new systems. Instead it opted for exploiting the entrepreneurial skills of its own workforce to find ways of improving the acquisition, storage and exploitation of knowledge by linking together existing company IT systems using low cost, commercially available products such as groupware platforms and client servers. In 1992, for example, Marshall Industries launched QOBRA (quality order booking and resell application) based around an IBM-DB2 platform, and internet/EDI front end and a Sun-Unix warehouse transaction management system.

The next stage was to link together all of the knowledge contained within the organisation such that the organisation could exploit internal knowledge management capabilities as a route through which to deliver superior levels of service to its customers. All field sales staff were equipped with laptop computers which permitted them in real time to check inventory, product specifications, data sheets and orders in process. The system also allowed the sales force to communicate with other employees who had specialist knowledge which might be used by the sales force in making presentations to customers. The core element of this intranet system is Compass which acts as a marketing encyclopaedia containing over 2500 documents about the product lines and suppliers for whom Marshall Industries acts as a distributor.

In 1994, Marshall Industries began to implement the next phase of its strategy to become a superior knowledge provider by creating an on-line browser that provided customers with a 24-hour, automated, order fulfilment process system. This system was complemented by an EDI automatic replenishment channel for large customers plus a fax and telephone-based order entry system. The following year, the company launched an object-relational database, which provides customers with a dynamic picture of the products, that Marshall Industries can supply. Behind the system is a database containing information about almost 200,000 parts, over 100,000 data sheets and a real-time inventory system. The site allows the customer to order parts and request samples. To assist customers track the progress of their orders, Marshall has linked its systems with that of its logistics partner, United Parcels.

The system offers an extensive range of additional knowledge provision services. RealAudio broadcasts news about the electronics industry. Visitors can also talk to Marshall engineers on-line 24 hours of the day to obtain assistance in the selection of products, troubleshooting problems and product design. The NetSeminar element of the system links together customers and suppliers to assist in the design of new products. It also offers after-sales training on new technologies. From a studio in El Monte, the firm broadcasts product information in real-time video and audio streams. Viewers and listeners can pose questions to the presenters of these programmes using a GlobalChat system. The success of NetSeminar has subsequently led the company to create a separate consulting business called the Education News and Entertainment Network. This system permits clients to hold real-time seminars over the internet for purposes such as publicity announcements, sales training and after-sales service. Hence it can be concluded from these case materials that the only effective strategy for e-commerce brand differentiation is to operate integrated information systems superior to those utilised by competition (Young et al. 1997).

ALTERNATIVE CUSTOMER NEEDS

In considering customer needs, over recent years a number of researchers have come to question classic strategic marketing theory on the grounds that it places undue emphasis on the management of single transactions. Studies of the marketing process in service sectors such as finance and retailing have revealed situations where customers do not exhibit a strong transactional orientated buying behaviour. This situation has thereby permitted supplier firms to exploit opportunities for building long term relationships based on working in close partnership with purchasers.

During the 1970s and 1980s, there was a massive expansion in companies dedicated to the provision of services in sectors as diverse as finance, fast food and management consultancy. Marketers hired by these organisations encountered significant problems when attempting to apply classical concepts such as influencing customer demand through application of the 4Ps. The conclusion of both practitioners and academics was that because of features such as the intangible nature of goods, difficulty in separating production from consumption and the heterogeneous nature of customer need, effective service marketing would require the evolution of new paradigms.

Similar to the marketer in industrial markets, many service marketing theorists focused on the fact that firms which were placing emphasis on single transactions should in fact be attempting to build long term relationships with customers. A strong impetus to this alternative philosophy was provided by Reichfeld and Sasser (1990) who demonstrated that a transaction orientation could result in focusing excessive resources on attracting new customers when in fact the real benefits of marketing come from programmes directed at retaining existing customers (or in their terminology ensuring achievement of 'zero defections').

As a result of studies of the marketing processes employed by both industrial and service firms, a new school of thought has emerged which examines how the firm can orchestrate internal resources and processes to create and sustain customer loyalty. Collectively this new orientation, which has both American (Berry 1982) and Nordic (Gummesson 1987) roots, is known as *relationship marketing*. Supporters of this new form of marketing argue that in order to survive in markets which have become

TABLE 5.4   CONTRASTING MARKETING PHILOSOPHIES

Transactional marketing	Relationship marketing
Orientation towards single purchase.	Orientation towards repeat sales.
Limited direct customer–supplier contact.	Close, frequent customer–supplier contact.
Focus on product benefits.	Focus on value to customer.
Emphasis on near term performance.	Emphasis on long term performance.
Limited level of customer service.	High level of customer service.
Goal of customer satisfaction.	Goal of 'delighting the customer'.
Quality is a manufacturing responsibility.	Quality is a total organisation responsibility.

more competitive and more turbulent, organisations must move away from managing transactions and instead focus on building long lasting customer relationships (Webster 1992).

Advocates of relationship marketing will typically support their views through a comparison of processes of the type shown in Table 5.4.

Some disciples of the 'new marketing' have suggested that traditional concepts based around the approach of focusing resources on the 4Ps, which may have been appropriate in North American consumer branded goods markets of the 1950s and 1960s, are no longer relevant in today's world. Gronroos (1994), for example, proposes that 'the usefulness of the 4Ps as a general theory for practical purposes is, to say the least, highly questionable'. A somewhat less extreme position would be for firms to adopt a segmentation philosophy ranging from building strong relationships with key customers through to continuing to utilise the traditional 4Ps approach for those customers seeking a standardised, generic product proposition. A similarly balanced view is presented by Anderson and Narus (1991) who recommend that firms weigh both customer orientation towards closer relationships and the cost/benefit implications of sustaining close relationships when selecting the most appropriate strategy to suit prevailing market conditions.

Jackson (1985) has presented a similar view about the need to recognise that only certain market scenarios will permit application of a relationship marketing orientation. For her, transactional marketing is probably more appropriate in those cases where the customer has a short time horizon and switching suppliers is a low cost activity. Thus a customer seeking a standard specification microchip can purchase this item from a number of manufacturers and the purchase decision will be heavily influenced by which supplier is offering what are perceived as the best terms and conditions at the time of order placement. In contrast, where the customer has a long time horizon and the costs of switching are high, then the purchase decision will involve a careful search for a supplier who is prepared to invest time and money to build a strong, lasting relationship with the customer. An example of this latter type of situation would be an automobile manufacturer seeking to purchase a 'state of the art' robotic, car assembly line who will carefully review the project bid specifications and commitment to partnership exhibited by potential suppliers of robotic machine tools.

If one accepts Jackson's perspective, then the debate between transactional versus relationship marketing is one of choice. Thus in virtually every industrial and/or service sector situation there are price orientated customers who respond well to a transactional marketing philosophy and there are other purchasers with whom a strong long term relationship can be created. The objective for the marketer under these circumstances is to select the marketing philosophy for their organisation that is most suited to their firm's internal capabilities and/or the nature of the product proposition they desire to offer to the market.

Knowledge-based Positioning

6

CHAPTER SUMMARY

Porter proposes the variables of price versus performance and focused versus mass market coverage can be used to select an optimal market position. Large firms usually adopt a position that permits the offering of a standard product across the entire market. Smaller firms tend to occupy niche positions. The advent of on-line trading is increasing the knowledge firms can acquire about markets. As large firms acquire such knowledge they are tending to enter niche markets and hence there is a blurring of the market boundaries between large and small firms. To determine if the firm is using knowledge to develop an optimal market position, a market knowledge audit is advised. The audit will cover issues such as customer knowledge, process knowledge, technology knowledge, relationship knowledge and strategic knowledge. For firms wishing to acquire further market knowledge, one solution is to become a member of a business network.

INTRODUCTION

Marketers have long accepted that success demands identification of some form of competitive advantage capable of permitting the organisation to be positioned differently from other firms operating in the same market sector. By combining the concepts of niche versus mass marketing and the nature of product proposition to be offered to customers, Michael Porter (1985) evolved the theory that there are four possible generic competitive advantage options available to organisations namely:

1 Cost leadership.
2 Differentiation.
3 Focused cost leadership.
4 Focused differentiation.

Cost leadership is based upon exploiting some aspect of internal organisational processes that can be executed at a cost significantly lower than the competition. There are various sources of this cost advantage. These include lower input costs, lower in-plant production costs and/or delivery costs reduced by the proximity of key markets. *Focused cost leadership* exploits the same proposition, but the company decides to occupy a specific niche(s) servicing only part of the total market. Porter has proposed that focused and overall market cost leadership represent a 'low scale advantage' because it is frequently the case that eventually a company's advantage is eroded either by rising costs or by a competitor identifying a mechanism by which to enter the market offering lower priced goods or services.

The generic alternative of *differentiation* is based upon offering superior performance. Porter argues that this is a 'higher scale advantage' because (a) the producer can usually command a premium price for output and (b) competitors are less of a threat, for to be successful they must be able to offer a higher performance specification product. *Focused differentiation*, which is typically the preserve of smaller, more specialist firms, is also based on a platform of superior performance. The only difference is that the firm specialises in serving the needs of a specific market sector.

An alternative perspective to the theory of low versus high scale advantage is the level of knowledge demanded to sustain a selected market position. Typically low scale advantage such as access to low cost raw materials (for example, the Middle East oilfields compared to Alaskan Slope fields) or low cost labour (car plants in the Czech Republic versus Germany) does not require superior knowledge capability to exploit them. This contrasts with high scale advantage where the acquisition of unique, specialist knowledge is usually demanded if the firm is to offer a superior product proposition to the market. The other facet of high scale advantage is that there are a multitude of different forms of knowledge which can be exploited in seeking to differentiate a product or service from the competition. Garvin (1987), for example, has proposed that in relation to superior quality there are seven different knowledge dimensions which might be considered, namely: the knowledge required to offer different features, better actual performance, greater conformance to quality expectations specified by customers, better durability, higher reliability, superior style and advanced design. In addition to the knowledge dimensions associated with the physical product, organisations can also exploit other aspects of the purchase and product utilisation process by developing superior knowledge management capabilities that will support offering outstanding service across the areas of ease of ordering, delivery, installation, customer training, maintenance, repair and post-purchase product upgrades.

Although a very useful conceptual tool, a very major risk associated with the Porterian competitive advantage option model is that if users exhibit blind allegiance to theory, they may incorrectly decide that the four alternative positionings are mutually exclusive. Available case materials would suggest that in the past many Western nations assumed that one should strive to be either a low cost leader or a producer of superior,

Performance

	Single benefits		Combined benefits
Mass market	Cost leadership*	Differentiation*	Value and performance differentiation
Mass customisation	Customised cost leadership*	Customised differentiation	Customised value and differentiation
Niche	Niche cost leadership*	Niche differentiation*	Niche value and differentiation

Market coverage

| Low | Average | High |

Knowledge management capability

(* = the original four porterian strategic options)

FIGURE 6.1 AN EXPANDED STRATEGIC OPTIONS MATRIX

differentiated goods. Thus, for example, in the 1980s, in response to the high labour costs associated with delivering the country's social charter, German firms concentrated on premium priced, superior goods market sectors, whereas in Spain, the lower labour costs stimulated the establishment of factories orientated towards serving down market, price sensitive sectors.

This situation can be contrasted with Pacific Rim firms whose Confucian approach to decision-making appears to result frequently in the generation of superior, holistic solutions. In the case of competitive advantage, the knowledge acquired in developing flexible manufacturing technologies and processes permitted Pacific Rim firms to develop products which concurrently offer high standards of performance and low prices. Their abilities to achieve this goal in areas such as video cameras, cars and televisions was a key factor in contributing to achievement of major global market share gains during the 1980s. Thus it seems reasonable to suggest that marketers can significantly increase the number of competitive advantage options available to them by considering the opportunities offered by directing knowledge management capabilities towards developing products that offer the options of (a) combining cost leadership with differentiation and (b) product customisation. As shown by Figure 6.1, this action increases the number of competitive advantage options from four to twelve.

Sustaining a Global Position

The Honda company is positioned as a supplier of vehicles in the mass car market. Underpinning this positioning is the business strategy of 'Small Is Smart' which reflects the goal of maintaining the flexibility and efficiency of a small company while operating as a large company in a global market (Sonoda 2002). In order to achieve this goal the company is critically dependant upon ensuring employees in all operations around the world can access the vast pool of knowledge which exists inside the organisation.

The global headquarters in Japan is the source of knowledge about manufacturing technology. Managers in the firm's five regions, North America, South America, Europe, Japan and Asia, have autonomy sufficient to respond to local changing customer needs and prevailing economic conditions.

In expanding globally Honda needed the ability to produce virtually any of its products in more than one market using a manufacturing model which could be adopted in all major factories. To achieve this goal the company has focused on ensuring that knowledge acquired in one location can be shared rapidly by other car plants around the world. An essential element in manufacturing flexibility has been the use of robots for welding. The robots are programmable and when any plant identifies a way to enhance the operation of their robots, this knowledge is shared with all other plants.

To maximise the benefits of knowledge sharing the company has defined a global standard layout for all main assembly lines. In this way process locations, times and work processes are common to all factories producing the same model type. This approach minimises the time it takes to introduce new models around the world. For example, in the case of the Honda Civic this model was introduced into twelve plants in just nine months. Just as importantly the standard layout means that as a lesson is learned in one location, the knowledge can be introduced immediately at the firm's other factories.

An important aspect of the Honda operating philosophy is the belief that employees, whether designing, manufacturing or marketing products, should use their own capacity to think and to resolve problems. This is achieved by the company encouraging a 'challenging spirit' within the workforce. As a result many of the ideas for change come from employees analysing how day-to-day tasks can be enhanced and improved.

Learning from Markets

The vision of the founder of IKEA, Ingvard Kamprad, was to go beyond Sweden and democratise the furniture industry across Europe by making new products affordable to mass market customers (von Krogh and Cusumano 2001). The initial strategy of market expansion was that of seeking to duplicate standard processes across all markets. The company would buy land on the outskirts of cities, build simple, functional two-storey buildings with displays on the floor and warehousing on the ground floor. IKEA also standardised documentation, logos, personnel selection and training. Employees acquired common knowledge through studying manuals and attending training courses.

When IKEA entered the US market it soon found, however, that knowledge which formed the basis of European operations did not immediately translate into a successful marketing philosophy in North America. Customer tastes and employee backgrounds were found to be very different. Customers had different needs and products specified for the European market were not appropriate in the United States. As a result IKEA had a slow start there until new knowledge was acquired about how to implement actions such as adapting product design concepts to suit American tastes.

Redeploying Knowledge

Daido Metals is one the three major suppliers of engine bearings to the Japanese car industry. The company market positioning is to outperform competition in the areas of both cost and quality (Nobeoka et al. 2002). To sustain this positioning the company relies heavily on acquiring knowledge from interactions with one customer that can then be redeployed across projects for other customers.

Customers typically conduct numerous engineering tests after integrating parts supplied by Daido into a system product or vehicle product. Daido is then provided with feedback on the technical performance of the part. It also receives data on performance in the final market such as customer satisfaction ratings and defect reports. Daido then distributes this new knowledge across the organisation to stimulate new or revised practices that can further reduce costs or improve quality.

Another Japanese manufacturer which also makes use of redeployable knowledge is Keyence, a supplier of sensors for car plant automation projects. The firm is positioned as being the lowest cost provider of customised products. The development of completely customised products for a single customer is an extremely expensive proposition. In order to overcome this cost obstacle the firm works with multiple customers, analysing each customer's needs and then developing a family of product sensors to solve the customer problem. Importantly the knowledge acquired for one customer is then redeployed across other sensor development projects. In this way the customer can be supplied with a customised solution but because development costs are reduced by exploiting existing knowledge, the customer solution can be delivered at a price approaching that which the customer would normally expect to pay for a standardised solution.

LARGE VERSUS SMALL FIRM POSITIONING OPTIONS

Richard Tedlow (1990) formulated some generic guidelines concerning effective strategies for establishing successful mass market brands. These guidelines clearly demonstrate why a firm with limited knowledge management capabilities and/or financial resources would in most cases be wise to avoid a confrontation with a larger firm. Firstly, the large firm can out-compete the small firm because the former has the knowledge and financial resources to be able to exploit the economies of scale of mass production to generate high absolute profits by selling large volumes of low margin goods. Secondly, the large firm can use its massive level of generated profits to invest in high levels of promotional activity as a mechanism through which to shape and mould market demand. Thirdly, the large firm has the knowledge to be able to create a vertical system in which raw materials are sourced, production operations managed and products delivered to the final consumer. Finally, having achieved market dominance through being the first company to exploit a strategy of high volume/low unit prices, firms such as Nestlé and General Foods are able to create economies of scale barriers to ward off attacks from virtually any source of competition.

In the early years of the internet, some of the first entrants into the market were small firms offering specialist goods. This trend caused some industry observers to predict that cyberspace trading at last provided a low cost, market knowledge delivery system that could threaten the long term existence of large companies which had achieved market dominance through using traditional mass marketing information channels such as television advertising. However, over the last few years it has become apparent that many major brands are now exploiting the internet effectively to further consolidate their market position. When one analyses this situation it is apparent that e-business is a market channel that tends to favour the brand leaders in many industrial sectors. A prime reason for this is that when customers start to use the internet they are often very concerned about the potential risks associated with this new way of executing the purchase transaction process. As a way to reduce risk, this type of customer will usually select the company or brand name about which they have greatest knowledge and product usage experience.

Many major companies have used their financial resources to offer a very broad range of products to consumers. Thus upon entry into cyberspace, these brands can exploit both the long standing purchase habits of customers shopping in terrestrial markets and their ability to offer breadth of product choice. Under these circumstances, the issue arises of whether small, less well known companies can survive in an on-line world. Analysis of the situation would tend to indicate that web sites featuring long established, broad product line propositions and category expert web sites will co-exist in cyberspace for the foreseeable future. This is because they are serving different customer needs. For example, in the case of medical products in the United States, some customers who have a limited need for new knowledge, because they know what they want, will probably visit the large company, broad line web operation such as *www.kmart.com*. Other customers may require additional knowledge about what is the best available treatment. In this latter case they will probably contact a smaller, but knowledge-rich, specialist web site such as *www.planetrx.com*. Similarly in the business-to-business market for computer servers, some customers with extensive prior experience of purchasing servers will be happy to buy on-line from the broad line, value-based supplier, Compaq. If, however, the customer feels that they need additional knowledge because they are in the market to buy a sector-specific, specialist server-based system, they are more likely to select a specialist provider of server technology in that market sector. This is because they will probably believe the specialist server supplier will provide the new knowledge they require in order to make an optimal purchase decision.

Christensen and Tedlow (2000) have suggested that in the debate over the depth or breadth of knowledge which on-line firms should make available to customers, one should recognise that possible outcomes may be similar to those which were seen in the battle between national retailers and small independent stores in the 1960s and 1970s. By exploiting their economies of scale in operations and procurement, plus using a high turnover inventory model, the former could offer products at 20% lower prices. The survival response of the small retailer stores was to move up-market and to exploit their in-depth market sector knowledge to offer superior customer service and product expertise. Thus if the small e-retailer is now facing this type of competition in cyberspace markets, yet again the solution is to move up-market. The market position to occupy should be that of being a superior knowledge source capable of offering the customer a much more informed, in-depth source of information about alternative product selection options.

Even before the advent of e-business, firms have had to give consideration to how their market positioning would influence the nature of the knowledge to be made available to customers (Evans and Wurster 1999). Essentially the issue has always been one of *reach* versus *depth*. Large firms tend to opt for reach because this maximises the number of customers who will receive information that can influence purchase decisions. Mass market producers have tended to rely on massive expenditure on promotional channels such as television. Major retailers base their operations around maximising the number of outlets which they open across a country.

This situation can be contrasted with specialist firms that tend to focus on contacting fewer customers but delivering to each potential purchaser a much more extensive volume of information. One example of depth in the place of reach is provided by specialist clothing manufacturers which use catalogue-based direct marketing campaigns to merchandise their sector or product-specific fashion goods. In the retail sector specialist outlets tend to be well staffed with sales personnel who can provide expert one-to-one guidance to potential customers.

The advent of e-business has raised new opportunities for firms debating the issue of reach versus depth of information that can be made available to customers. This is because web sites potentially offer an ability (a) to reach any individual who has access to an internet connection such as a PC, a television or a WAP telephone and (b) by using multiple web pages, to provide the contacted individual with huge quantities of information. Thus in the small firms sector, an independently owned hotel which previously was restricted to media such as an insertion in a tourist board brochure or a limited number of newspapers can now go on-line to make contact with potential visitors from anywhere in the world. In the large firm sector, music firms are complementing their mass marketing campaigns with information-rich web sites carrying performer biographies, chat rooms and downloadable sample video and music clips.

An interesting trend in e-commerce is the appearance of new on-line knowledge providers willing to assist the customer gain access to more extensive and, even more importantly, totally unbiased information. Thus, for example, American consumers are no longer reliant upon the information available at the local dealer showrooms. They can now go on-line and visit Microsoft's CarPoint site to obtain comparative data on both product specifications and prices being offered by all the major car manufacturers. The dilemma facing on-line suppliers of products and services is how they should respond to this alternative mechanism whereby customers can access alternative knowledge sources. Some firms have already decided that the only solution is to expand their knowledge provision activities by offering information about their competitors. In response to on-line travel agents offering consumers access to search engines listing all available airlines and prices, some of major airline web sites are also beginning to provide a similar breadth and depth of information about all carriers on a specific route. In the computer industry, Dell has expanded its on-line product configuration service to include computer peripherals from other manufacturers.

The Sabre Story

How the majority of firms will cope with a world where there will be increasing pressure from customers for suppliers to expand the volume of knowledge provision is as yet extremely unclear. However, one lesson that can be learned from an early example of exploiting electronic technology is American Airline's development of their SABRE computer-based routing and seat reservation system. Initially developed as an in-house product for the company's own use, the developers rapidly realised that the system could be made more powerful by embedding data on competitors into the system. Having validated the power of the system, SABRE was spun off as an independent company to offer the technology to the rest of the airline industry. This new company, which essentially is one of the first examples of a firm created as an electronic plat-form, knowledge management systems provider, is now valued by the stock market at twice the value of the originator, American Airlines. Similarly *www.priceline.com*, an internet auction site offering deep discount travel bookings, was valued at its April 1999 stock market offering at $10 billion. At the time this valuation was made it was higher than the combined stock market valuation for United, Northwest and Continental Airlines.

THE BLURRING OF STRATEGIC BOUNDARIES

Many years ago marketers in large companies recognised that in some mass markets customers were beginning to exhibit variation in their product needs. In analysing this situation, Tedlow (1990) concluded that long term survival of many leading mass market companies necessitated them moving from a profit-through-volume strategy towards an operating philosophy based around segmenting the market and offering a variety of goods to the now more sophisticated and experienced customer. This move into market segmentation was the beginning of a blurring between the strategic positioning of many smaller firms and their large firm counterparts.

Many large multinationals have accepted that market segmentation is more advantageous than merely offering a single, standardised product to all areas of the market. For example Coca-Cola and Pepsi-Cola have launched low calorie products for weight conscious consumers. One of the key driving forces in such moves has been the ability of these large firms through the use of sophisticated computer-based analytical tools to acquire much more detailed knowledge about the specific needs of identifiably different customer groups. Once acquired, such detailed knowledge can then be exploited to position products effectively to appeal to specific target market audiences and to select the best media vehicles through which to deliver promotional information.

Further blurring of the strategic positioning boundaries between large and small firms occurred as the former acquired the knowledge to use lean manufacturing technologies to cost effectively serve the specialist product needs of smaller and smaller customer segments. The ultimate possibility offered by this scenario is that in some market sectors, companies could consider the idea of one-to-one or mass customised marketing.

Before the 1990s, a major drawback for large firms wishing to expand into one-to-one or mass customised marketing was the limited knowledge that these firms had about microvariations in customer need. This barrier was removed because companies became able to acquire data on individual customer purchases due to the advent of electronic shop tills which permitted the monitoring of purchase patterns of individual consumers. Further knowledge could be accessed by large firms exploiting data generated from consumers using credit cards to make purchases and the information available from customers joining loyalty schemes which utilise 'smart cards' to record individual purchase behaviour. These data sets, when studied using computer-based statistical analysis tools, permit the identification of much smaller, distinct customer clusters. Baker and Baker (1998) have proposed that this new approach has permitted large firms to compete more effectively with smaller specialist firms because the former are now able to move much closer to their customers using the knowledge they have which permits them to:

- Classify customer into distinct groups based upon their purchase behaviour.
- Model relationships between possible variables such as age, income, location to determine which of these influence purchase decisions.

- Cluster data into finite clusters that define specific customer types.
- Use this knowledge to tailor products and other aspects of the marketing mix such as promotional message or price to meet the specific needs of individual customers.

Customers' increasing use of electronic purchase platforms in both business-to-business and consumer goods markets has greatly added to the ability of large firms to use data mining to gain in-depth insights into the behaviour of their customers. The reason for this situation is that when customers start surfing the internet they are asked to provide detailed information to potential suppliers. One can link together information on what pages they visit, data provided to questions asked as they register to be considered as customers, their e-mail address and data from their credit card (*Business Week* 1999b). In commenting on this new world, Jeffrey Bezos, the founder of Amazon.com, has proposed that the e-retailer can now behave like the small-town specialist shopkeeper because large firms have in-depth knowledge about everybody who comes into their on-line stores. Armed with such knowledge, the large retailer can compete with small shops because they have the capability to personalise service to suit the specific needs of every individual customer across a widely dispersed geographic domain.

Even before the advent of e-commerce, in commenting upon the increasing value of exploiting technology to gain a deeper understanding of individual customers, Porter and Miller (1985) forecasted that the future market winners would be those organisations that recognised ahead of the competition the value of managing knowledge as the core asset of the business. As firms have begun to exploit the data-rich environments which are associated with the e-commerce transaction process, a new concept has arisen in the marketing literature, namely CRM. This involves using data about customers to ensure a firm offers an optimal product proposition and customer-specific prices. Additionally the firm can tailor all aspects of service quality such that every point of contact from initial enquiry to post-purchase service is perceived by the customer as a trouble free, seamless service (Vowler 1999). In the past only small firms believed they were sufficiently close to customers to be effective at CRM. The advent of e-CRM technology being adopted by large firms has radically changed this scenario. This technology, by blurring the strategic boundary between large and small firms, represents a major threat to the latter. This is because many are deluding themselves into believing they are still able to offer a level of customised service that is superior when compared to what they perceive as 'faceless', impersonal multinational corporations.

In his analysis of the strategic implications associated with operating in the knowledge-rich world of e-commerce, Glazer (1999, p. 61) has proposed that the current winners are the 'smart companies'. He defines these as organisations which have realised the power of IT to totally transform business practices within their market sector and are the 'first movers' to exploit every advance in computer and telecommunications technology ahead of their 'dumber' competitors. He suggests that the key objective of the smart firm, whether it is large or small, is to offer the benefits of:

- One-stop shopping such that customer needs can be satisfied by the knowledge available from a single supplier, thereby saving the customer time in searching out a range of goods.
- Providing the customer with a menu of knowledge concerning modes of product form and different delivery options.
- Proactively anticipating the changing market needs and developing even more effective knowledge delivery systems for more rapidly and more efficiently satisfying the customer.

A critical variable in the execution of a mass customisation strategy is an ability to produce the customised product when required by the purchaser (*The Economist* 2000c). This aim has already been achieved by large firms such as Dell Computers which permits customers to design an individualised computer on-line that is then manufactured by the company. Many small hi-tech manufacturing firms can only look with envy at this approach. To aspire to such levels of on-line sophistication will usually require a complete redesign of virtually every operating system and knowledge management process within the organisation from procurement through to post-purchase provision of service support.

THE KNOWLEDGE AUDIT

For the firm wishing to move closer to customers through one-to-one marketing it is critical that prior to such a positioning decision being reached the organisation already has the capability to manage the knowledge required to implement such a marketing strategy. To assist the firm it is useful to undertake a knowledge audit. This audit will need to examine the following areas of organisational activity (Pepper et al. 1999):

A Customer knowledge management

1 Ability to identify the company's different customer groups.
2 Ability to categorise customers by the value of business each group represents.
3 All customer data is stored on accessible electronic platforms.
4 Where the firm markets products in B2B markets, data is accessible about the different personalities who constitute the purchase decision process within each customer organisation.
5 Ability to rank customers in relation to the revenue flow which each represents.

6   Ability to use databases to classify different customer groups within each market sector.
7   Ability for effective personalised interaction with each customer.
8   Ability to collect data on customer interaction and to store this data in a readily accessible form.
9   Ability to exploit different media such as personal, impersonal, fax, telephone, web site.
10 Ability to customise products and services to meet specific customer needs.
11 Ability to individualise products and services to totally fulfil variance in customer needs.
12 Ability to individualise pre- and post-purchase services to fulfil variance in customer needs.

B Process management

1   Appropriate structured service quality systems already exist.
2   Quality is a formalised critical aspect of delivering the firm's marketing strategy.
3   Quality management is orientated towards the specific needs of different customer groups.
4   Full understanding of the relationship between managing internal processes and fulfilling the needs of customers.
5   Full understanding of how to assess how business processes can impact individual customer expectations.

C Technology management

1   Orientation is towards technology selection aimed at satisfaction of customer needs.
2   Effectiveness of technology is evaluated through research involving customers.
3   New technology is being sourced continually to further enhance the effectiveness of managing interactions with customers.
4   New technology is being sourced continually than can enhance the way employees interact with customers.

D Knowledge management

1   The company has a clear strategy about how to acquire and analyse information about customer needs.
2   The company is extremely effective at analysing knowledge acquired about customers.
3   All employees are encouraged to identify every opportunity to acquire new customer information.
4   The company is able to analyse the interaction which occurs between the company and the customer.
5   The company is able to acquire and integrate knowledge from all areas of the company operation.

E Market relationships

1 The company selects market partners who can complement knowledge management capabilities.
2 The company selects market relationships on the basis of how potential partners perceive the importance of using knowledge to serve customer needs.
3 The company continually evaluates the effectiveness of its partners' knowledge management strategies.
4 The company has a detailed understanding of the relationships which exist between market partners and customers.

F Customer relationships

1 The company is able to build relationships by differentiating between the needs of different customer groups.
2 Data is being acquired continually to generate new knowledge about the needs of different customer groups.
3 The total experience of customers from pre-purchase through to post-purchase product utilisation is analysed to generate detailed understanding of customer needs.
4 All points of customer–company interaction are analysed to generate knowledge about customer needs.

G Strategy

1 The views and opinions of customer groups influence company strategy.
2 Substrategies are evolved to respond to variation in customer needs across different customer groups.
3 Knowledge acquired from customers drives new product and service development strategies.
4 Product and service development strategies utilise knowledge to drive the individualisation of customer need provision.
5 Customer needs provide the basis for the development of customised marketing programmes.
6 Knowledge of competitor behaviour continually influences the evolution and development of the firm's ongoing marketing strategies.
7 Using all sources of knowledge to achieve the aim of being perceived as 'best in class' across all customer groups.

NICHE MARKETING

It is usually assumed that niche marketers rarely have to worry about being confronted by competition from larger firms. The assumption is based upon the view that larger organisations lack the specialist skills and flexibility in manufacturing and other value-added processes to compete with smaller, more specialist providers. In recent years, however, the advent of lean manufacturing has resulted in large firms in some market sectors now being able to switch from long production runs of standard goods to limited runs of a diversity of products without incurring any cost penalties. This has happened, for example, in the electronic components industry. Global firms such as Cisco are successfully entering niche markets for specialist sector-specific switches and routers which in the past tended to be supplied by small manufacturing firms selling to customers located 'down the road' from their factories.

One of the constraints facing niche players wishing to implement a growth strategy is that the revenue generated on sales is often insufficient to permit the level of investment in knowledge provision to customers using multiple channels that is required to continually grow the size of the firm's base of new customers. The advent of e-business has clearly changed this situation because by establishing a web presence, niche firms can now offer the product or service across the entire globe. This niche player may be able to avoid promotional expenditure on building awareness of their web address because potential customers are often prepared to spend hours using internet search engines to find the knowledge required to solve a specialist problem or satisfy a very specialist need.

Business-to-business Niches

The tendency of the popular media, when seeking to run a story on e-commerce, is to feature firms operating in consumer goods markets. In reality, however, the volume of e-commerce niche marketing is significantly much higher in business-to-business markets (Stackpole 1999). The reason for this situation is that many business-to-business markets contain highly fragmented groups of buyers and sellers, many of whom encounter problems finding each other because of time and/or geographic constraints.

An example is provided by Weldcraft, a small UK firm which specialises in complex welding problems created by variations in materials being welded or the adverse physical environment in which the weld has to survive. Initially the company created a generic advisory web site to provide information about techniques for solving complex welding problems. The site generated a vast number of enquiries about specific welding problems from other companies around the world, some of which ultimately resulted in the acquisition of new contracts to undertake welding jobs outside of the UK. These events have subsequently led the company into a diversification strategy involving the launch of an international cyberspace and terrestrial world welding consultancy business.

Another example of on-line diversification is provided by SeaFax in the United States (Stewart 1998). The business was started by Neal Workman who opened a debt collection agency in Portland Maine. His primary customer group consisted of small-scale fishermen who faced the problem that repossessing goods had little point because by the time this could take place, the product would have gone rotten. One day Workman

---

realised that an invaluable aspect of his business was his knowledge of which businesses were poor credit prospects. He decided to create a knowledge-based business to market credit worthiness information. His first move was to establish SeaFax which offered a subscription service, with subscribers being faxed a 'flash report' providing the latest information on which buyers in the seafood industry were slow payers or which businesses might be heading into trouble. The next product extension was to develop a credit rating bureau providing a 48-hour response to clients wishing to investigate potential customers before actually shipping the product.

Initially the company used computers to manage internal databases that underpin an ability to rapidly update and process new information. Having established such an effective internal system, the company's first move into electronic business was to publish annual CD-ROMs providing data on specific market sectors such as seafoods, meat and poultry. Then in 1998, with an aim to further enhance customer service levels, the company established a web site which permits subscribers to acquire instant information at the click of a button.

NETWORK-BASED POSITIONING

Miles and Snow (1986) proposed that the 1990s will be characterised by a deintegration of large firms as these organisations begin to establish 'dynamic networks' based on new forms of contractual relationships with other independent firms. At the core of the Miles and Snow network paradigm is a lead organisation fulfilling the role of a 'broker' orchestrating the interfirm collaboration exchange of knowledge. Jarillo (1993), although reaching a similar conclusion about the potential for business networks in a changing industrial world, believes the overwhelming pressure to reduce operating costs further would be the primary factor underlying the creation of these new entities. Subsequently Piore and Sabel (1984) developed their value added partnerships (VAPs) theory of networking in which independent companies collaborate in the exchange of knowledge to support the effective management of transaction costs associated with the flow of goods and services along the entire value added chain. Examples of this approach were provided by Biggiero (1999) in his study of regional clothing networks in northern Italy.

During the 1980s in Denmark, the government working with the Danish Technological Institute sought to encourage growth in the small and medium size enterprise (SME) sector through the creation of business networks. In those industrial sectors and/or geographic regions where there are no large firms to fulfil the role of hub facilitator, there was a need for independent network brokers to manage the processes of identifying potential opportunities for small firms to acquire knowledge through networking, to seek potential network members from within the local business community and to act as a mentor/facilitator in the creation of a new, commercially viable, trading entity.

Studies of economic development initiatives which utilise business networks to stimulate SME sector growth have revealed that sharing of knowledge and resources to achieve greater scale in the execution of marketing processes is one of the most common reasons for smaller firms to enter into a partnership with other organisations. The following are illustrative examples of some of the networks which have been created:

- Ten Danish landscape gardening firms interested in the opportunities available in the construction of golf courses which realised that by acting individually, none of them had sufficient knowledge to manage major contracts in overseas markets such as the United States.
- A group of Danish organisations including fishermen, processing companies and a hospital which came together to pool their various areas of specialist knowledge to develop new health products which use the sea as the primary source of basic ingredients.
- Eleven Danish textile manufacturers which produce different products have formed a network called 'CD-line'. While continuing to operate independently in their traditional markets, the firms pooled their knowledge to form a consortium to enter West Germany, marketing a complete range of image clothing for employees in large corporations such as banks and car makers.
- Four Danish furniture companies which shared knowledge to design a new range of furniture for the Netherlands market and jointly resourced the opening of an export sales office to market the range in that country.
- Three Norwegian furniture firms which formed a network to share knowledge as the basis for successfully bidding to supply all of the equipment needs for the Winter Olympics in Lillehammer.
- Four Norwegian producers of kitchen equipment which formed a knowledge network to offer total system catering solutions for oil platforms in the North Sea.
- Four Norwegian fish farming equipment manufacturers which collaborated in the exchange of knowledge that permitted them to develop a fish farm management system to support expansion into new overseas markets.

On the basis of these and other examples, it is appears there are two dimensions associated with the formation and operation of small firm marketing networks. One is the sharing of knowledge and resources to manage more effectively the marketing processes directed at (a) increasing sales to current customers, (b) gaining access to larger customers in existing markets or (c) entering completely new markets. The other dimension is sharing knowledge to revise product offering through either (a) the combination of existing products to offer an enhanced proposition or (b) the development of an entirely new range of products.

By combining these two dimensions, as demonstrated in Figure 6.2, one can generate the following nine different knowledge collaboration pathways from which firms can then select the best option for enhancing their marketing operations (Chaston 1999b):

1 Where sales of existing products to existing customers are increased by a pooling of knowledge (for example, a group of small furniture manufacturers creating a single sales force to represent all of their products in the marketplace).
2 Where pooling of knowledge permits access to new customers for existing products (for example, a group of cheese producers already distributing their products through local retailers can now gain access to national supermarket chains because together they can offer a full range of cheeses from a single source).
3 Where sales of existing products can be increased by pooling of knowledge to permit entry into a new market (for example, a group of component manufacturers in the leisure craft industry pooling promotional resources to develop new export markets).
4 Where pooling of knowledge permits offering of an enhanced product to current customers (for example, a group of accountants drawing upon their various areas of specialist expertise to offer a complete financial management services portfolio to their clients).
5 Where pooling of knowledge leads to the creation of an enhanced product proposition which can assist in gaining access to new customers (for example, a group of specialist management trainers creating a 'complete training solution' package which means they will now be considered as viable potential suppliers to large, multinational corporations).
6 Where pooling of knowledge to enhance an existing product permits entry into a new market (for example, a group of specialist computer software designers, who normally work as subcontractors for system provider firms, combining their skills to move into the systems provision market).
7 Where pooling of knowledge permits the creation of a new product marketed to existing customers (for example, a group of hotels creating their own package holiday operation).
8 Where pooling of knowledge creates a new product for sale to new customers in an existing market (for example, a group of fresh juice processors who distribute their product through small retailers, developing a new longer shelf-life product which means they can now market their output to national retail chains).
9 Where pooling of knowledge leads to the development of a new product to create access to new markets (for example, a group of civil engineering firms each specialising in specific aspects of construction creating a total project design and management system which permits them to enter overseas markets offering a complete tourism infrastructure project management capability).

Market	Existing market(s)		New market(s)
Product	Existing customers	New customers	New customers
Existing product	**1** Sharing market management knowledge and resources to increase existing customer sales	**2** Sharing knowledge and resources to achieve scale effect to gain access to new customers	**3** Sharing market management knowledge and resources to execute new market entry strategy
Merged product line to enhance product position	**4** Increased sales to existing customers by sharing knowledge to offer an enhanced product proposition	**5** Access to new customers through sharing knowledge to offer an enhanced product proposition	**6** Gaining access to new markets through sharing knowledge to offer an enhanced product proposition
New product	**7** New sales to existing customers through sharing knowledge to develop a new product	**8** Gaining access to new customers by sharing knowledge to develop a new product	**9** Gaining access to new markets through sharing knowledge to develop a new product

FIGURE 6.2   ALTERNATIVE STRATEGIES FOR KNOWLEDGE-BASED BUSINESS NETWORKING

Networks Are Not a New Phenonenon

There is a tendency in the academic literature to perceive networks as a relatively new organisational form which uses knowledge exchange between members to enhance business capability. In reality, however, the philosophy of firms working together has been around for many years. Ville and Fleming (2000) have demonstrated this fact through their analysis of business networks in Australia and New Zealand.

In the late nineteenth century in New Zealand, the agriculture sector witnessed the emergence of pastoral networks. The focal point of such networks was pastoral agents who acted as expert intermediaries linking farmers to providers of supplies and financial services. These networks emerged because farmers required access to services such as produce consignment, finance, sale of property and sale of livestock. Many of New Zealand's farmers were new to the industry at this time. In consequence the pastoral agents were a key source of knowledge about farming techniques, market trends, new products and financial management. These networks were further enhanced by the entry of the freezer companies. The pastoral agent sought to protect the interests of the small farmers in their collaboration with the much larger freezer companies. This was achieved by the agent offering credit to the farmer and ensuring the freezer companies paid the farmers in a reasonable time period.

When the effectiveness of the pastoral agent networks began to decline, in order to sustain the knowledge exchange and marketing benefits associated with network participation, farmers began to form co-operatives. Some of the earliest co-operatives were formed in the dairy industry and led to the construction of dairy factories to process milk output in a specific geographic area.

The co-operative and pastoral agent networks tended to operate on a geographically restricted basis which meant producers had insufficient knowledge of how to operate effectively in the increasingly global market for agricultural output. To overcome this knowledge gap in the 1920s the government entered the sector to create various marketing boards. These boards sought to ensure that New Zealand producers received the highest possible returns on overseas sales by minimising transportation costs and managing overseas marketing activities to maximise prices received for products.

Constructing Knowledge Plans

CHAPTER SUMMARY

Alfred Sloan of General Motors introduced the idea of examining existing knowledge as the basis for planning future marketing activities. Knowledge can be used to answer the three key questions: where are we now? where are we going? and how do we get there? The resource-based view of the firm stresses the importance of assessing internal knowledge relative to market opportunity. This activity can be undertaken by constructing a knowledge management resource planning matrix. Firms cannot be good at everything. Hence it recommends that an organisation concentrates on those areas of knowledge exploitation related to optimising performance of the organisation's core competencies. An example of a disguised case is provided to illustrate the knowledge management marketing planning process.

INTRODUCTION

As the dominant trading nation for most of the twentieth century, it is understandable that over the last 100 years, the United States has become the primary source of many of the new theories of management. America's initial success in world markets was based upon the principle of exploiting the scale benefits of mass production to supply low priced, standardised goods such as automobiles, refrigerators and televisions.

Alfred Sloan, who rescued General Motors during the 1920s recession, held the view that the secret of successful management is grounded in the concept of applying rational planning to achieve the single-minded goal of maximising profits. To assist in the formalisation of this theory, Sloan and his supporters from within the academic community such as Chandler and Ansoff drew upon the conceptual rules of business established by the economist Adam Smith (author of *The Wealth of Nations*) and the militaristic principles of the Greek and Roman empires. Described as a *classical approach* to business, the principles of rational planning models as a path through which to optimise organisational performance have subsequently become the foundation stone upon which the syllabi of many business schools around the world have been constructed (Whittington 1993).

America's loss of market share to the new economic tiger nations of Japan and Taiwan in the latter years of the twentieth century caused a radical re-examination of the management principles being taught in Western nation business schools. Some researchers have focused their efforts on seeking to understand the nature of Pacific Rim managerial practices in the context of assessing how such nations are utilising classicist managerial philosophies. Their conclusions are that within Pacific Rim organisations, success can often be attributed to a classicist approach to planning linked to a 'work ethic' commitment.

Other Western researchers such as Mintzberg have adopted the view that there is a need to place greater emphasis on observing actual management practices when seeking to evolve new theoretical paradigms of how managers use knowledge in the formulation and execution of business plans. From such thinking, alternative schools of management thought have begun to emerge. Mintzberg (1989), for example, has questioned the basic premise of classicist management theory that strategy formation is a controlled, conscious knowledge acquisition process undertaken by an individual acting as a rational, economic thinker. He, and others such as Cyert and March (1963) believe the rational, economic thinker is a figment of mythology rarely found outside of textbooks. Their perspective of the manager is of an individual who is reluctant to embark on unlimited searchers for new knowledge and instead is more likely to form an opinion on the basis of the first satisfactory option that is presented for consideration. These academics would also argue that as members of an organisation, managers survive by being willing to accept compromise in return for achieving acceptance of an opinion. Known as the *Processual approach* to management, this school of theorists downgrades the importance of rational analysis and instead perceives management as creating strategies through selecting those routines which within the organisation can be identified as contributing to success.

Another perspective, which again questions the ability of senior managers to act as rational planners, is that posited by the *evolutionists*. This school of thought, which has been strongly promoted by Bruce Henderson, the founder of the Boston Consulting Group, believes the destiny of the firm is determined by 'the laws of the commercial jungle'. Hence in the real world, despite whichever plan is adopted by managers, ultimately the winner will be the organisation most suited to surviving in the face of prevailing market conditions. The evolutionists' view of strategic planning is to urge the manager to accept that markets control destiny and that the emphasis should be given to selecting industrial sectors which are compatible with the identified capabilities of the organisation.

In contrast to the processualist and evolutionist approaches to management, the *systemic school* of management supports the idea of organisations placing faith in a structured planning process through which to evolve a strategy compatible with the external environment in which the firm is required to operate. Although this is clearly a philosophy which in part is compatible with the classicists' view of the world, the systemicists feel that the actual behaviour of organisations is to a large degree determined by specific sociological contexts. This implies that decision-makers are strongly influenced by the social networks of which they are a part. Thus in examining alternative approaches for developing an effective planning philosophy, the systemicist will seek to comprehend the social roots from which the organisation has emerged.

In terms of the degree to which alternative management philosophies are based upon highly formalised activities, within with the processual or evolutionary planning schools, the approach is to adopt a less routinised, less formalised planning philosophy. This can be contrasted with the classicist and systematic planning schools' highly structured, carefully regimented knowledge acquisition activity. In relation to which managerial philosophy is most appropriate in the field of knowledge management, insufficient research has been undertaken to permit any certain conclusions to be reached. What is known, however, is that translation of tacit knowledge into explicit knowledge does require the application of relatively formalised processes if the firm is to evolve systems which support effective utilisation of knowledge across the organisation. Hence at the current time it would appear that knowledge management planning might best be implemented by adopting a classicist orientation. If one accepts this perspective then it seems reasonable that one can utilise a sequential planning model of the type shown in Figure 7.1.

The aim of organisational learning is for firms to enhance performance by combining new knowledge with existing experience as the basis for evolving new solutions to encountered business problems. The critical importance of learning within the planning process was noted by Castogiovanni (1996). He feels that the most important goal in the marketing planning process is not the generation of a formal document. Instead managers should perceive planning as an opportunity to use organisational learning as the basis for reviewing recent events and determining a future direction for their organisations.

When reviewing the development of a knowledge management marketing strategy for the firm it is necessary to ensure that both existing and new knowledge sources are exploited when assessing various alternative market management scenarios. The implications of this conclusion is that in utilising a planning model of the type shown in Figure 7.1, the firm should seek to learn more about (a) the knowledge issues currently confronting the organisation, (b) the direction in which the organisation wishes to go in relation to the future exploitation of knowledge and (c) the selection of the most appropriate actions associated with how to achieve specified future knowledge management performance goals.

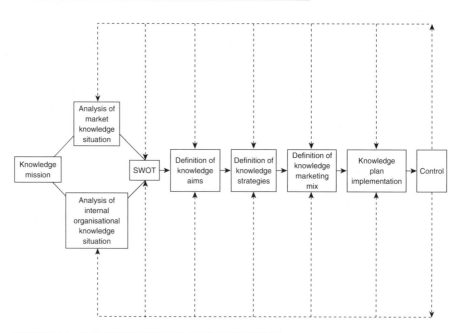

FIGURE 7.1   THE KNOWLEDGE PLANNING PROCESS

It is suggested that there should be three groups involved in the learning process. These are the firm's stakeholders (for example, customers, suppliers, the financial community), the management and the employees. The most productive form of learning is where there is interaction between all three groups as this maximises exposure to sources of new knowledge. In relation to learning about where the firm is now, it is proposed in Figure 7.1 that two areas of information will need to be reviewed, namely identified signals of potential change in the market environment and recent internal organisational activities.

It is understandable that the activities surrounding determination of future aims will tend to be dominated by the values and attitudes of the management. These individuals can, however, acquire a much broader perspective about the future by drawing upon the opinions of stakeholders, for example, by the firm's customers providing data on the benefits associated with being given expanded access to knowledge provision by the firm in the future. Another source is the firm's employees' perceptions of what actions may be necessary in relation to upgrading their access to knowledge which could enhance their execution of assigned tasks.

All three of these stakeholder groups' sources of opinion should also be involved in the processes associated with determining what actions will be required to deliver the future knowledge management marketing performance aims which have been agreed for the firm. It may be useful to generate a template to summarise these agreed actions. This template should not be in the form of a huge document so beloved by management consultants and the boards of companies. The recommended format is a very simple record of proposed actions which is probably no more than a few pages in length. The critical issue about this template is that all employees are made aware of its content. They are able to use this knowledge source to guide them in the fulfilment of their future job roles. The other benefit of the template is that it provides a control system that permits rapid evaluation of actual events against specified aims when the new knowledge management plan is being implemented.

THE RESOURCE-BASED VIEW OF KNOWLEDGE

Hamal and Prahalad have suggested that 'competition for the future is competition to create and dominate emerging opportunities ... to stake out new competitive space'. They further recommend that 'a firm must unlearn much about its past ... recognise that it is not enough to optimally position a company within existing markets ... develop foresight into the whereabouts of tomorrow's markets' (1994, p. 23).

In offering guidance on how to achieve this aim, Hamal and Prahalad rely very heavily on the concept of exploiting new and existing knowledge to understand the probable nature of future market conditions and to ensure the organisation has acquired competencies appropriate for achieving ongoing success. Their definition of a successful firm is one which is able to envisage the future accurately, acquire knowledge which can underpin the development of core competencies ahead of competition and thereby become the dominant player within an industrial sector.

Clearly this is a conceptual philosophy which in practical terms only a minority of firms can ever aspire to achieve. Nevertheless exploiting the knowledge management capabilities of the firm as the basis for defining how knowledge can provide a potential source of competitive advantage does seem to be an extremely appropriate start point in the formulation of a knowledge management marketing plan.

Day (1994) has developed an eloquent argument which proposes that a capability-based approach to planning is likely to be a more productive source for determining competitive advantage than the competitive forces model tabled by Michael Porter. In defining capabilities, Day suggests that they are complex bundles of skills and accumulated knowledge which, when integrated with the firm's organisational processes, permit the optimal utilisation of assets.

A similar perspective on the utilisation of distinctive capability to provide the basis from which to evolve a marketing plan has been presented by Hunt and Morgan (1995, 1996) in their resource advantage theory of competition. They posit that the internal resources of the firm determine market position and financial performance. In tabling their model, Hunt and Morgan have specified some observable variables which they feel overcome many of problems associated with applying neoclassical economic theory to explaining the management of the marketing process. Firstly, they suggest that customer preferences are rarely homogeneous because customers usually exhibit variation in their choice of product features. Secondly, as most customers have imperfect knowledge, this will lead to variances in buyer behaviour. Thirdly, firms, in seeking to achieve superior financial performance, do not act to maximise profit but instead use the benchmark of other firms in the same market sector to determine the exact definition of financial performance superiority. Fourthly, they feel that firms have a multiplicity of expertise, knowledge, competencies and resources which results in organisations adopting very different approaches to achieving alternative routes to competitive advantage in the same market sector. Fifthly, it is usually the distinctiveness with which firms utilise their knowledge, resources and competencies that results in firms being able to occupy different market positions.

Hunt and Morgan have proposed that their model can be used to define alternative competitive positions by using the dimensions of (a) *relative resource costs* (the degree to which a firm's operating costs are higher or lower than the competition and (b) *relative resource-produced value* (the degree to which the firm's financial performance is better or worse than the competition). Although this a very effective model, one potential risk is that the marketer using the concept as a decision model might be directed towards placing too great an emphasis on financial performance. Hence if one considers that the purpose of marketing is to deliver products or services which are perceived to offer the highest possible level of knowledge content to customers, it seems reasonable to propose that the 'value customers place on knowledge' is preferable in a planning model to the concept of 'relative resource-produced value'. Similarly it seems logical to replace 'relative resource-produced value' with the alternative of variable of 'internal knowledge management capability'.

These two redefined knowledge variables provide the basis for a start point in building a knowledge management resource planning matrix. Step one is to determine which factors influence the degree to which customers value knowledge within a portfolio of products or services. Factors influencing relative perceived importance of knowledge will vary by both industrial sector and nature of marketing style being utilised by the organisation. Examples of reasonably standard factors which might be considered in virtually any situation include:

- Level of actual knowledge associated with the product or service being delivered to the customer.
- Range of benefits offered by knowledge content contained within the product or service.
- Role of knowledge content in fulfilling service quality expectations.
- Price.
- Effectiveness with which knowledge is made available to the customer.
- Relative knowledge provision capabilities of competitors.

Similar to perceived value of knowledge, factors influencing knowledge management capabilities relative to competition will also vary by industrial

Value customers place on knowledge

		Low	Average	High
		1 Immediately terminate operations	**2** Phased business withdrawal	**3** One-off investment to significantly upgrade knowledge management capability
Internal knowledge management capability	**Low**			
	Average	**4** Phased business withdrawal	**5** Sustain current level of knowledge management	**6** Investment to upgrade knowledge management competencies
	High	**7** Reduce resources committed to knowledge management	**8** Knowledge management diversification	**9** Investment to sustain knowledge management leadership

FIGURE 7.2   KNOWLEDGE MANAGEMENT RESOURCE PLANNING MATRIX

sector and marketing style orientation of the organisation. Examples of standard factors which are applicable in virtually any situation include:

• Cost of knowledge provision.
• Cost of knowledge acquisition and storage.
• Impact of knowledge on employee productivity.
• Cost of internal and external distribution of knowledge.
• Cost of fixed assets required to support a knowledge management system.

Having defined key factors, the next stage in the process is to rate these factors on some form of scale. Possibly the simplest approach is a scoring system ranging from a low of one through to a high of ten. Where a score approaches ten for each dimension respectively this indicates (a) the high level of value customers place on knowledge and (b) the high level of internal knowledge management capability. Having executed the scoring, the average total score is found by dividing summated total scores by the number of factors used in the analysis. This generates an overall score for value placed on knowledge and knowledge management capability. Data can then be interpreted by entering scores on a knowledge management resource planning matrix of the type shown in Figure 7.2.

As can be seen from the diagram in Figure 7.2, resultant positions in the matrix guide the organisation towards the possible adoption of the following generic strategies:

1 Where the low perceived value customers place on knowledge and poor knowledge management capability suggest the firm has minimal opportunity for success. Hence the company (assuming it also has operations in other, more successful, sectors) should withdraw from this market sector immediately.

2 Where the average perceived value customers place on knowledge and the low knowledge management capability infer poor future prospects, but where withdrawal should be a phased process because this will permit avoidance of major financial write downs for redundant capital assets.

3 Where the high perceived value that customers place on knowledge means that the company is confronted with an opportunity which, if at all feasible, it must exploit. Hence the strategy is to initiate a major internal process revision project that can lead to a significant upgrading in knowledge management capability. If, however, this project does not deliver the required acquisition of higher knowledge management capability, then a market sector departure strategy would be the next action.

4 Where, similar to 2, low perceived value customers place on knowledge and only average knowledge management capability infer poor future market prospects. Again market withdrawal should be a phased process because this will permit avoidance of major financial write downs for redundant capital assets.

5 Where both perceived value customers place on knowledge and internal knowledge management capability are both at parity with other firms in the marketplace. For many organisations this type of classification applies to a core business area generating a major proportion of total revenues. Hence the existing operation should be managed to sustain current market performance (for example, if the competitors begin to offer increased levels of knowledge to customers, actions should be taken to match these increments). Similarly if competitors appear to be making gains in the internal knowledge management capabilities, action should be taken to ensure parity of capability is sustained.

6 Where knowledge management capability is only average but perceived value of knowledge among customers is high. The organisation should initiate a knowledge management capability improvement programme with the eventual aim of achieving much greater internal operating competencies than the competition.

7 Where knowledge management capabilities are high, but perceived value customers place on knowledge is below average. The firm's advantage in the area of internal knowledge management should be examined to determine whether this situation can provide the basis to reduce internal operating costs without impacting customers' perceptions about the value of knowledge being made available by the firm (for example, moving from a telesales operation providing knowledge to making such knowledge available via a web site).

8 Where the firm can use higher than average knowledge management skills as the basis for moving into new market sectors where achievement of offering customers an appropriate level of knowledge is a viable option.

9   A highly attractive position for the organisation because both a high perceived value customers place on knowledge and high knowledge management capability have been attained. This will probably mean that the company has already achieved a market leadership position and, therefore, this mandates ongoing investment in order to protect the operation from any new competitive threats.

KNOWLEDGE MANAGEMENT ASSESSMENT AT LUKES' GARAGE AND ENGINEERING SERVICES LTD

This is a disguised case about a company which is a family owned business based in the UK. Over three generations the family has built up an operation comprising garages offering car sales, vehicle servicing and repairs, petrol sales, forecourt shop sales, a car dealership specialising in 4-wheel drive sales and servicing plus a specialist car restoration components distribution business. A recent acquisition, aimed at beginning to diversify away from the car industry, has been an engineering firm which specialises in the repair and servicing of marine leisure craft engines.

In the UK independent garages selling petrol used to have to compete only with garages owned by the large petrol companies. Then the supermarket chains moved into petrol retailing, competing on price. They now have a dominant market share of the UK petrol business and Lukes', like other independents, is having a very hard time achieving even a minimal level of profit. As customer petrol purchasing levels have fallen, this has been accompanied by a corresponding decline in the sale of goods from the forecourt shop.

Lukes' has no major main dealership franchises for new cars. This situation has meant that generation of vehicle sales is heavily dependent upon offering a superior level of service to potential customers. Over the last two years, EU legislation aimed at forcing uniform car pricing across Europe by the major car manufacturers has meant that main dealerships have become very price competitive. An added pressure on Lukes' profitability has been increased competition created by the entry of on-line car sales operations into the UK market. The only area which has been relatively unaffected by these external influences has been Lukes' specialist 4-wheel drive operation where product expertise of the management team has permitted the establishment of a very successful market niche.

On average, the UK consumer is not served very well by the majority of garages offering servicing and repairs. Evidence exists that many consumers perceive garages are not very honest, over charge for services, undertake unnecessary repairs and are not interested in resolving complaints. Lukes' genuine commitment to the provision of high quality servicing and repairs has gained the company a strong reputation for delivering extremely good value to customers.

The car restoration business evolved out of the family's hobby of buying and restoring classic cars. Over the years the family has acquired expertise both in locating rare car component spares and, where these appeared totally unavailable, using their engineering skills to build replicate parts. Five years ago, one of the sons persuaded the family that this expertise offered a new business opportunity and convinced them to invest in the creation of a car restoration components business. The sourcing or manufacturing of rare parts not only proved commercially viable, the operation's expertise soon resulted in the son becoming involved in providing a restoration consultancy service to both private collectors and car museums. Two years ago the firm established a brochure-ware, newsletter and chat room web site.

Another family hobby is boating and over the years the family has owned and maintained a diverse range of boats all kept at a local boat yard. Three years ago, the owner of the yard and associated marine engineering business decided to retire and offered the Lukes' family first refusal on the business. One of the sons now runs the yard and, to avoid direct competition with the growing number of marinas in the area, has reduced the yard's involvement in offering on-river berthing and on-land boat storage facilities. Concurrently he is endeavouring to expand the engineering side of the business by seeking to build a reputation for the servicing and repair of marine leisure craft engines. The family has assumed that their extensive mechanical expertise would be sufficient to resource their marine engine repair activities. It has become apparent in the face of a number of cost over-runs on engine rebuilding contracts, however, that they need to improve their understanding of how to operate successfully in the boating industry.

In the face of ongoing difficulties across some areas of the Lukes' operation, the board has decided that it is necessary to re-evaluate the future direction of the company. Their perception of opportunity is that confrontation on the basis of price is extremely dangerous and that the focus of the business should be where (a) customer demand is for products and services accompanied by knowledge provision and (b) the company has the ability to support knowledge provision activities effectively.

In the face of this perspective an assessment of current operations was undertaken using the knowledge management resource planning matrix approach. The outcome of this analysis is illustrated in Figure 7.3.

It can be seen from Figure 7.3, that new/used car sales, petrol sales and forecourt operations are three areas where a phased withdrawal of trading activity is indicated as advisable. The marine leisure craft engine business is a sector where customers value knowledge provision by suppliers, but where Lukes' currently lacks expertise. Hence the indicated decision rule is that the company will need to make a significant investment in upgrading internal knowledge management capability.

Car servicing is an important 'cash cow' for the company. The position of this business sector in the planning matrix indicates that the operation should be

Value customers place on knowledge

		Low	Average	High
		1 None	**2** New/used car sales	**3** Marine leisure craft engines
Internal knowledge management capability	Low			
	Average	**4** Petrol sales and forecourt operations	**5** Servicing cars	**6** None
	High	**7** None	**8** Specialist car sales	**9** Specialist car restoration components and consultancy service

FIGURE 7.3   APPLICATION OF PLANNING MATRIX TO LUKES' GARAGE
AND ENGINEERING SERVICES LTD CASE

retained but no change in knowledge provision or knowledge management capability is necessary unless subsequently customer needs or competitor behaviour undergoes change. Results for the 4-wheel drive business indicate that car sales in specialist sectors can be successful. The decision of the company is to examine other specialist market niches (for example, sports cars) into which to diversify the business.

The fastest growing and most profitable area of the Lukes' operations is the car restoration components operation. The position in the Figure 7.3 matrix indicates further investment in seeking to ensure the firm can sustain this level of business performance is an advisable activity. The company currently tends to focus on the UK market. An indication of overseas interest based upon customers making contact from other countries suggests there may be a significant new opportunity from seeking to implement a major expansion into other countries around the world.

SELECTING CORE KNOWLEDGE COMPETENCIES

Having matched markets to capability using an analysis tool such as the matrix shown in Figure 7.2, the next issue confronting a firm is to select which core knowledge competencies will be the driving force upon which to build future market success. A frequently quoted example of an organisation which illustrates this approach is the Japanese computer giant, NEC (Kobayashi 1986). Originally a supplier of telecommunications equipment, the firm realised that the communications and computer industries are on a convergent path because both exist to serve the needs of customers wishing to manage information electronically. The identified opportunity was that of becoming a global provider of systems which simultaneously handle voice, data and image traffic. To be successful, the firm recognised that knowledge management excellence would be required in three areas, namely: distributed data processing using networked computer systems, evolving electronic components from simple integrated circuits to ultra large scale integrated circuits and the move from mechanical to digital switching. By internal knowledge development and accessing new knowledge sources through the formation of both technology and marketing alliances, the company has been able to develop core knowledge competencies that have supported revenue growth from $3.8 billion in 1980 to over $30 billion in the 1990s.

A useful tool for assisting the selection of core knowledge competence is to apply conceptual modification of Porter's (1985) value chain concept. The modified model, as shown in Figure 7.4, proposes that opportunity for adding value comes from exploiting knowledge across (a) the five core processes of inbound logistics, process operations, outbound logistics, marketing and customer service and (b) the four support processes of management capability, HRM practices, exploitation of technology and procurement.

Jarillo (1993) has posited that analysis of the precise role which an organisation will undertake within a market system supply chain is a crucial step in the determination of future strategy. A fundamental objective in this process is to ensure that the organisation is able to maximise the exploitation of acquired knowledge to ensure optimisation of the organisation's value added activities within the system. He further points out that the exact nature of the knowledge needed to exploit market opportunity may change over time. An example he uses to illustrate this point is the computer industry where in the past the producers of hardware were able to enjoy a major proportion of the profits generated by value added activities. More recently, however, as the knowledge of the technology associated with the assembly of 'boxes' has become more widely available, then greater profits have begun to accrue to those who have retained a 'lock on key technologies' (for example, Intel knowledge about the manufacture of microchips; Microsoft's knowledge of operating systems and software applications).

Jarillo also proposes that now that advances in IT permit firms to exchange information rapidly and efficiently, then many firms should be examining how their more peripheral activities might be sourced by other organisations with higher levels of internal knowledge. Thus firms operating in transactional markets might assess their value chain to determine if any

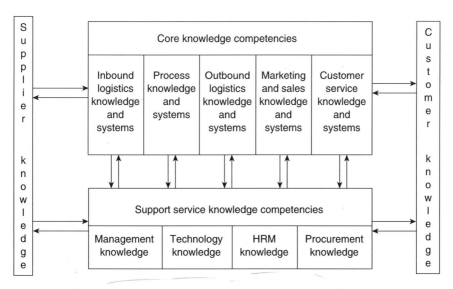

FIGURE 7.4 A KNOWLEDGE CHAIN MODEL FOR SUPPORTING ADDED
VALUE GENERATION

activity such as sourcing raw materials might be assigned to a more knowledgeable outside supplier. In relationship orientated markets, firms might examine how horizontal knowledge exchange partnerships with other firms at the same level in the market system and vertical knowledge exchange partnerships with suppliers can be utilised to identify how their specific value added activities when linked with others can optimise achievement of competitive advantage.

The arrival of e-commerce has created a technological framework in which firms can genuinely evaluate how IT can be used to effectively manage outsourcing certain aspects of their value chain in order to lower operating costs. Alternatively knowledge-based IT systems might permit delivery of increased perceived customer value. Whichever route is taken, this action can release the managerial resources of the firm to concentrate even more attention on optimising those core knowledge management competencies associated with maximising added value activities from activities retained within the firm. Such ideas lead to the emergence of a management paradigm in which the firm becomes a hub containing core knowledge competencies critical to generating internal added value while being surrounded by a satellite of other firms performing outsourced activities. This alternative paradigm is sometimes referred to as the 'virtual organisation'. Indications are that as firms become involved in e-commerce, then more organisations will increasingly transform themselves into a virtual knowledge management entity in order to maximise competitive advantage within their supplier–customer value chain.

BIO-CELL LTD

In the world of diagnostic medicine, biological research and bio-technology, one of the ways of trying to understand the complex interactions which occur within organic systems is to keep as many variables constant as possible. All three of these disciplines use animal cells, bacterial cultures and strains of viruses in their laboratories. One way they achieve constancy in their experiments is to use the same cell, bacteria and viral cultures over many years because this then results in the production of 'pure strains' which have a known biological history.

Bio-Cell Ltd is the disguised case of a UK firm which specialises in the supply of pure strain biological cultures. Started as a small laboratory in the 1950s supplying universities, over the years the business has expanded. The firm now has customers in medical establishments, commercial research centres and university laboratories across all of Western Europe. The firm operates by growing pure strain cultures which are then frozen and stored in the firm's warehouse. Customers are serviced through a network of local sales staff and a central telesales centre in the UK. Shipments are arranged by the company's distribution department which utilises the services of various parcel express and air freight operations. Although long since retired, the founders of the business have left an accepted heritage that the firm's leading market position is due to the extensive pool of knowledge which exists in the organisation that is heavily relied upon by their customers in their successful design and operation of experimental techniques in their respective laboratories.

Unfortunately over recent years management have found it increasingly difficult to retain effective control over the business because sales have been increasing very rapidly. Inside the firm, more and more time is spent sorting out inventory problems, shipment errors and delivery mistakes. Additionally the sales force staff, whose intended role is to act as technical consultants to the laboratories in their respective areas, are also finding they are spending inordinate amounts of their time 'fire fighting' shipment problems and placating angry customers.

The management of Bio-Cell is aware that the pharmaceutical industry in the United States has exploited the opportunities offered by e-business to radically revise its structure and operation with the intent of (a) permitting manufacturers to concentrate on exploiting internal knowledge in order to focus on further developing the technologies associated with the manufacture of new drugs and (b) outsourcing other activities in order to improve customer service levels. Hence a small project team was sent on a study tour with the assignment of utilising their observations of the American scene as the basis for recommending how Bio-Cell might be restructured.

The project team's visit to the United States confirmed both the logic and feasibility of outsourcing non-core business activities. The company was able to identify another firm that produces and stores frozen vaccines which are distributed to a customer base very similar to Bio-Cell. It was also apparent that distribution could best be handled by contracting the whole activity to an international delivery operation which has superior knowledge management capability in the fields of distribution and logistics. Improving knowledge exchange with the customers can be achieved by launching a web site which offers information, an order-entry facility and an automated technical knowledge search system database. This latter system is easy to evolve because for some years the company has been using Lotus Notes as an internal groupware product for accumulating internal expertise from all departments. The American vaccine firm already has a totally automated, computer-based scheduling and inventory knowledge management system. Hence by linking both the Bio-Cell web site that provides order placement information and the Bio-Cell cell production and freezing operation to the American vaccine company's automated system, Bio-Cell would be able to confirm orders placed and, by balancing available inventory on-hand versus sales patterns, to determine production schedules automatically to ensure on-hand inventories are adequate. By providing electronic links between the international delivery services offered by FedEx, Bio-Cell, the vaccine company and customers, all parties could gain immediate real-time knowledge concerning the status of goods in transit.

Fortunately both Bio-Cell and the vaccine firm had already established internal integrated databases and intranets to manage knowledge interchange between departments. Also FedEx's extensive experience in IT meant integration of their shipment management system into the Bio-Cell and vaccine company operations was a simple process. The only major investment was in the creation of the Cell-Tec web site. By hiring the services of an American internet development company with extensive experience in the pharmaceutical industry and basing the system within a major UK internet service provider site, it was possible to complete the development and launch of the web site in less than nine months. After only six months into the new operation, inventory control and all aspects of customer service quality have improved dramatically. Even more importantly, sales staff and Bio-Cell technical staff have been able to return to their primary role of utilising knowledge to offer superior products and advisory services to their customers across Europe.

DEVELOPING THE KNOWLEDGE MANAGEMENT MARKETING PLAN

The format and contents of business plans depend upon the size of the organisation (most small firms, for example, produce very short plans, whereas in multinational branded goods companies the plan can approach the size of a small book), the attitude of the organisation to the degree of formalisation required within the annual planning cycle process and accepted sector conventions (for example, consumer goods companies

TABLE 7.1   ISSUE COVERAGE IN A KNOWLEDGE MANAGEMENT
MARKETING PLAN

 1 Situation review
 2 Strengths/weaknesses/opportunities/threats (SWOT) analysis
 3 Summary of key issues
 4 Future objectives
 5 Strategy to achieve objectives
 6 Marketing mix for delivering strategy
 7 Action plan
 8 Financial forecasts
 9 Control systems
10 Contingency plans

typically produce much more detailed plans in comparison to their counterparts in many industrial markets).

Knowledge management marketing, especially when utilisation of e-commerce technology is envisaged, is usually based around applying established marketing management principles as the basis for defining how new technologies are to be exploited (Bradbury 1999). Additionally in many organisations, knowledge management projects will usually involve building upon existing off-line activities as the basis for providing new sources of information, customer–supplier interaction and/or alternative purchase transaction channels. In view of this situation, it seems logical to propose that a knowledge management marketing plan will be similar in structure to that used in the conventional marketing planning process. Hence the areas which should be covered in a knowledge management marketing plan are summarised in Table 7.1.

Within the situation review there should coverage of the strategic situation facing the organisation. This will be based on a description of market size, market growth trends, customer knowledge and product benefit requirements, utilisation of the marketing mix to satisfy customer needs, knowledge management activity of key competitors and the potential influence of changes in any of the variables which constitute the core and macroenvironmental elements of the market system. This review should include analysis of whether the firm is merely going to service end user market needs or will concurrently seek to integrate knowledge management systems with those of key suppliers.

The internal knowledge management capabilities of the organisation are reviewed within the context of whether they represent strengths or weaknesses which might influence future performance. One of the key issues will be whether staff have appropriate knowledge management operational skills, whether new staff will need to be recruited or aspects of the project outsourced to specialist data management providers.

Market circumstances are assessed in relation to whether knowledge management trends represent an opportunity or, threat. Consideration will need to be given to whether the move is proactive or, alternatively, a reactive response to initiatives already implemented by the competition. Other issues are (a) the degree to which new knowledge management practices might be used to enhance activities within existing markets and (b) whether knowledge management can be used to support entry into new markets. Combining the external and internal market analysis will permit execution of the SWOT analysis. The SWOT analysis, when linked with the situation review, will provide the basis for defining which key issues will need to be managed in order to develop an effective knowledge management marketing plan for the future.

The degree to which knowledge marketing objectives will be defined can vary tremendously. Some organisations will merely restrict aims to increasing the effectiveness of their provision of promotional information. Others may specify forecasted increases in sales or desired market share. Some organisations may extend this statement by breaking the market into specific target market segments as the basis for specifying detailed aims for sales, expenditure and profits for each product and/or market sector.

The knowledge management marketing strategy will define how, by positioning the company in a specific way, stated marketing objectives will be achieved. The marketing mix section will cover how each element within the commerce mix (product, price, promotion and distribution) will be utilised to support the specified strategy. In relation to the product, it will be necessary to determine the degree to which knowledge provision can enhance product benefits to be made available to customers. Such actions might include upgrading service quality, improving product utilisation and broadening the nature of the product line. Concerning pricing, thought must be given to how the scale of knowledge provision might influence future prices. The promotional mix will be reviewed in relation to how knowledge can most effectively be communicated and the degree to which such activities will enhance customer awareness of the company offerings. Distribution needs to be examined in the context of how the company can enhance customers' understanding of the status and location of their products within the order–shipment cycle.

The action plan section will provide detailed descriptions of all actions to be taken to manage the knowledge marketing plan, including timings and definition of which specific individuals and/or departments are responsible for implementing the plan. The financial forecasts will provide a detailed breakdown of revenue, cost of goods, all expenditures and resultant profits. Many organisations will also include forecasts of fund flows and, via a balance sheet, the expected asset/liability situation. Finally, after the knowledge management issues have been resolved, then the plan should specify how control systems will be evolved to support assessment of actual knowledge delivery versus the level of knowledge provision envisaged in the marketing plan.

Contingency plans exist to handle the fact that actual events rarely happen as predicted by the plan. If the organisation has already given thought to alternative scenarios prior to the beginning of the trading year, then if actual events are at variance with the plan, management is more able to implement actions immediately to overcome encountered obstacles. The usual approach for achieving this goal is that during the planning cycle the marketer examines the implications of alternative outcomes (for example, the impact of actual sales revenue being 25% higher and 25% lower than forecast). Having reached conclusions from this analysis, the marketer then includes alternative plans as a component of the overall actions for which senior management approval is being sought.

EXTRACTS FROM THE DRAKE TYRE COMPANY KNOWLEDGE MANAGEMENT MARKETING PLAN

Situation Review

The world tyre market is estimated to have an annual turnover in the region of £68–70 billion. It is a mature industry exhibiting annual growth in the region of approximately 3% per year. The two largest markets are North America and Europe, which together probably represent some 60% of total world demand. Within both these markets, approximately 30% of sales are for fitting tyres to newly manufactured vehicles. The balance of sales are replacement tyres for use on existing vehicles. The top three manufacturers are Bridgestone, Goodyear and Michelin.

For many years, an alternative to buying new tyres has been to purchase a remould. These are manufactured by taking a used tyre casing and bonding on a new tread. When remoulds were first introduced, quality was poor, the tyres had a somewhat short road life and, consequently, prices were much lower than for new tyres. Over the years, however, as tyre manufacturing technology has advanced, remoulds increasingly have been able to challenge new tyres in the areas of quality and durability. Despite this trend, however, most remould customers have remained extremely price sensitive.

Drake Tyres is a disguised case of a UK company which specialises in the provision of remoulds for lorries in both the business-to-business and public sector markets. The company has managed to create and sustain a premium quality/premium price position by exploiting knowledge to:

1 Undertake R&D to support the development of remoulds which have a higher durability, and therefore longer mileage life, than offerings from the leading multi-national producers.
2 Provide a technical support service to companies operating long-haul lorry fleets, which involves analysing returned tyre casings and advising customers on how changes in aspects of lorry fleet operations (for example,

tyre pressures, rectifying suspension and brake system faults) can extend tyre life.
3 Develop customised designs to suit specialist usage applications (for example, tyres for brewery lorries, van fleets for national/international delivery services and off-road tyres for waste haul fleets).

The company operates a manufacturing facility in southern England. Using their own lorry fleet, Drake delivers products directly to the depots of those customers who operate their own truck maintenance sites and also to national tyre distributors who fit remoulds to their customers' lorries. Drake's primary promotional activity is the use of a national sales team who call on both primary customers and tyre distributors. The sales force and/or the customers place orders with Drake head office via telephone, fax or mail.

Over the last few years, the company has been enjoying a year-on-year growth in sales of over 10 per cent/annum. Increasingly, however, their market success is attracting the attention of the bigger manufacturers. These latter organisations, unable to match Drake on technically advanced products or providing technical support services to customers, are approaching major Drake clients offering extremely low prices. Drake has been forced to respond by reducing prices on standard lorry remoulds and, as a result, net margins are gradually being eroded.

The other factor which needs response is that some of Drake's major long-haul fleet customers are moving into pan-European operations and to simplify their procurement procedures wish to purchase their remoulds from a single source in all countries. To date Drake has stayed out of mainland Europe because of the perceived high costs of establishing an overseas sales force and a European product distribution system.

Key Knowledge Management Issues

1 Can further investment in knowledge management provide a route to counter price competition through enhancing customer service levels or reducing operating costs?
2 Can knowledge management platforms assist any move into mainland Europe?

Knowledge Management Objectives

1 To utilise knowledge management both within and outside the firm to sustain current net profit margins.
2 To use knowledge management to support a cost effective entry into mainland Europe and contribute towards the attainment within three years of incremental sales of at least £2 million/annum (which equates to 10% of current UK sales).

Knowledge Management Strategy

1   While retaining an overall strategy of providing premium quality/premium price remould tyres, to exploit knowledge management to (a) further deepen relationships with customer service, (b) optimise internal operating costs in and (c) support entry into mainland Europe, which is not reliant upon using price to achieve projected sales targets.

Knowledge Management Marketing Mix

UK Product

The proposal is to create a web site which provides customer knowledge about product specifications, a searchable database covering the technical aspects of tyre usage optimisation, prices, an order-entry system and a system that permits customers to track tyre shipments in transit. As different customers receive different prices depending upon both purchase volumes and other services provided by Drake, the standard price list will have to be accompanied by confidential extranets to provide customer-specific pricing terms. Virtually all of the customers to whom Drake delivers direct have access to the internet from their respective offices. National tyre distributors tend to authorise their individual outlets to order their own remould requirements and most of these firms do not provide internet access at depot level. Hence Drake will have to continue to service this latter customer group using the existing off-line product ordering system.

Pan-European Product

In mainland Europe, most UK long-haul fleet operators either have their own in-country maintenance depots or authorise a major national tyre distributor in each country to provide tyre maintenance services. Initially Drake intends to offer a web site facility, similar to the UK site, to permit long-haul fleets who have their own in-country maintenance operations to order tyres on-line. This will mean that tyre delivery will be relatively simple and the sales force will only have to be expanded to include a small team to cover these European maintenance operations. A specialist multi-language extranet will also be made available so that staff at these European operations can dialogue with Drake's technical staff over resolving encountered problems. At a later date, Drake will examine how to handle the marketing and logistics problems of servicing the needs of long-haul operators who use national tyre distributors to take care of their lorries across Europe.

Technology Product Services

The web site will draw upon Drake's years of expertise to offer generic guidance on the selection and optimal utilisation of remould tyres. At the moment the customer is provided with feedback from Drake's tyre inspection and usage service team when this group sends the customer a written report on tyre casings that have been returned to the Drake plant. The returned tyres are held at the Drake manufacturing plant for three months in case the customer wishes to visit Drake, see the casings and review the technical report with the Drake inspectors. To improve the effectiveness of this service, the company wishes to investigate whether it is feasible for the inspectors to video the casing to highlight areas of identified damage. These visual materials and inspectors' reports could be made available on-line through customer extranets. Customers could then download these materials in the comfort of their own offices and use e-mail to pose questions the inspectors. It is hoped that this procedure will increase the volume of knowledge about resolving tyre operating problems that can be shared with customers and also will reduce the need for customers to visit the Drake plant to inspect tyre damage. Once a reasonable video library has been accumulated, Drake will then add these materials, suitably edited to protect customer anonymity, to enhance their product information knowledge pages.

Pricing

Although the move to e-business trading is expected to reduce operating costs, Drake will attempt to sustain the same pricing policy for both on-line and off-line customers.

Promotion

Drake will continue to use traditional promotional tools including attendance at trade exhibitions, trade advertising, press releases, a company newsletter and a sales force. It is hoped that the advent of the web site facility will permit the sales staff to spend more time involved in knowledge management tasks such as acting as tyre remould product selection advisors. Concurrently it is intended that the sales team will spend much less time 'fire fighting' problems such as incorrect orders, invoicing errors and product shipment delays.

Distribution

The company will continue to use its own delivery lorries to service UK customers. Upon entry to Europe, the services of a long-haul fleet provider will be used to deliver tyres across Europe. Selection of a fleet operator will be dependent upon the selected supplier being prepared to share operating knowledge by automatically linking into the Drake on-line order entry/product shipment delivery system.

Knowledge Management Infrastructure

Last year Drake completed a major upgrading of the IT operation to create an integrated enterprise resource planning (ERP) system which already permits real-time data exchange between sales, manufacturing, production scheduling, quality control, procurement, shipping and accounting databases. This will simplify the construction of the on-line knowledge management infrastructure because the main elements required for the new system will be the construction of an on-line front-end for displaying product information, permitting on-line ordering, downloading of specific data to key customers via extranets and providing customers with access to check on the status of tyre shipments in transit. In the case of the off-line orderentry system, this will be integrated into the on-line operation by providing office sales staff with terminals and an intranet via which to enter orders received by telephone, fax or mail. Given Drake's limited expertise in the design of IT-based systems, the front end will be developed by an American software firm which has experience in the US tyre manufacturing industry. The actual system will be installed off-site at a major ISP which is based in the same town as Drake's head office. Preliminary costings suggest the new system can be developed and implemented for a total cost of £250,000. On-going annual operating costs are estimated at £75,000 per annum.

Financial Forecast

Although the new system is expected to halt any further erosion in the UK operation net profit margins, this factor is not budgeted into the cost analysis. Hence the financial forecast is based entirely upon net incremental revenue generated from the proposed new European operation.

£000

	Yr 0	Yr 1	Yr 2	Yr 3
European revenue	0	500	1000	2000
European profit*	0	50	100	200
Project investment	250	0	0	0
Annual costs	0	75	75	75
Net profit	(250)	(25)	25	125
Accum. profit	(250)	(275)	(250)	(125)

*profit before deduction of e-commerce operating costs

The above forecast suggests that break-even will not occur until year 4 of the project. This situation is not unusual because most organisations find that an investment in computer-based knowledge management systems is not an immediate pay-off proposition. Similar to other companies facing this scenario, Drake judges the financial projections as acceptable because long term sustained business growth can only occur if the firm successfully avoids price competition by building strong relationships with customers who value working with a supplier committed to using knowledge to more effectively satisfy customer needs.

8

Product Knowledge and Innovation

CHAPTER SUMMARY

Firms must accept that products have a finite life cycle and hence survival is dependent upon continuous innovation. Product portfolios should regularly be evaluated. Innovation involves the application of knowledge to create new products and/or services. One approach is to use a linear sequential product development model to minimise new product failure rates. Time-to-market is becoming a crucial issue and firms need to exploit knowledge as a path to reducing development times. Organisational culture may cause new knowledge to be rejected. One solution is to consider going outside the firm for new knowledge sources. Complex innovation can be frustrated by inadequate knowledge sharing among the development team members. Another approach to product development is to acquire other companies as a source of new knowledge.

INTRODUCTION

Chaston (1999b) proposed that most firms will opt to select one of four possible areas of strategic product focus, namely: *product performance excellence, price performance excellence, transactional excellence* and *relationship excellence*. Given the high risks associated with virtually any form of organisational innovation, it is probably much safer for a firm to retain its existing strategic focus when considering the exploitation of new knowledge to enhance existing products or services or to develop new products or processes.

Nevertheless, prior to finalising the project specification for the incorporation of new knowledge into any product or process, the firm should revisit the issue of the commercial validity of retaining the current strategic positioning. This action is a risk assessment exercise designed to confirm that an appropriate decision has been made concerning the future strategic pathway along which to exploit new knowledge as a mechanism through which to add value to the firm's product line.

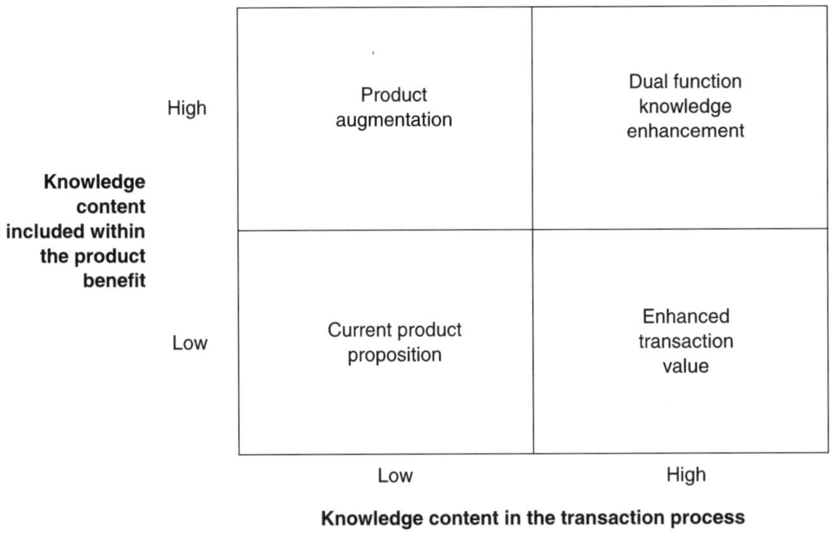

FIGURE 8.1 A KNOWLEDGE ENHANCEMENT OPTION MATRIX

In undertaking a product line risk assessment exercise, the firm has two product dimensions to consider, namely the functionality of the product (the benefit offered to customers) and the structuring of the purchase transaction process. As shown in Figure 8.1, these two dimensions generate four alternative options.

The lowest level of risk presented in Figure 8.1 is to change neither product functionality nor transaction process. There is only minimal risk in upgrading the knowledge content of the transaction process while leaving the product form unchanged. Upgrading the product form by addition of knowledge will involve a certain degree of risk because the change must be perceived as beneficial by the customer relative to competitors' product offerings. Finally the highest risk proposition is to introduce new knowledge into the product and concurrently revise the product transaction process.

ENHANCING PRODUCT FUNCTIONALITY WITH KNOWLEDGE

In the 1980s, Nestlé's baby food division in France was running an extremely poor second to Bledina. This latter brand had achieved its leadership position through aggressive promotional expenditure based around the conventional approach of spending heavily on television advertising (Rapp and Collins 1994). Nestlé France was not prepared to enter into the expensive and probably extremely risky process of a head-to-head promotional spending battle with

Bledina. Instead it re-examined the conventions of how the customer acquires information in the baby food market and the nature of the knowledge contained within conventional promotional messages.

Its solution was to identify ways of enhancing the delivery of knowledge about baby care. It opened rest-stops alongside the main autoroutes in France during the summer holiday season where parents at no charge could stop, feed and change their babies. At each location the parents could also visit the Relais Bébé Nestlé desk to be provided with knowledge about different baby food selections specially recommended to suit both different age groups and the time of day.

The next step in their move to increase the knowledge content of the product was achieved by Nestlé building a database of new mothers to whom the firm mailed a gift pack on a regular basis. Concurrently the firm established a toll-free number through which parents could obtain guidance, advice and reassurance from a Nestlé licensed dietitian. The impact of this entrepreneurial approach to knowledge management is demonstrated by the fact that in only a few years Nestlé's market share went from 20 per cent to over 43% of the total market in France.

Although most organisations are aware that customers undertake post-purchase evaluation, the majority of firms only tend to create minimal marketing structures to accommodate the provision of additional knowledge after the customers have made their purchase. A relatively standard approach to providing post-purchase service is to have a department for handling complaints and offering a contact point where the customer can be supplied with answers concerning any problems encountered during product usage. An effective example, however, of how one can exploit the knowledge marketing opportunities offered by the post-purchase evaluation phase is provided by the American motorcycle manufacturer, Harley-Davidson (Rapp and Collins 1994).

In the early 1980s this firm, whose name for many years has been synonymous with large powerful motorbikes, was faced with intense competition from Japanese firms such as Honda and Kawasaki, which had invaded the US market offering lower priced, well made, heavyweight machines. Having recognised the need to greatly improve build quality and thereby reduce defect rates, the next problem confronting Harley-Davidson was how to rebuild customer loyalty. The solution was to recognise that in the minds of its customers, along with apple pie, John Wayne and the Stars and Stripes, the name Harley-Davidson is also synonymous with the American dream of a free, democratic, wide open spaces lifestyle. Instead of attempting to promote this concept through the traditional approach of large scale pre-purchase promotions, the firm decided to adopt the entrepreneurial approach of exploiting the post-purchase evaluation phase. This it achieved by supporting the customers' dream in which their machine is part of both a special relationship between owner and motorcycle and a special social relationship which can only come from being a Harley-Davidson rider.

In 1983, they formed the Harley Owners Group, which rapidly became more commonly known as the HOG Club. Members were charged an annual fee of $35 for which they received an amazing range of knowledge benefits and the opportunity to participate in numerous social activities. Service and knowledge benefits included items such as an emergency pick-up service, a fly and ride rental programme, low cost insurance, touring handbook and the *Enthusiast* magazine. The firm also realised that its network of motorcycle dealerships had a critical role in both generating sales and, just as importantly, in assisting to sustain a positive post-purchase evaluation experience. The company formalised its aim of establishing an apparently seamless customer care network through persuading dealers to adopt a proactive knowledge provision role to Harley-Davidson owners in their respective areas of the country.

An example of simultaneous enhancement of knowledge content in both the product and the transaction process is provided by the Cisco Corporation. To upgrade product knowledge content functionality the firm moved to lean manufacturing accompanied by the creation of free advisory services for customers seeking design advice or assistance to customise product specifications. Concurrently the company moved to establish a telesales operation to enhance the speed and efficiency of its sales ordering and delivery systems.

PRODUCT PORTFOLIO MANAGEMENT

All firms should accept that their products and services have a finite life in the marketplace. This concept is described within the theoretical paradigm known as the product life cycle (PLC) curve, which proposes that products and services pass through the four phases of *introduction, growth, maturity* and *decline* (Heldey 1977). In recognition of the risks associated with a firm depending upon a single product which has a finite life, most firms will have a number of products positioned at different stages on the PLC curve. The objective is that such a portfolio will ensure long term revenue stability.

The Boston Consulting Group originated the idea of a decision matrix based around the two dimensions of market share and rate of market growth. The theories underlying the BCG matrix are that (a) high market share products generate large profits and (b) the earlier a product achieves market domination, the more likely is the case that this share will be retained as the market moves into the maturity phase on the PLC curve The tool was evolved by the Boston Group as a way of assisting their clients to manage product portfolios more effectively.

Academics such as Doyle (1998) expressed the concern that the BCG model exhibits the potential weakness that (a) market share is possibly a somewhat crude assessment of performance and (b) market growth rate may be an inadequate description of overall industry attractiveness. To handle the criticism about using market share as a performance measurement

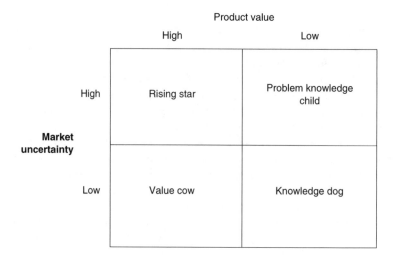

FIGURE 8.2   A MODIFIED VERSION OF THE BCG MATRIX

dimension, Slywotzky (1996) has suggested that firms should assess sales revenue of a product relative to proportionate share of the total financial value of all firms contained within a market sector. In his analysis of financial value he compared different valuations of firms in the computer industry. His explanation of why firm such as Microsoft have a much higher market valuation than IBM is that the former corporate operations are more firmly embedded in the exploitation of unique, proprietary knowledge as the basis for generating added value from internal operations.

In relation to market growth rate being an inadequate description of overall industry attractiveness Chaston (1999b) proposed that this variable within the BCG matrix might be replaced with the new dimension of product knowledge penetration. As suggested in Figure 8.2, it is then possible to determine appropriate marketing strategies for a product portfolio which is more reflective of the objectives of knowledge-based value maximisation and management of risk.

During the introduction and growth phases of the PLC, product knowledge penetration is low. Thus suppliers need to make available the educational information required by customers to convince them that adopting a relatively poorly understood product is the correct decision. By the time a market moves into the maturity phase, most customers have acquired a level of knowledge which causes them to be confident that they have made the correct decision about being loyal to a specific product. If a firm's product has achieved a dominant share of total market value by the time the market has reached maturity then, because customers are extremely confident about their purchase choice, the firm will only have to expend limited funds as a percentage of sales on promotional activity to sustain market position. Hence this product, the *value cow*, will contribute a significant proportion of the company's total value.

In contrast the *Knowledge Dog* product is in the unenviable position that (a) customers' knowledge of the product is low relative to more successful brands and (b) the profits needed to increase the company value can only come from stealing sales from a market leader. Because value cow customers are now highly certain about the correctness of their product choice, the company with a knowledge dog product will have to expend a massive level of funds and/or dramatically reduce price in order to stimulate customer switching. In most cases this strategy is not financially viable, which is why knowledge dog products are rarely able to overthrow value cows in most markets.

If a firm owns a low share product during a high market uncertainty phase (a *value problem knowledge child*), then this may be an appropriate time to act to attempt to stimulate brand switching. For this is when customers are still at the stage of not having sufficient knowledge to be certain about which supplier offers the best proposition. Consequently firms with a low share product are well advised to assess whether, while customer generic product knowledge is still low, action should be taken to (a) upgrade new product performance by exploiting new knowledge and (b) launch a promotional campaign to enhance customer knowledge. These actions might result in a product proposition capable of effectively attacking the *rising star*. An example of this approach was the decision by ex-IBM employees who utilised their extensive knowledge of computer manufacturing to start the new small business Compaq Corporation to market a PC with a specification equivalent to IBM products but which could be offered at a much reduced price.

INNOVATION

Innovation, whether directed towards the development of new products or the ongoing improvement of existing product production processes, is possibly the most important activity within any firm. In a world where other firms are seeking to expand their market share, successful firms often can only stay ahead of the competition by exploiting new knowledge to offer improved products or processes that deliver new forms of added value to their customers.

In specifying an appropriate innovation management strategy, management will need to determine the scale of innovation to be implemented by the firm. Reaching a decision on the scale of innovation requires the selection of an appropriate orientation to innovation at a point somewhere along a continuum. At one extreme is the decision to progress innovation based purely upon using existing knowledge to support a minor extension to the current product portfolio or production processes. The other extreme on the continuum involves the firm in exploiting new knowledge sources as

	3	4
Entrepreneurial	Focus on existing innovative products or processes	Focus on new entrepreneurial products or process
	1	2
Conventional	Focus on existing products or processes	Focus on conventional new product or new process development

Marketing style

Existing products　　　New products

Source of market revenue

FIGURE 8.3　PRODUCT KNOWLEDGE MANAGEMENT MATRIX

the basis for making available to the market a completely new product or production process.

Another necessary decision is whether the firm wishes to adopt a conventional market management approach or to opt for an entrepreneurial orientation. This matter also involves the selection of a point somewhere along a continuum. At one extreme is the decision to progress development based purely upon conventional thinking. The other extreme on the continuum involves the organisation in adopting a totally entrepreneurial approach to create an unconventional product or process.

Combining the dimensions of source of market revenue and marketing style generates the alternative medium term product knowledge management option matrix of the type illustrated in Figure 8.3. Cell 1 is associated with concentrating on exploiting existing knowledge to market conventional products or processes. Product or process improvement activity will have minimal impact on the organisation's future performance. This path is probably the most frequently utilised of all of the options proposed in Figure 8.3.

Cell 2 proposes the option of emphasising the importance of new knowledge to support product or process innovation, but retaining a conventional orientation to these innovative activities. Firms which adopt the Cell 2 position typically assume that as their new products or processes can assist in the generation of market revenue, they will be able to move back nearer to a Cell 1 situation with new applications of knowledge being a significantly less important source of revenue growth.

Cell 3 suggests that an entrepreneurial firm having previously developed a range of unconventional products or processes will, at least for the foreseeable future, concentrate on generating revenue growth without committing additional knowledge resources to the development of any new product or process concepts. Cell 4 positions the firm as concentrating the majority of knowledge resources upon entrepreneurial new product or process development. It is possibly the riskiest of all of the options available within the matrix. Accordingly, most firms will only adopt this position for a defined period of time with the hope that once the new products are launched, they can gradually move towards Cell 3 situation where this latest generation of company knowledge will come to represent a long term source of revenue growth. A possible exception to this scenario, however, is the firm run by an intuitive entrepreneur who only achieves real personal satisfaction from trading activities which continually involve exploiting totally new knowledge to develop radically different products or processes.

The proposed model in Figure 8.3 is posited as a dynamic process, changing over time depending upon the circumstances confronting the firm. What is possibly a very rare direction within the dynamic model, probably because it requires a fundamental shift in organisational culture, is for a firm to shift management style from an entrepreneurial to a conventional marketing style. One circumstance when this is likely to occur is when an entrepreneurial firm is so successful that its product strategy becomes the new convention within an industrial sector. One could argue, for example, this is exactly the scenario which faced Microsoft. Having applied its entrepreneurial knowledge management capabilities to develop its suite of windows-based programmes (for example, Word, Excel, Access, Powerpoint) as the global standard in the world of computing, it now spends a significant proportion of its time exploiting these products and, on a regular basis, acting in a very conventional way by issuing updated, more powerful versions of the same product concept.

Knowledge Sources

An important catalyst in the innovation process is the acquisition of new knowledge that identifies the existence of new opportunities. Possibly the richest source of such knowledge is the company's customers (Linneman and Stanton 1992). In some cases knowledge can be acquired through observation. Convarec Corporation observed that sales of Stomadhesive, an adhesive patch used to attach colostomy devices, were much higher than forecasted. Investigation revealed that doctors and nurses were cutting up the product and using the material in other forms of surgical repair. To respond to this situation the company launched pre-cut patches under the brand name of Duoderm.

Also in the medical market, DuPont observed that small hospitals and clinics rarely purchased the company's range of discrete clinical analysers. Research revealed that in addition to cost, these smaller operations lacked the skills to use such sophisticated technology and were unable to maintain the equipment. The solution was to accept

---

trade-ins from large hospitals, recondition these and offer them, accompanied by on-site training and service guarantees, to smaller medical facilities.

Knowledge of customer problems also permits evolution of a diversified product range to fulfil variation in need across a customer base. DuPont carefully studied the materials needs of aircraft designers, plant engineers and the boat construction industry. Aircraft designers wanted materials offering high strength-to-weight ratios, plant engineers wanted a long lasting durable material for use in pumps and boat builders wanted to create larger hulls capable of higher cruising speeds. From this knowledge DuPont was able to develop specific marketing campaigns directed towards the provision of sector-specific knowledge about how their new Kevlar-based products could fulfil these diverse market needs.

It can also be the case that knowledge is created but that nobody is totally certain how to exploit such knowledge (Coover 2000). The laser for a number of years was referred to by engineers as a solution looking for a problem. Another example of this scenario is provided by cyanoacrylate adhesives, better known as Superglue. The adhesive properties of cyanoacrylates monomers were first noticed as a technical problem plaguing the development of plastics for use in optical gun sites. Then in the 1950s, the Tennessee Eatman Company was involved in researching cyanoacrylate polymers for use in jet aircraft canopies. Again the amazing adhesive properties were noticed. One observed property was that the adhesive was so strong that it was capable of actually damaging expensive laboratory optical equipment. This second time the phenomenon was encountered, it was decided to determine whether this new knowledge represented a commercial opportunity. From this opportunity review was developed the well known Superglue product. The first application was in the construction of a joint in the atomic bomb. Numerous other opportunities subsequently emerged in car manufacturing, electronic board assembly and aircraft construction. More recently the technology has been adopted by the medical profession. Cyanoacrylates are used in various medical treatment situations such as sutureless surgery and repairing lesions in eyeballs.

Barriers to Knowledge Acquistion and Exploitation

A problem facing larger organisations is the tendency of management to rely on products and processes which utilise proven, well understood technologies (Loutfy and Belkhir 2001). A classic example of this scenario is provided by Xerox Corporation whose PARC R & D laboratory made a number of important discoveries in the areas of computing such as Windows and the computer mouse but then failed to commercialise any of these opportunities.

The reason why new knowledge may be ignored by large corporations is that in their struggle to grow revenue there is a preference to operate in large, well established markets where there is detailed understanding of how to grow the business by exploiting existing knowledge. Additionally many large firms are often under pressure from their customers not to introduce any new knowledge that might disrupt the latter's ongoing operations.

In order to ensure that new knowledge is regularly being imported into an organisation may require a revision in both structure and operational processes. Xerox Corporation, for example, having learned its lesson from the PARC episode, has created its Xerox New Enterprises (XNE) operation. This is assigned the task of supporting the exploitation of new knowledge that might permit entry into new markets or evolve new product solutions for existing markets. To assist this operation the company has created a team of principals co-located within the firm's research laboratories who are responsible for scanning the market for opportunities and screening internal activities as sources of new, emergent technologies. This team selects the most promising opportunities for further examination and research. Where further study validates that a significant opportunity exists, a new project team is formed to commence work to exploit commercially the new knowledge that has been identified.

OPTIMISING THE PRODUCT DEVELOPMENT PROCESS

A number of authors have undertaken research to identify factors influencing the success and failure of new products. One of the most prolific writers in this area, Professor Cooper (1975, 1986, 1988, 1990), has conducted numerous cross-sectional and longitudinal studies of Canadian firms. Application of factor analysis has permitted the development of his Newprod computer-based evaluation tool. The factors which form the basis of the Newprod predictive assessment of probable performance of a new product are:

- Utilising knowledge to achieve product superiority/quality in relation to competition.
- Utilising knowledge to offer greater economic value than existing product(s).
- Utilising knowledge to achieve good overall fit in terms of the product development project being compatible with the organisation's existing areas of production and marketing expertise.
- Utilising knowledge to achieve technological compatibility of the product within the organisation's existing areas of technological capability.
- Utilising knowledge to ensure the firm can draw upon existing expertise and will not be forced to learn completely new operational skills.
- Utilising knowledge to ensure the product offers opportunity to enter a large, rapidly growing market sector.
- Utilising knowledge to ensure the firm can cope with any competitive threats.
- Utilising knowledge to ensure the new product fits into a well defined existing market category as opposed to being a truly innovative idea providing the basis for a completely new market sector.
- Utilising knowledge to ensure the product development project is well defined and understood inside the organisation.

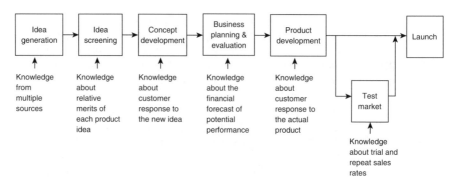

FIGURE 8.4 A TRADITIONAL LINEAR NEW PRODUCT PROCESS MANAGEMENT MODEL

Growing recognition of the costs of failure has resulted in the development of various systems to manage the new product development process. Traditionally these systems are of a linear sequential nature of the type illustrated in Figure 8.4. The ultimate aim within the model is to progress from idea generation to launch only those products for which success is guaranteed. As the firm moves through the process, at each stage knowledge is acquired and evaluated about whether the product under development should be progressed or terminated. Costs associated with development increase at almost an exponential rate while the product is being progressed from idea stage through to market launch. Hence the earlier the firm acquires knowledge that suggests project termination, the greater will be the savings made.

The classic view of entry point for the process model is idea generation. However, Li and Calantone (1998) posit that certain market and internal competences are key antecedent determinants of success at the idea generation stage. As illustrated in Figure 8.5, the greater the firm's knowledge of customer needs, the more probable it is that new ideas will be generated that offer the greatest potential for market success. Another possible success moderator is the degree to which the firm utilises knowledge about competition in the determination of new opportunities. In many markets, technological change can provide the opportunity to permit the development of radical new product forms. Hence as shown in Figure 8.5, the performance of the new product development team will also be greatly influenced by the firm's R & D knowledge competence in identifying and exploiting new technological opportunities.

The objective of the idea generation stage is to maximise the number of knowledge sources utilised such that a large number of new ideas become available for consideration. This is achieved by involving as many sources as possible. These may include customers, intermediaries, the firm's sales

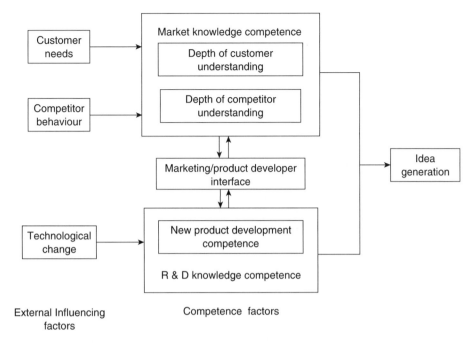

FIGURE 8.5 INFLUENCE OF KNOWLEDGE COMPETENCE ON THE
NEW PRODUCT PROCESS

force, employees from all areas of the organisation, studying competitors' products, the firm's R & D department and the firm's suppliers. At the idea screening stage, the objective is only to progress those ideas where available knowledge indicates that the ideas have genuine potential for success. The ideas approved for development then enter the concept development phase. New ideas are usually framed around phrases and descriptions used by individuals within an industrial sector, many of which are often not understood by the customer. Hence the first step in the concept development phase is to redefine ideas into customer-orientated benefit and product attribute statements. The resultant concept statements can then be tested to generate knowledge about customers' reactions to the new idea. This knowledge generation is achieved using techniques such as focus group meetings and one-to-one interviews.

Knowledge generated from focus groups and interviews permits the firm to assess purchase probability, appeal of product benefit and customer price expectations. This provides the basis from which to forecast sales and then to evolve a business plan for the new product. The sales forecast, when linked with knowledge about cost of goods, marketing expenditure, operating overheads and fixed asset requirements, permits estimation of expected profits and return on investment (ROI) for the project.

Understanding of specified customer benefits identified during the concept development stage, when linked to forecasted production costs in the business plan, permits the creation of a detailed specification for use during the product development phase. Once prototypes have been produced, market research can commence to generate knowledge about whether the actual product is capable of fulfilling customer needs. In consumer goods markets, this research is often based on activities such as blind side-by-side comparisons and in-home placement tests. In industrial markets, firms often involve potential customers in the evaluation activity through a technique known as Beta-site testing. In this situation, the customer is kept closely involved in all aspects of the prototype development programme. Through usage of the test product in their organisation, they are able to provide detailed feedback about possible significant modifications for improving the final product.

In industrial markets the small number of customers, the high unit value of purchases per customer and the use of one-to-one personal selling as the primary promotional vehicle usually means that following successful completion of the prototype development phase, the company has sufficient knowledge to decide if the new product can be launched. Virtually none of the market research undertaken during all of the new product development phases will, however, answer the question of whether a new product will survive in the self-service environment characteristic of many consumer goods markets. This means that prior to the launch decision, many consumer goods will need further testing using the medium of a test market.

The objectives of the test market are, in a geographically restricted area, to generate knowledge about the performance of the product when placed alongside competitive offerings in end user outlets. During the test, research studies are undertaken to measure variables such as product awareness, trial rate, repeat purchase rate, market share attainment, achieved level of in-store distribution and behaviour of the competition.

There are four possible outcomes for a test market, each of which has different implications. The first outcome is the knowledge that the product has achieved a high trial and a high repeat rate. This will usually mean the test market has been successful and the product should be launched immediately. The second outcome is the knowledge acquired about a low trial and a high repeat rate. This outcome will require further investigation. It usually indicates that there is a need either to achieve higher customer awareness or to expand the level of achieved distribution.

The high trial and low repeat of the third outcome is a little more worrying because it usually infers that having tried the product, consumers remain unconvinced of the merits for adding the item to their 'shopping basket' of regularly purchased goods. The worst scenario is the fourth outcome where the test market reveals that the new product achieved both a low trial and a low repeat rate. Here one must assume fundamental organisational problems exist and, therefore, serious questions need to be posed of the project team to find out what exactly has been going on at all stages within the new product development process.

NEGATING KNOWLEDGE TO CREATE A NEW STRATEGY

Any small firm which enters into head-to-head confrontation with a brand leader should rarely have the expectation that such a marketing philosophy will generate a major increase in sales revenue. If the firm wishes to gain a significant share of sales in an established market, it is usually necessary to acquire new knowledge that can support the innovation needed to achieve this aim. By acquiring and exploiting new knowledge the firm may identify an opportunity to steal significant market share from the competition. To achieve the share increase objective, however, this new knowledge must be capable of providing the basis to support a viable attack strategy (Smith 1995). The most likely path to success is to evolve a strategy which negates a significant aspect of the existing knowledge used by incumbent firms to manage the marketing processes which currently prevail within a market sector.

Evolution of an effective attack strategy will require a careful appreciation of how the incumbent firm utilises knowledge and capabilities to generate sales. In this way the newcomer may be able to identify a vulnerability in the brand leader's operations. In the American industrial oxygen industry, Union Carbide had focused upon exploiting knowledge to permit them to manufacture gases using high fixed cost production plants and then distribute the gas using a sophisticated rail-based distribution system. To defeat Union Carbide, Air Products Corporation exploited its knowledge of small system gas generation to develop a machine which customers could use to generate their own oxygen on-site. By removing distribution from the cost equation, the company was able to dominate that sector of the market which used large volumes of oxygen in the production processes.

In the PC industry at one stage knowledge of managing direct sales forces and distributor operations was a critical capability which underpinned the success of firms such as IBM and Compaq. However as time passed, customers became more price sensitive. Dell recognised the implications of this trend and established its direct marketing mail-order business thereby negating the need to have a detailed understanding of how to manage sales forces and distributor networks.

In the photocopying industry, the success of Xerox Corporation was based upon a knowledge model consisting of an in-depth understanding of how to manufacture expensive, high-volume output machines and then to generate rental income by leasing the equipment to end users. Canon's response to this scenario was to seek new knowledge to permit it to drive down the costs of low volume copiers. The outcome was solutions such as (a) using fibre optics to replace conventional lens and mirror systems and (b) developing a solution to toner formulation that vitiated the need for users to have to mix the toner chemicals. Then the company developed the knowledge required to appoint and then train dealers in selling versus seeking to lease their machines. To ensure potential customers had adequate knowledge of Canon's extremely reliable, low cost products the company also invested heavily in television and print advertising at a time when Xerox still relied heavily on a direct sales force to fulfil the role of customer communication.

ACCELERATING THE INNOVATION MANAGEMENT PROCESS

Linear product development models of the type shown in Figure 8.4 are essentially orientated towards using knowledge to minimise mistakes. Assuming that a firm is prepared to take risks then a possible alternative approach to innovation is to revisit the classic stage gate process described in Figure 8.4 and to recognise that this is essentially a linear system which can lead to rigid and inflexible decision-making within the firm.

Cooper (1994) has proposed that greater creativity within the stage gate process can be achieved by permitting progression to the next stage in the development even though knowledge may still be missing about certain issues. Essentially what drives Cooper's new vision is a fact repeatedly validated by Japanese corporations, namely organisations must find ways of reducing the time taken from idea generation through to product launch. In an increasingly competitive world when seeking to reduce 'time-to-market', managers will have to balance the risks of not proceeding to the next phase until knowledge becomes available against being pre-empted by a more entrepreneurially orientated competitor.

An extremely important tool for reducing new product development times is the process known as concurrent engineering (Hartley 1992). This involves cross-functional teams using available knowledge to initiate parallel activities possibly even while the concept is still at the preliminary idea stage. For example, the manufacturing team begins to design a new production line, suppliers commence work on the development of machine tools to manufacture components that will be required by the new product and the advertising agency begins to evolve an appropriate promotional campaign.

The modern computer has made an almost immeasurable impact on accelerating time-to-market. Designers can now use computer-aided design (CAD) systems to acquire knowledge that permits the virtual reality evaluation of prototypes. By linking these systems to computer-aided manufacturing (CAM) systems, engineers can be provided with the knowledge needed to assess the feasibility of manufacturing a new product idea prior to construction of a new production line. Furthermore if the firm is willing to overcome reservations about project confidentiality, the firm can provide suppliers with knowledge about new product plans using real-time data links. These permit suppliers to remain totally informed about all new product projects as they progress from idea through to manufacture of early prototypes.

CULTURE BLOCKS

Over the last 20 years, as more research has been undertaken on the factors influencing the performance of firms, some theorists have suggested that senior management need to pay greater attention to the nature of the prevailing culture within their organisations. Unfortunately these various writers rarely appear to agree on exactly what they mean by the concept of culture. Hence for the purposes of the following discussion it is assumed that culture is a reflection of the dominant attitudes and values exhibited by the majority of the workforce.

Large multinational companies usually offer superior value, standardised goods across a diverse range of transactionally orientated markets around the world. It is perhaps understandable, therefore, that many of these firms find that the most effective operational culture is that based on closely defined employee job roles, permitting minimal variation in personnel policies between departments and using detailed, performance indicator-type monitoring systems to identify financial variances rapidly. The risk with highly regimented internal environments is that employees are unable to gain access to the knowledge that will permit them to exhibit creativity and flexibility when responding to new situations.

THE 3M STORY

Many firms have found that as markets have become more competitive, there is a need for a culture shift towards becoming more entrepreneurial in their approach to the generation and utilisation of new knowledge. The 3M Corporation provides some effective guidelines for stimulating innovative behaviour in any size of firm. The cornerstone of its success is to strive to retain an entrepreneurial culture directed towards new ways of delivering customer satisfaction. Rigid operating policies are kept to a minimum, salaries are tied to the success of new products and employees are encouraged to be inventive. The 25% rule requires that a quarter of a division's sales must come from products introduced within the last five years. Any barriers to success such as turf fights between departments are kept to a minimum and the 'not invented here' syndrome is actively discouraged.

At 3M, staying close to the customer to acquire new knowledge is an ingrained cultural trait. Researchers, marketers and manufacturing personnel are actively encouraged to spend time in the field and customers are routinely invited to join brainstorming sessions organised by 3M. Once an employee comes up with an idea, they are encouraged to accelerate the sharing of knowledge through the creation of multi-disciplinary teams to progress new concepts from the idea stage through to market launch. To give people time to access and process new knowledge, there is a 15% rule which permits virtually anybody to spend up to 15% of their working week engaged in any activity that can enhance their capability to contribute to the firm's innovation programmes.

The 3M company seeks to reinforce the vision of continuous innovation by making this philosophy a core component of company tradition (Brand 1998). Additionally, by focusing upon HRM policies to minimise staff turnover, the company actively strives to reduce the loss of knowledge that accompanies the departure of experienced employees. This commitment to employees is accompanied by a tolerance for mistakes. This reflects the knowledge that some of 3M's best products (for example, ceramics; the Post It Notes) were outcomes of technological mistakes. The firm also has sufficient tolerance to permit employees unofficially to progress the R & D activities even though formal permission for project continuation has been revoked.

There are two fundamental approaches to innovation within the company. Knowledge by design involves top management identifying important technologies where the corporate strategy seeks to promote active R & D effort. These projects are often progressed by involving key customers in the sharing of knowledge to determine more rapidly how to exploit a new source of technology. This approach was taken with the Thinsulare material originally developed for ski jackets. By involving customers in the textile and clothing industries a diverse range of other opportunities for further exploiting the materials across such usage areas as camping gear, uniforms and cars was identified. The second approach is known as knowledge by emergence. Here the company accepts that developments may occur which for some time do not indicate any immediate opportunity or alternatively that developments will occur through an unforeseen event. For example, a scientist dropped some chemicals on a tennis shoe and found the coating provided resistance to dirt. The result was the Scotchguard range of chemicals for the protection of textiles and paper products.

GOING OUTSIDE FOR KNOWLEDGE

In the face of both the increasing complexity of modern technology and the requirement to reduce time-to-market, the more enlightened firms have become aware that they lack all of the knowledge necessary to develop new products and processes rapidly. The solution to this knowledge gap is to go outside the firm and develop links with other knowledge sources. Quinn (2000) holds the view that no one company acting alone in the twenty-first century can ever hope to out-innovate the competition and hence is a strong proponent of outsourcing innovation.

Depending upon the nature of internal knowledge within the firm, an organisation can outsource virtually any aspect of the new product development process described in Figure 8.4. At idea generation stage many of the large drugs companies have already moved to provide research grants to universities and independent laboratories. Once fundamental research has indicated the potential for a new source of opportunity, the applied research to evolve commercially viable product ideas can also be outsourced. Millennium Pharmaceuticals is a firm which undertakes this type of work. The organisation has developed software models that can analyse virtual chemicals to determine their potential to solve agricultural disease problems.

Some companies are prepared to outsource major components of their value chain activities. Dell outsources virtually every aspect of the design and development of new components and software. Intel avoids involvement in undertaking the R & D required to create the final end-product production facilities that are required once the company has developed its next generation of microchips. In the car industry, companies such as Ford have delegated a significant proportion of the work required to develop new subsystems. For example, in the case of the development of new concepts for automotive interiors the firm delegates this entire task to the world's leading supplier of interiors, Johnson Controls Corporation.

For innovation outsourcing to succeed, the partners in the process do need to share a common vision about both the future and the best approach to exploiting market opportunities. Additionally all participants should already have a strong track record in the use of new knowledge to support innovative activities. Another critical issue is that of ensuring knowledge sharing definitely results in innovation synergy. One risk that may be perceived by the initiator of the innovation partnership is that the firm to whom the project is outsourced will need to be provided with knowledge about the market and the future plans of the outsourcing firm. Under these circumstances the outsourcing firm may need to give consideration to the creation of strategic blocks that prevent suppliers bypassing the firm and moving to make direct contact with the firm's customers. Nintendo, for example, has expertise in the mass marketing, mass production branding and distribution of computer games. The company outsources product development to external game designers who in theory could use their acquired knowledge about the Nintendo operation to become a future source of competition. To avoid this eventuality, Nintendo uses both dominant knowledge of game marketing and patents to protect itself from such a threat.

Quinn notes that most cases of outsourcing success are critically dependent upon the creation of effective communication systems that permit the rapid interchange of knowledge between participants in the product development process. Increasingly firms are exploiting advances in communications software to create knowledge interchange platforms. An identified benefit of computerising communications systems is that it forces participants to adopt common language platforms, performance measurement systems and rules to guide knowledge interchange effectively. The other benefit is that knowledge management can be a fully distributed process allowing the firm to develop outsourcing relationships with other organisations based anywhere in the world.

MANAGING COMPLEX INNOVATION

In projects involving the management of complex innovation, firms are increasingly using computer-based systems to store, exchange and manipulate knowledge inside the organisation. An accepted obstacle in the effective operation of these systems is (a) the need for everybody to be linked into every database within the organisation and (b) data interchange being on a real-time basis. Achievement of this goal demands that all departments are orientated towards giving priority, not to their own information needs, but to the effective operation of the organisation's entire IT system. Even in off-line companies, efficient interdepartmental communication during execution of an innovation project is rarely an easily achieved goal. Once the communication requirements are for real-time data interchange, seeking to establish effective communication flows usually becomes at least a hundred times more difficult.

In the e-commerce sector, an additional issue in complex project innovation management is that in many cases the product developers will need to draw upon new technologies from a very diverse range of sources such as computing, telecommunications and opto-electronics. Although the Japanese have yet to emerge as dominant players in the e-business industry, their achievements as leading innovators in other hi-tech industries does suggest that their new product and process management techniques can provide some useful lessons. Bowonder and Miyake (1992) in their research on Japanese innovation management have used a number of sources to evolve a model in which the following factors are perceived as critical in achieving success:

1   There is a clear purpose of seeking to maximise the level of activity associated with fusing together knowledge across a broad range of different technologies.
2   Firms are willing to collaborate with each other to gain access to critical core knowledge sources.
3   Multiple knowledge sources about different technologies are used in order to lower the risk of failure by one single technology frustrating progress across other elements within the project.
4   Concurrent engineering is utilised to exploit knowledge interaction that can come from parallel activities, which offers the potential drastically to reduce time-to-market development cycles.
5   There is emphasis on involving the entire workforce in organisational learning to ensure new ideas, knowledge and skills are spread throughout the operation.
6   There is emphasis on seeking new knowledge about technological innovation external to the organisation to ensure the latest scientific thinking is incorporated into the organisation's core knowledge base.

Innovation at Hitachi

Hitachi (*www.hitachi.co.jap*) is a world leader in developing the low powered chips demanded of laptops and e-commerce devices such as internet linked telephones and 'smart' domestic devices. To acquire knowledge about software design back in the 1980s, the firm entered into a development alliance with Texas Instruments. It then applied their knowledge of electron beam lithography to test manufacture the world's first low power 64MB-DRAM chip. Experience then permitted it to move onto making 256MB, 1024MB and 4000MB chips. Underlying this rapid innovation pace is a philosophy based around (a) investing in knowledge acquisition of technological intelligence from outside the firm, (b) very rapid internal organisational learning, (c) the ability of the workforce to assimilate knowledge about new technologies, (d) using alliances to enhance knowledge acquisition and (e) exploiting concurrent engineering to minimise product development time.

Other researchers have examined the influence of organisational structure on effective innovation management. In a seminal review of this extremely diverse area of the academic literature, Nakata and Sivakumar (1996) examined the issue of the degree to which an orientation towards individualism versus collectivism within a national culture can influence successful innovation activities. They conclude that, especially in high-technology industries, outstanding new ideas tend to come from firms where individualism is both valued and nurtured. It appears that this type of orientation towards the exploitation of new knowledge provides the innovator with sufficient freedom and autonomy to permit them to evolve totally new visions for products and organisational processes. The potential problem with this orientation is that although it can be the source of outstanding new ideas, it may not be favourable for managing the latter stages of new product development. For in this subsequent phase it is necessary to bring together the contributive, but diverse, knowledge sources contained within all of the departments in the organisation which have a role to contribute in the latter stages of product development, prototyping, scaling up manufacturing systems and product launch. Nakata and Sivakumar conclude that during the latter stages of an innovation project reduction of development time scales and overall scale of success is likely to be higher in organisations which exhibit a collectivism orientation towards the management of knowledge.

It would, therefore, appear to be the case that there are two phases in the optimal management of a knowledge which provides the basis for an innovation project. During the idea search and identification stage, developers should be granted extensive freedom to maximise the number and range of knowledge sources that should be considered. Once, however, a specific idea has been selected as offering the optimal way forward, then in moving into the innovation implementation stage, a successful outcome is more likely if there is a shift to a team-based approach based around close co-operation, cohesion of effort and single-minded purpose in the exploitation of the knowledge required to achieve success.

Shifting to a group orientation approach in the latter stages of innovation projects is usually achieved by the formation of a cross-functional team. In their study of these structures Jassawalla and Sashittal (2001) concluded that in teams which had achieved a high level of co-operative working, costs are decreased, creativity enhanced, time-to-market reduced and profitability optimised. A critical factor influencing this outcome is that high levels of co-operation cause knowledge to be more effectively transferred between participants. Achieving effective knowledge transfer occurs because participants have a high awareness of the agendas, interests and objectives of other team members. Additionally knowledge exchange stimulates synergy between team member contributions and performance is greater than the sum of the individual contributions.

The need for a high level of co-operation should be recognised by senior management and these latter individuals are critical in establishing an organisational culture which values collaboration. These senior managers must also be active in selecting team leaders who possess appropriate experience to direct the development of an effective team operation. Senior managers must also ensure these leaders are free from any functional departmental affiliations in order to signal that interdepartmental equality is the only acceptable behaviour trait within the organisation. Finally it is the responsibility of senior managers to ensure teams have access to all necessary knowledge sources and are granted permission to act independently in seeking creative solutions, taking risks and implementing bold initiatives.

In turn the team leaders must be able to create an appropriate learning environment for their team. This will usually mean ensuring team members are collocated away from the functional departmental groups where they have previously been based. Another critical issue is to ensure that functional department heads do not have any control over the team formation process. In this way the team leader is free to ensure that the new team is constituted only of top performing employees.

A Diverse Approach to Knowledge Acquistion

In 1998, after ten years of more than 30 per cent compound annual growth, Intel the world's leading chip manufacturer found industry consolidation and increased competition resulted in revenue growth slowing to 5 per cent annum (*Electronics World* 2000). In response to this situation, Intel's chief executive Craig Barrett has sought to implement a diverse range of knowledge acquisition innovation capable of moving Intel from being a chip manufacturer to an organisation heavily involved in exploiting the internet.

In order to get acceptance of a very different strategy, Intel has faced the need to persuade staff to drop their 'knowledge not from here' attitude to acquiring new understanding of emergent technologies. To assist this process, in 1999 the company spent $6 billion to gain access to the knowledge held by twelve companies already operating in the internet sector. Concurrently the company has expanded its knowledge acquisition activities by using its venture capital operation, Intel Capital. In 1999 this operation invested approximately $1.2 billion in more 350 software and internet companies.

Internally the company has sought to evolve a more entrepreneurial spirit among employees by offering funds to support the exploitation of new knowledge to stimulate the proposal of new start-up business ideas proposed by employees. These range from a scheme to equip doctors with secure IDs to encourage on-line medicine through to installing information terminals in the backs of seats in Madison Square Garden. One idea which emerged was to move the company into the web hosting business and in 1999 the company's first net centre was established in Santa Clara, California. Early success has caused Intel to start planning to build more computer centres around the world to host e-commerce operating services for other companies. At the same time the firm is not seeking to leave the world of microchip manufacturing. What is happening, however, is that the company is investing heavily in the acquisition of new knowledge using R & D to pioneer the creation of new generations of chips for use in the networking, telecommunications and information appliances markets.

KNOWLEDGE MANAGEMENT AND R & D

Within all of the activities associated with innovation, possibly the most important area to optimise knowledge management is within an organisation's R & D operations. In recognition of this critical issue Armbrecht et al. (2001) were sponsored to examine this important topic by the Industrial Research Institute in America. In their view the key aspect of knowledge management within the R & D process is to ensure that knowledge flow extends beyond storage and retrieval to embrace creation, capture, retrieval and reuse. Knowledge sharing between R & D staff is also perceived as critical.

R & D strategies are usually driven by corporate strategies and goals which are cascaded downwards within the organisation to stimulate the development of new products and processes. The first phase in the research process is to initiate discussion and review of available knowledge. Both tacit and explicit knowledge sources should be accessed. As comprehension is gained over the nature of the proposed research programme, knowledge acquisition will usually need to be expanded to access new sources. In some cases this new knowledge will be located elsewhere within the organisation, but frequently the knowledge search will have to be expanded outside the boundaries of the firm.

A critical aspect of effective knowledge flow is to break the 'knowledge is power' syndrome that may exist, which can result in knowledge not being shared with others. This often requires action by either management edict or through moves to create a culture shift towards a higher level of collaborative learning. The speed with which knowledge can be accessed will have a dramatic impact on the rate of progress for any R & D programme. To accelerate the rate of knowledge exchange many firms have migrated from crude electronic systems such as e-mails and are establishing web-enabled knowledge centres. These sites will usually feature descriptions of individuals within the organisation who have expertise. Concurrently searchable catalogues are created through the documentation of earlier projects which have been undertaken by the firm. In many instances these formalised systems are complemented by networks of experts from diverse backgrounds who can be consulted by researchers seeking specialist, tacit knowledge sources. As such individuals are often geographically or functionally dispersed there is a need to promote the idea of individuals frequently finding opportunities to come together in what are known as 'communities of good practice'.

Few employees exhibit any natural skills in the accessing and exploitation of knowledge. Thus formalised training schemes will be necessary to assist new people within a R & D team to become proficient in the utilisation of available knowledge. Formalised development can often be enhanced by providing new staff with access to mentors who can guide individuals through the process of acquiring the 'softer skills' of acquiring tacit knowledge from others. These actions are necessary because evidence suggests that where knowledge management practices are poorly understood then this will act as an inhibitor to the successful execution of the innovation process.

Another inhibitor to progress is where employees are disconnected from each other due to organisational structure or geography. This situation can be further exacerbated where certain employees seek to retain personal rights to knowledge and are unwilling to share data with others. Senior management will usually have to intervene to resolve this latter problem. The sharing of dispersed knowledge can usually be overcome by the creation of organisational 'silos' which can be electronically visited by employees during their search for relevant information. Concurrently there is need to avoid structural hierarchies causing communications barriers to be created. To overcome this latter scenario the usual solution is to create multidisciplinary teams who operate within a matrix management structure.

In summarising their research, Armbrecht et al. (2001) have proposed the following six imperatives:

1 Ensure full participation in innovation across an organisation's entire workforce.
2 Seek ways of promoting easier access to tacit knowledge.
3 Create effective search and retrieval tools to access internal and external knowledge.

4 Focus on promoting the development of a creative organisational culture.
5 Capture all learning in order that it can be reused.
6 Establish a culture that is totally supportive of the knowledge management needs of everybody engaged in innovative activities.

Mathews (2001) has examined the degree to which firms exploit external knowledge. He posits that within a firm there are distinctive capabilities which may not remain appropriate if market circumstances undergo fundamental change. In his view firms which are more likely to survive in such circumstances are those whose structures are orientated towards creating relationships with other firms through participation in knowledge networks. In this way firms can rapidly access complementary knowledge and more rapidly determine new approaches for using innovation as a source of competitive advantage. He illustrates this view by a describing the network organisation TCG, a cluster of interacting IT firms based in Sydney, Australia. The approach is for each firm, having determined internal competence relative to the overall competences required to execute an innovative activity, to seek other small firms which can provide the identified areas of missing knowledge.

Rycroft and Kash (2000) have examined the role of networks in relation to the type of innovation that is demanded by participants. They suggest there are three innovation patterns. *Incremental innovation* is associated with a gradual improvement in current core technology. *Transition innovation* involves the integration of new technology into existing processes. *Transformation innovation* is characterised by a dramatic shift in fundamental technology.

The easiest knowledge management process occurs within incremental innovation networks. Here the focus is upon enhancing existing core capabilities by acquiring knowledge that complements existing expertise. Speed is of the essence and this requires acceptance of the need to implement actions with the minimum possible level of new knowledge. The network must focus on building upon existing knowledge and not get diverted by accessing new knowledge that is not immediately useful.

Within transition networks the focus is upon expanding core competences that can complement existing knowledge assets. The network can often rely upon the reservoir of knowledge that is contained within the participant pool. In enabling change, however, there is a need to understand that certain competences may become more critical while others may become marginal or even redundant. Integration of newly combined knowledge sets demands there are efficient systems for optimising knowledge flows between the project participants. In some cases although learning will remain within the same technological boundaries, knowledge priorities can be expected to change and to some degree 'unlearning' will need to occur.

Transformation projects involve the acquisition of completely new core competences. Under these circumstances the network may have to accept periods of apparent chaos as new ideas are imported, new knowledge assimilated and determination made of the best path of direction as the project progresses. It is often the case that participants will have to learn how to fuse new knowledge into their existing knowledge frameworks. Furthermore as new core competences are being established, the network must be prepared to accept that new knowledge may be located in unrelated or unfamiliar areas outside the boundaries of prior experience. Another obstacle is that transformation projects often commence prior to there being strong signals from the market of the need for fundamental change. Hence sustaining commitment and enthusiasm in the early phases of any learning activities is often a difficult objective to achieve.

INNOVATION BY ACQUISITION

In some cases firms, having identified a significant knowledge capability gap, may decide to resolve this problem by seeking to use an acquisition strategy to gain access to new sources of competence. In an analysis of the implications associated with acquisitions in knowledge-intensive scenarios, Birkinshaw (1999) has determined that the most immediate problem following acquisition is the human resource implications of seeking to integrate staff and to avoid negative attitudes arising among employees concerned about an uncertain future. He suggests that the first step must be for the management of the acquiring company to reassure employees of the acquired firm that they will be involved in all decision-making in the merged organisation. This should be followed by a period of activity designed to integrate operational aspects and build a unified corporate culture. Such actions should not be initiated, however, until the objective of making employees comfortable with the new operating environment has been achieved.

Birkinshaw has concluded that all acquiring firms should accept realistic time frames for knowledge transfer to occur and recognise that this will not occur until cultural and employee behavioural convergence has begun to emerge. One of the apparent obstacles for the acquiring firm is the need to avoid moving too rapidly in implanting a new culture upon the employees within the organisation which has been purchased. It will take time for these latter employees to begin to accept that a revision in corporate identity is necessary and some years may pass before they cease to identify with their old, autonomous operation. Thus effective management of the post-merger phase will involve (a) creating a visible integration leader, (b) convincing employees of the acquired company that they have a valuable role to play and (c) clearly defining the new responsibilities for knowledge management exchange which now exist within the acquired R & D oper-sations. These processes should be seen as vital because knowledge workers such as scientists and engineers do need to be treated with care if they are to continue to work to the best of their abilities in the new organisation.

Chemical Industry Acquisitions

Eka Chemicals acquired the paper chemical business of Albright and Wilson, a UK firm, in 1990. A critical objective was to then integrate knowledge generation activities across laboratories in Sweden, the UK and the United States. To ensure the acquired employees felt secure, Eka announced that all five technical research centres would remain in operation, each focusing R & D activities upon different areas of technology. To encourage networking, however, research staff were rotated through the various laboratories to stimulate knowledge exchange. These actions were subsequently followed by moves to create multisite research projects to further accelerate the rate of knowledge transfer between employees.

Alfa Laval faced a somewhat more challenging task because its acquisition of Sharples in the United States was through the mechanism of a hostile bid. To rebuild employee morale at Sharples the decision was made to sustain research centres in both Denmark and America. To a large degree in the early years following the merger, the two units were left to operate independently of each other. Only after it had been determined that Sharples employees had recovered from post-merger events did Alfa Laval slowly move forward to establish integrated research programmes to stimulate knowledge transfer.

The Swedish firm ABB, in acquiring Combustion Engineering of America, had the view that knowledge transfer needed to occur somewhat rapidly. Hence the firm created a new business team composed of representatives from both sides of the Atlantic. By setting common standards, regular meetings, video conferencing and regular exchange visits ABB sought to minimise the time between acquisition and R & D knowledge exchange commencing. To further accelerate the exchange process, the firm announced 20 interconnected development programmes to be completed within three years. Unfortunately it soon became apparent that the expected pace of change was based upon exceptionally optimistic targets. Hence aims were revised with management shifting towards accepting parallel development instead of totally integrated project structures.

9

Knowledge Provision Through Promotion

Promotion is the marketing process for providing customers with the knowledge that can influence their purchase behaviour. Numerous different promotional techniques are available for knowledge distribution. The role and importance of promotion is influenced by the position of the product on the product life cycle curve. The advent of the internet has greatly increased organisations' abilities to provide both educational and product-specific knowledge to customers. On-line knowledge distribution has been important in the development of effective CRM strategies. Internal promotion is also critical in terms of distributing information that permits employees to have a deeper understanding of tasks and job roles inside their organisation.

INTRODUCTION

An important role within the marketing function is to assist the customer to acquire sufficient knowledge that they are persuaded to purchase a company's goods or services in preference to an offering from the competition. A simplified model describing the stages of the buyer behaviour process which leads to the customer reaching a purchase decision is presented in Figure 9.1. The entry point into the model shown in Figure 9.1 is when the customer first recognises a need to purchase the product or service. The next stage is the customer acquiring understanding about potential products or services which might fulfil their specified needs. After understanding has been achieved by the customer, then a purchase decision is reached. As the customer moves through the early phases of the purchase process, understanding which has been acquired will create expectations about actual product performance. These expectations are tested in the post-purchase evaluation phase. If the product lives up to or exceeds expectations, positive feedback ensues, thereby raising the probability

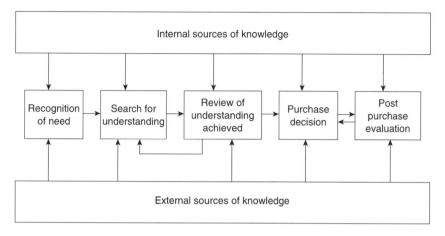

FIGURE 9.1 A BUYER BEHAVIOUR MODEL

that the customer will purchase the same product in the future. Conversely, if the product fails to meet expectations, negative feedback occurs which reduces the probability that the customer will consider purchasing the same product in the future. In Figure 9.1, acquisition of understanding comes from two sources of knowledge. One source is external knowledge which is made available through the promotional activities of the supplier or any intermediaries who might be involved in the product distribution process. Internal knowledge comes from those sources which are beyond the direct control of supply chain members (for example prior product purchase experience; product experiences communicated by friends or relatives; recommendations made by colleagues at work).

Firms operating in terrestrial markets have long understood the critical importance of achieving post-purchase satisfaction, especially in relation to the management of logistics activities to ensure delivery satisfaction. Given this heritage it seems somewhat surprising that such understanding is frequently not exhibited by e-commerce firms. The ease with which the customer can come on-line, place an order and receive order acceptance confirmation is known to raise customer expectations about the speed of all other aspects of the purchase process (Schuette 2000). Yet even today, many on-line customers will be dissatisfied, for example, finding their orders for Christmas presents will often remain undelivered until well into January of the following year. In some cases the cause of the problem is that firms new to e-business have only terrestrial market experience of managing the bulk shipment of products to intermediaries. Hence such firms face a knowledge gap in terms of lacking the capability to ship individual items to multiple locations. Other firms face the need to undertake product assembly activities where previously the knowledge to fulfil this role was vested in their terrestrial market intermediaries. Another knowledge gap in some firms is a total lack of back-office experience in managing real-time customer requests.

Understanding the On-line Customer

Hilton owns over 1,800 hotels across the world and has been in the forefront of exploiting the opportunities offered by the internet (Wagner 2000). The company has found that in telephone conversations the potential guest will only talk for about two minutes. This is contrasted with on-line visitors who spend five to six minutes using the web site to obtain information about facilities, services and prices. Its understanding of this situation has caused the hotel to break with the industry convention of using a third party to handle on-line bookings and instead has established its own web site to manage customer contacts.

In addition to creating an extensive on-line information provision system the company has moved to create extranets to communicate with companies that have contractual agreements to use Hilton facilities. The customer is linked to a specific system which is customised to carry data on contractual prices and travel limitations. This service permits their B2B clients more effectively to control their employees' travel costs.

The company is very aware of the need to provide maximum ease of access for its on-line customers. Hence it has been a pioneer in developing systems which permit bookings using wireless connections such as mobile telephones and Palm computers.

/ THE ROLE OF KNOWLEDGE PROVISION

Promotion can be considered as all of the activities associated with the provision of knowledge about a product or service. The aim of these activities is to achieve the outcome that this knowledge convinces the customer to purchase the organisation's output. Marketers have a variety of alternative knowledge delivery systems available to them which can be used to construct an appropriate *promotional mix strategy*. These include (Kotler 1997):

- **Advertising** which permits the delivery of a non-personalised message through the action of renting time and/or space within an advertising channel (for example, radio, television, cinema, newspapers, magazines and billboards).
- **Collateral promotion** which covers a variety of message delivery approaches including brochures, packaging, merchandising materials, logos/company information on delivery vehicles, layout of office areas where service providers have contact with the customer and the corporate clothing worn by company personnel.
- **Direct marketing** which exploits advances in technology to create an ever increasing portfolio of techniques to interact with individual customers

(for example, mail shots, tele-marketing, e-mail, fax, voice mail and internet home pages).

- **Personal selling** which involves a one-to-one, personalised interaction between the customer and the producer's sales force (and/or the sale staff of intermediaries) within the marketing channel.
- **Public relations and publicity** which is constituted of a broad range of activities designed to promote the organisation and/or the organisation's products (for example, an article about the organisation in a trade magazine; sponsorship of a popular sporting event such as a round-the-world yacht race).
- **Sales promotions** which involve activities that offer the customer some form of temporary, increased value (for example, a coupon good on next purchase; participation in a competition offering the chance to win an overseas holiday).

Given the critical role which knowledge provision plays in the effective execution of a promotional campaign, extensive research has been undertaken by academics seeking to determine exactly how promotional activities can influence customer attitudes and values. A large proportion of these studies have focused upon the effectiveness of advertising, but many of the conclusions which have been reached are equally applicable to other activities such as personal selling and public relations.

One of the issues that has concerned researchers is the degree to which involvement in the product influences customer response to promotion campaigns. Houston et al. (1987) have suggested there are three types of involvement:

1 **Product involvement** which is the influence of the customer's prior purchase and consumption experience on their individual needs and values.
2 **Situational involvement** which describes the individual's concern for their behaviour at each stage in the buying process.
3 **Response involvement** which refers to the persuasiveness of the knowledge which is provided to the customer.

Munch and Hunt (1984) feel response involvement is a critical variable in terms of determining the effectiveness of a promotional message. They propose that 'involvement is the level of perceived personal importance and/or interest evoked by a stimulus (or stimuli) within a specific situation' (1984, p. 46). From this definition it can be concluded that in cases of low involvement goods (for example, the decision to purchase household goods such as tea or coffee) the customer will very rapidly progress through the problem solving model of the type shown in Figure 9.1. Over time, however, the repeated consumption of a product will evoke memory patterns that create feelings which ultimately may influence future purchase patterns. Many long established brands such as Maxwell House coffee and

Kellogg's cornflakes recognise the importance of using promotion to reinforce the memory patterns evoked by regular product usage. They have remained successful over the years by using an unchanging promotional strategy based around communicating a conventional message restating brand knowledge already known to the customer delivered via a mass marketing channel such as television advertising to sustain customer loyalty.

Other researchers feel it is also important to recognise that both cognitive and emotional reactions can be generated by promotions. Thorson and Friestadt (1989), for example, maintain that emotions triggered by a promotional message will 'condition' customers' feelings and thereby influence subsequent purchase decisions. By the 1980s, the issue of emotional content has resulted in the emergence of a school of thought which believes that whether the customer finds the knowledge content within a promotional message likeable or unlikeable will influence their attitudes towards the level of effective persuasion which is achieved by a promotional campaign. Brown and Stayman's (1992) research demonstrated that attitudes towards an advertisement have a distinct effect on brand cognition and a positive impact on customer attitudes towards a brand.

It is also felt by some academics that in assessing potential response to knowledge provided by suppliers, it is also necessary to recognise the influence of customer personality. Wilson (1973) defines personality as a 'general disposition to behave' and contrasts this with attitude which he describes as 'opinions on something in the world outside'. He further posits that personality is a continuum, with at one extreme there being customers who seek consistency in their lives through purchase of items which are familiar, comforting and reassuring. At the other extreme, there are customers who continually seek to be exposed to new and different experiences. Foxall and Goldsmith (1994) have concluded that this latter group are more likely to respond to entrepreneurial (unconventional) promotion because they are flexible thinkers, can tolerate a higher level of ambiguity, have high self-esteem and a positive attitude towards seeking out new knowledge.

In planning a promotion, most organisations opt for following the current knowledge provision conventions which prevail in their industrial sector. There are, however, two potential problems with this philosophy. Firstly, if one or more competitors decide to act aggressively and increase their level of promotional expenditure, then the conventional firm is typically forced into also up-weighting their own promotional activity in order to avoid losing market share. Secondly, smaller brands rarely have the scale of financial resources required to support the same level of promotional expenditure as the larger brands and hence find it extremely difficult to grow their market share.

Given these potential drawbacks of following prevailing conventions, a very feasible alternative is for a firm to adopt a more entrepreneurial attitude towards its promotional activities. The four alternative options are:

1 To deliver knowledge to completely new target customer groups.
2 To find an alternative approach to the delivery of knowledge.
3 To identify a new method of using knowledge to guide the purchase process.
4 To find an unconventional way of managing the flow of knowledge provision within the market system.

Towards Knowledge-based Promotion

A potential problem with conventional, limited content promotion is that this can easily be replicated by the competition. Some companies have responded to this threat by accepting the benefit of becoming more customer focused and adopting a relationship orientation (Vandermerwe 2000). Having adopted a customer focused philosophy, success can only ensue if the knowledge provision within the promotional message reflects this desire to build a long term customer relationship.

An example of a knowledge provision promotional approach following strategic repositioning is provided by Baxter Renal UK. The company decided to move from being a producer of dialysis bags to become perceived as a dialysis patient care-giver. To achieve this aim, having researched the market, the company recognised the need to provide expanded educational support to patients. This was achieved by expanding patient understanding through the creation of a Web site, Kidneywise.com, referral through mobile diagnostic centres and a seminar programme for general practitioners. The company also realised that many patients choose hospital treatment rather than home treatment because they lack the knowledge required to reach an optimal decision. Baxter's response was to establish pre-dialysis clinics where educators can take the patient through all of the issues associated with the treatment options available to them. Having commenced dialysis, patients are offered guidance on treatment and lifestyle modification. This guidance is available by a 24-hour technical and clinical guidance service which can be contacted by telephone or via the internet. Special telemedicine devices have also been developed that can capture information on at-home treatment with the data disseminated via the internet to those supervising the care programme.

A failure to recognise the benefits of adopting a knowledge provision strategy is demonstrated by IBM in the late 1980s. This company became so fixated by using conventional promotional strategies to maximise the transactional volume for PCs and mainframes, they left the market open to knowledge providers such as consultants and value added resellers (VARs). Upon appointment as the new president of IBM, Louis Gerstner immediately recognised the hazards of perpetuating a transactional orientation. Through a revised philosophy knowns 'New Blue', the company was repositioned as an IT knowledge advisor and this capability formed the basis of all mainstream promotional campaigns. The outcome is that IBM has now become the largest provider of IT knowledge services in the world.

Offering More Knowledge

Recreational Equipment Inc. is an American retailer of outdoor sporting goods. Even before the advent of the internet the retailer had created a catalogue operation as a means of increasing the level of knowledge that can be made available to customers (Kemp 2001). The company was an early mover to exploit the benefits for knowledge exchange offered by electronic communications.

The company perceived the internet as permitting an opportunity to offer customers a more personalised view of products based upon their tastes and recreational needs. This was followed by the move to create a common database for both on-line and off-line operations. This was followed by the creation of web kiosks in all stores to assist customers more rapidly to locate products that could meet their individual needs.

Recreational Equipment is a co-operative which means customers can become members of the business and receive an annual dividend based upon their level of purchase activity. By tracking members' on-line and off-line purchase behaviour the company can use this knowledge to develop a deeper understanding of customers' spending habits and product preferences. Access to cross channel buyer behaviour has shown that actions to stimulate purchases such as customised promotions will lead to increase purchase frequency by customers.

PROMOTION AND THE PRODUCT LIFE CYCLE

The nature of customer behaviour in relation to the growing importance of price as customers gain knowledge through usage of the product over time does mean that the role of promotion should be expected to change depending upon the product's position on the PLC curve (Wasson 1978). As can be seen from Table 9.1, in the early stages of the PLC, generic promotional activity is directed at educating the customer about the new product and thereby building market understanding. As the product enters the growth phase, promotional activity, although still aimed at generating trial by educating new potential customers, now also has a concurrent role of making available knowledge capable of stimulating repeat purchase. Maturity is typically the most competitive period during the life of the product and promotion activity is very much concerned with defending the product against competition. Typically this will require a promotional strategy involving the provision of knowledge concerning the nature of the benefit superiority offered to the customer relative to the claims made by the competition. Once the product enters the decline phase, price usually becomes the dominant factor influencing demand and, therefore, knowledge provision via promotional activity is drastically reduced.

Sales promotion is an activity designed to offer higher temporary value to the customer. Examples of sales promotions include price packs, free product, money-off coupons and competitions. As such, sales promotion management is as much concerned with providing a tool to supplement the

TABLE 9.1 MARKETING MIX AND THE E-PRODUCT LIFE CYCLE

	Introduction	Growth	Maturity	Decline
On-line sales	Low	Rising	Maximum	Falling
On-line marketing objectives	Trial and awareness	Ongoing trial and initiate repeat purchase behaviour	Maximise sales by defending market share	Sustain required sales volume
Product strategy	Offer basic product proposition	Increase variety by product line expansion	Maximise by choice of available product types	Scale down breadth of product line
Pricing strategy	Price to meet innovator value expectations	Price to increase market penetration	Price to support chosen product positioning	Reduce price to sustain sales
Generic promotion strategy	Educate potential customers and build market awareness	Expand awareness and stimulate repeat purchase using a dual knowledge campaign	Communicate product benefit superiority claim	Reduce to minimum level to sustain loyalty
Sales promotion strategy	Stimulate trial	Stimulate repeat purchase	Use to defend against competitor activities and price competition	Use as an alternative to price reductions
Distribution strategy	Selective, restricted to full service intermediary outlets	Enter new outlets to expand market coverage	Act to maximise market coverage	Return to selective distribution

product pricing strategy as it is a mechanism for communicating product benefit knowledge to customers. In most cases, price becomes a more dominant influencer of customer purchase behaviour the further one progresses through the PLC. Consequently, as shown in Table 9.1, sales promotion only begins really to dominate the promotional mix during the late maturity and decline phases of the PLC.

Promotion involves encoding knowledge about the organisation's product or service into a message for delivery to the customer (Crowley and Hower 1994). Following message delivery, there are two possible feedback responses, which can be initiated by the customer. Firstly, in those cases where reaching the product purchase decision and/or subsequent usage of the product requires a high level of knowledge, it is very probable that the customer will seek more data from the supplier. Whereas, secondly, where reaching the product purchase decision and/or subsequent usage of the product requires only a low level of knowledge, the customer will not usually attempt to acquire more data from the supplier. As dialogue is possibly the most effective form of communication it is likely, prior to the advent of call centres and the internet, that the supplier will rely heavily upon the use of a sales force to deliver the majority of the promotional message.

Unfortunately personal selling is possibly the most expensive method per customer contact to deliver knowledge to the market (Anderson 1994). Hence although all firms would probably like to include a large sales force in their promotional portfolio, it only becomes cost effective where the average unit of purchase per customer is very high. Consequently one tends to find that personal selling dominates the promotional mix in industrial markets, but that it is replaced with lower cost per customer delivery systems such as advertising (a) in industrial markets where the value of the unit purchase per customer is quite low (for example, office supplies such as printer ink or paper clips) and (b) in the majority of consumer goods markets. Even in industrial markets, firms are continually striving to find new ways of minimising the costs associated with the delivery of knowledge to the customer. Thus promotional planning must be perceived as a dynamic process which is continually being adapted to suit identified changing circumstances in the external market environment.

TECHNOLOGY AND THE PROMOTIONAL PROCESS

The early application of IT, especially in service sector firms, was directed towards the automation of administrative processes. More recently IT has been recognised as being capable of automating the complex tasks of a firm's knowledge workers. One of the first areas where this type of innovation has emerged is in assisting sales personnel fulfil their role within the promotional process of delivering knowledge to customers (Sviokla 1996). In his study, the researcher examined how various insurance companies have sought to incorporate an expert system known as Profiling into the provision of knowledge services to clients.

Profiling is a software platform which captures data on the customer such as demographics, financial position and personal circumstances. The expert system component of the software then utilises these data to generate a comprehensive review of the customer's insurance needs including recommendations on how to enhance their personal financial plan for the future. Developers of the software felt that those firms adopting the software would recognise that by providing greater knowledge to their clients this would move their sales operation from a transactional to a relationship orientated operation. Such a move was perceived as offering a consequent improvement in customer loyalty levels. The transactional orientation exhibited by sales staff prior to the advent of the Profiling software is indicated by the fact that in most insurance companies these individuals tend to concentrate on selling a single product to the client without any emphasis on knowledge interchange to acquire a real understanding of customer needs.

Four firms were studied by the researcher, namely Lutheran Brotherhood, National Mutual, Sun Alliance and Prudential. The approach to software adoption at Prudential was that the expanded knowledge provision role of their sales staff would require a total restructuring of the selling process. Sales personnel were provided with resources to hire assistants to take care of day-to-day activities such as answering telephones, making appointments and general administration. Sun Alliance did not feel the software demanded a complete revision in the structuring of the sales process. Nevertheless Profiling was perceived as demanding a complete change in the culture and skills of sales personnel. Hence significant resources were allocated to developing sales personnel as knowledge workers and senior management worked to persuade all concerned that the company was moving from 'policy selling' to the creation of 'advice relationships' with customers.

The attitude of these two firms that their promotional activities were faced with fundamental change can be contrasted with the situation at Lutheran Brotherhood and National Mutual. Within these organisations Profiling was perceived as an interesting way of using a new computer-based tool for assisting the sales force to fulfil their current role. Hence minimal resources were allocated to trying to revise sales force selling practices.

The difference in implementation strategy was reflected in the subsequent assessment of the effectiveness of Profiling across the four firms. Within Lutheran Brotherhood and National Mutual, the sales force did not perceive the software as altering their role as knowledge providers. Selling techniques remained virtually unchanged and the outcome was that the new technology was considered to offer minimal enhancement to existing promotional practices. This conclusion can be contrasted with that at Sun Alliance and Prudential. Both management and sales personnel concluded that Profiling offered an opportunity to alter radically the sales role from selling policies to that of becoming professional knowledge workers capable of offering a much higher quality of financial advice to customers. Hence these latter organisations perceived the software as a medium through which to use knowledge provision as the basis for acquiring a new source of competitive advantage.

Building On-line Brands

IT companies such as Microsoft, Intel and Sun Microsystems have long recognised the benefits of establishing strong brand identities in an e-commerce world. Nakache (1998) has proposed that there are four basics steps for providing the knowledge customers require that can move a company from unknown to becoming a household name in a short period of time. The first, and possibly most important, is to find ways of giving the product away to as many people as possible. America Online is the giant in the give away business, appearing in places such as breakfast cereal packets, in-flight meal trays and on music CDs.

The second step is to communicate knowledge by conducting an aggressive public relations war against potential competitors. Sun has used this approach to build a global awareness for their flagship software platform Java. In many cases they have exploited 'techies" strange aversion to Microsoft products as a platform upon which to suggest that a move to Java is a move to avoid Microsoft dominating cyberspace.

The third step is to exploit the internet to deliver knowledge that can provide the basis for building a strong relationship with the customer. Amazon.com is master at this technique using tools such as BookMatcher to deliver knowledge automatically to customers about new titles which may be of interest to them. Complementing this knowledge provision approach, the fourth step is to communicate that your firm is an organisation full of fun loving people who want their customers to share in their laid back approach to life. The Java team at Sun is a leader in this approach as illustrated by the creation of Duke, the Java mascot that is part penguin, part tooth, 'battling to keep the internet safe for everyone'. Another positive image about the fun to be had in cyberspace is that portrayed by Yahoo's dynamic founding duo Jerry Yang and David Filo.

THE INTERNET AND THE COMMUNICATIONS MIX

The advent of the internet has added new dimensions to the promotional management process. One dimension is that the internet is a medium which combines the features of both broadcast and publishing to facilitate two-way exchange of knowledge. Berthon (1996) has suggested that the internet might be considered as a cross between an electronic trade show and a community flea market. As such it faces the same dilemma as conventional trade shows or a flea markets, namely how to provide the knowledge required to convert web site visitors from being browsers to becoming purchasers.

A somewhat different perspective is provided by Leong et al. (1998) who used mail surveys followed by cluster analysis to gain the views of Australian marketing practitioners about where the internet fits in relation to other media. They concluded that most practitioners consider the internet to be similar to direct mail because many web sites in their early stages of development are used to deliver knowledge through what are essentially on-line catalogues. Similar to direct mail, the internet has the ability to precipitate the action of causing the visitor to purchase. Perceived advantages over direct mail are that the costs of reaching target markets are much lower on the world wide web.

Most marketing practitioners do not see the internet as replacing other media. Instead most felt that it complements other knowledge provision channels such as television or magazine advertising. Furthermore most respondents have adopted the approach of adding the internet to the range of channel options being considered during the process of deciding which media mix offers the most cost effective approach for achieving the aims which have been specified for a promotional campaign.

Berthon (1996) provides an alternative perspective of the internet as being a mix of personal selling and broadcast advertising. He suggests it can be used to generate awareness, passively provide knowledge, demonstrate the product and, if required by the customer, support interactive knowledge exchange. Acceptance of this perspective permits the evolution of a customer purchase behaviour model in which the internet can be used to move customers through the successive phases of the buying decision process. This phase movement commences with attracting site visitors. Making contact with interested individuals, converting some into customers and then supporting the purchase/post-purchase phase of the supplier–customer relationship follows this initial contact.

McLuhan (2000) feels that many advertisers are still struggling to learn how to utilise the internet as an effective element within their marketing mix. Because many firms have not evolved internet strategies capable of differentiating their offering from the competition or building long term on-line relationships, many customers are just switching between web sites looking for the lowest possible price. Already in the United States, almost 80% of on-line shoppers admit that price is the main motivator in causing them to revisit a web site. To overcome this problem, McLuhan believes advertisers must develop on-line provision of knowledge that establishes the availability of offerings which are more personalised and of real interest to their customers. This can sometimes be achieved by using the internet to offer specialist knowledge to specific customer groups.

Stauffer (1999) has posited that the advent of on-line promotion means that firms need to re-examine carefully the aims of their sales force strategy, implementing revisions where these are required. He suggests that e-business is causing the emergence of two product categories. The first category is commodity sales. Products and services within this group are virtually identical which means that purchase decisions will be based mainly on price. If customers for these items are using the internet to acquire pricing information, Stauffer feels that companies really have little need for a sales force as a channel through which to deliver product knowledge.The second category is products or services which are of sufficient complexity that customers will often require access to a one-to-one interactive discussion to acquire detailed product knowledge to assist them reach a purchase decision (for example, advanced machine tools; complex specification components).

187

Customers will be able to use the internet to acquire comparative information. Hence they will no longer require the services of a sales person to provide basic data about the relative merits of alternative propositions. Instead the role of the sales force becomes that of acting as a knowledge provider, assisting and guiding the customer to make the optimal purchase decision most suited to their specific needs. Stauffer feels that this new selling orientation requires (a) a sales force with in-depth product knowledge, (b) that all members of the selling organisation are able to offer learning services to the client and (c) a workforce totally proficient in the utilisation of multimedia channels.

On-line Knowledge Provision

Some of the earliest recognition of the opportunity provided by the internet to expand knowledge provision within promotional campaigns has occurred within the US banking industry (Weinstein 2000). Traditional media such as television or magazine advertising are very restrictive over the volume of information that can be delivered in a single advertisement. This constraint is removed once a firm moves on-line.

The US banks have known for years that if contact can be made with children this will increase the probability that such individuals will subsequently provide a new source of customers. Having created web sites to service adult customer transactions, a number of banks have moved to create web sites aimed at children. The focus of these latter Web sites has been to use them to offer knowledge-based educational programmes to children aimed at developing their basic understanding of how to manage their personal finances. FleetBoston Financial Corporation established FleetKids (*www.fleetkids.com*). The site provides knowledge on issues such as setting financial goals, saving and financial budgeting. These skills are communicated by embedding them in computer games that can be played on-line. First Union (*www.firstunion.com*) has a similar web site offering a savings calculator, a budgeting game and tools to help children improve their abilities to handle money.

When any new media form is established, it will take time before operating experience permits marketers to gain a detailed understanding of how to obtain optimal benefits from using the new promotional channel to deliver knowledge to customers. Until recently, the narrow bandwidth of the internet meant that advertisements were restricted to very simple text and graphics. Advances are now being made in 'rich-media technology'. This permits the advertiser to enhance the volume of knowledge provision by incorporating high-grade graphics with audio and interactive capabilities (Reed 1999). This approach to upgrading web site technology has, for example, permitted firms to provide customers with video clips about their companies' product lines.

Over time it can be expected that ongoing improvements in technology will permit improvements in both the content and sophistication of internet advertising. Virtual reality technology will permit the site visitor to 'experience' the brand totally before purchase. Firms will also be able to customise their advertisements to deliver knowledge designed to meet the needs of individual customers. The Ultramatch technology launched by Infoseek already makes it possible to target those internet users who are most likely to respond to a certain advertisement. The system uses neural networking to observe users' on-line behaviour when they seek out information on the internet. Ultramatch ascertains which individuals are responding to which advertisements, thereby permitting advertisers to select internet users who have been pre-screened as being a suitable target group (Cartellieri et al. 1997).

Concurrent with the emergence of more effective electronic customer–supplier interfaces, companies are also recognising that their intellectual capital can provide the basis for enhancing the promotional process by the provision of personalised knowledge to customers. This advance has been made possible through the exploitation of large relational databases to support the provision of customer value-added services (Hu et al. 1998). The approach known as *knowledge mining* permits the abstraction and validation of data from a diversity of company information sources. Techniques utilised include clustering, classification, value prediction, association discovery, sequential pattern discovery and time sequence discovery.

In their article, Hu et al. draw upon a case study to illustrate how knowledge mining can enhance customer support provision. The example company is a producer of about 20 office products which are sold through a diversity of distribution channels to over 10,000 customers. In the company's mass market operations, customers are classified into distinct knowledge need categories, which are then utilised in the provision of targeted promotional activity using both terrestrial and electronic media. In those sectors where the company relies upon a sales force, these staff are provided with detailed guidance on how to use knowledge in the customised provision of selling messages to specific clients. This latter system also provides sales personnel with knowledge about each customer's order patterns, key decision personnel within purchasing organisations and business events which will be of specific interest to the client.

The effective storage of knowledge to support knowledge mining activities is known as *data warehousing*. As pointed out by Parzinger and Frolick (2001), a data warehouse does not create value. Instead value comes from using the available knowledge to enhance marketing activities such as customer communications. This is because businesses are more able to access and customise information to fulfil the knowledge needs of individual customers. Warehouses clearly offer benefit to firms involved in high intensity transaction markets. Thus on-line firms can use a warehouse to analyse customer buying patterns and then send a personalised promotional message concerning a product which is likely to be of high interest to the customer. Similarly in a terrestrial environment, banks are able to rapidly analyse purchase behaviour patterns and then create carefully targeted promotions offering additional services known to be of appeal to a specific type of customer.

Some firms have also recognised that warehouses can generate information of use to other members of the supply chain when the latter are planning future promotional campaigns. Wal-Mart, for example, adopts this philosophy and freely shares sales data from 2,800 stores with the company's 4,000 suppliers.

The entire process of capturing, storing and exploiting a diverse range of relational databases to optimise the delivery of value-added services is now often referred to as CRM. Sowalski (2001) has presented some guidelines on effective management of CRM in a review of the process within the US insurance industry. He recommends that firms need to adopt a holistic view by integrating all of the technologies available for the provision of knowledge to the customers. Thus a call centre needs to be transformed into a multimedia interface using both old (for example, fax, telephone) and new technologies (for example, interactive voice response, speech recognition, Internet call-back and live internet discussions) capable of offering the customer a wide variety of communications options.

Concurrently back-office systems need to be reconfigured to provide a 360 degree CRM operation. This is achieved by drawing upon available databases to provide communication services such as personalised scripting and automated identification of new sales opportunities. To optimise exploitation of 360 degree CRM the firm needs to provide sales staff and intermediaries with sales automation and workflow management tools. In this way knowledge interaction with the customer can be synchronised across multiple promotional channels and customer contacts can be routed to the most appropriate service response interface.

At the heart of such systems are integrated databases and automated decision-support systems. These provide the capability for knowledge mining to assist employees understand how best to serve the needs of customers. Wherever possible such systems should be linked with other organisations with which the firm has formed alliances or which act as market intermediaries. This latter action is critical if the firm wishes to maximise the number of promotional channels through which to deliver knowledge-based communications to the maximum number of customers.

Exploiting New Market Opportunities

United Parcel Service (UPS) was an early beneficiary of the internet age because most on-line operations use third party suppliers to manage the delivery of the products sold to on-line customers (Violino 2000). The company rapidly realised that customers wanted the ability to track all packages from the point of shipment through to the point of final delivery. Hence the company has created a software system which customers can access on-line to obtain knowledge about the status of all shipments.

As the company acquired knowledge of their customers' logistics operations it soon realised that such knowledge permitted it to offer a new service aimed at optimising supply chain systems. The company has used this knowledge to cut out processes such as billing, accounts receivable, inventory management and warehousing for major clients such as the Ford Motor Company. Wherever possible the company forms partnerships with software suppliers such as Oracle to create systems which are integrated into its clients' internal, existing database management activities.

As knowledge of specific industries has grown this has permitted UPS to offer tailored logistics services to an industrial sector offering supply chain re-engineering, transportation network management and service parts logistics to manufacturers and their distributors. Another opportunity is that of offering the delivery of digital documents. Through the UPS Document Exchanger clients can avoid the need for the delivery of paper-based documents and instead download text documents, accounting information and legal documents from the UPS server.

UPS also realised that e-commerce offered new opportunities in the provision of financial services. They created a subsidiary, UPS Capital Corporation, to provide services such as electronic funds transfer and collection of accounts receivables. This has subsequently led the company to become the financial guarantor in e-commerce transactions; UPS was able to access this market because, having the knowledge of when a package has been delivered, it is in a unique position to know whether the purchaser's payment should be released to the supplier.

ON-LINE COMMUNITIES

Traditional fmcg brands have managed their promotional relationship by the provision of communication flows to the customer via the medium of mass marketing promotional channels. Consequently these mass marketing operations have faced significant obstacles in seeking to find ways of unlocking the potential for using the internet to expand their knowledge provision activities. An emerging solution which appears to be gaining in popularity is for major brands to seek to stimulate the creation of on-line communities constituted of their customers (McWilliam 2000). This they are achieving by the sponsorship of chat rooms either on their own web site or by acquiring space on a more universal site such as America Online.

The marketer must take care to ensure that the on-line consumer does not perceive the sponsor is attempting to manipulate the interactive dialogue which is occurring. They have found, however, that by acting to assist in threading conversations and hiring non-affiliated web masters to guide debates, it is possible to create brand sites where participants can be the recipients of knowledge that can assist in building stronger brand–consumer relationships.

The concept of sponsoring on-line communities is already well established in B2B markets. The Elsevier Science Group, for example, has established BioMedNet, a virtual community for biologists and medical personnel. The site features specialist discussion groups, a regular forum on a topical issue, a research database Medline, a job exchange and a daily newsletter. By creating this knowledge-based community the company has found that sales commissions can be earned by the firm's on-line bookshop and through selling e-mail lists to other advertisers.

In the UK, Reed Personnel Services funded the creation of Red Mole (*www.redmole.co.uk*) to attract the attention of college students. The users of this virtual community can access the Reed graduate recruitment database and also information of college courses available in UK universities. The students can also use the community notice board to post requests seeking assistance with their college coursework. Within the Working Mole system, students can search for part-time employment and vacation employment opportunities.

Firms adopting the virtual community approach to promotional knowledge provision do need to recognise that customers are more interested in some products than others. Thus, for example, Bosch, a manufacturer of power tools, has found that attraction of trades people to its site where they can seek information and swap solutions to problems has been a relatively easy task. Similarly the US Pentax site has a very active community of photography enthusiasts who exchange information on all aspects of photography and photographic equipment. Consumer goods companies, on the other hand, have often found that their product will not provide the core interest sufficient to construct a viable virtual community. Under these circumstances an alternative traffic building mechanism may be required. Canada's Molson beer has achieved this goal by sponsoring a site for ice hockey enthusiasts. Johnson and Johnson has created the Your Baby site where mothers can exchange ideas, suggestions and advice on bringing up children.

For consumer goods firms which feel unable to create and lead their own communities, a alternative opportunity is to form links with existing on-line communities which have already established a high level of active membership. Possibly the easiest route to linkage formation is to seek an alliance with the numerous electronic publications which have been launched in recent years (Dysart 2001). One such example is an e-mail delivered newsletter produced by the Canadian Association of Retired Persons (*www.fifty-plus.net*). This organisation has over 70,000 members, which provides a subscriber base for firms engaged in the promotion of services in sectors such as health, finance and travel.

Another example is provided by Computerists International based in Palo Alto, California (*www.computist.com*). The organisation distributes a newsletter and has a web site where members can access a searchable archive system. In this case the site would be of interest to firms seeking to communicate knowledge to a community composed of individuals known to be interested in computing and software. Similar opportunities exist in B2B markets where many trade associations have also established on-line communities. Membership of such communities will mean that readers will have very distinct interests and hence represent a well defined target audience for the provision of knowledge-based promotional campaigns.

INTERNAL ELECTRONIC PROMOTION

A key objective in any promotional strategy is to ensure that all forms of communication are consistent and that information imparted is supportive of the desired overall company or brand image. The advent on intranets has been especially effective in assisting this aim (*Business Week* 2001a). An example of this approach is provided by the ShareNet system established by the German company, Siemens. The system is designed to create a virtual community linking together the firm's 12,000 sales personnel. Since inception in 1999, the system has proved invaluable in sharing knowledge that can enhance sales personnel's interaction with customers. For example, ShareNet was used by the firm to land a $3 million contract to build a broadband network for Telekom, Malaysia. The in-country sales team lacked the expertise to develop a proposal but through ShareNet accessed appropriate knowledge from a team in Denmark which had already successfully bid on a similar contract. In Switzerland Siemens won a contract even though the bid was 30% higher than the competition. In this latter case sales staff in the Netherlands provided technical data that was used to validate a claim of greater equipment reliability for the Siemens product. Siemens is now considering the utilisation of ShareNet to provide its customers with access to the firm's vast range of technical knowledge databases.

A similar perspective on the benefits of intranets is exhibited by Xerox (Wah 1999). It has established Eureka which is a 'social tactical system' for linking together the knowledge contained within the experiences of the company's 25,000 field service representatives. The aim of the system is to persuade technical staff to share experiences acquired while repairing and servicing clients' machines. It is estimated that the knowledge exchange has resulted in a 5% annual saving on both parts and labour. Service staff access the system at the rate of 5,000 enquiries per month and new ideas are generated at a rate of approximately one new tip per 1,000 service calls. Although the software was originated in the United States, Xerox is a global business. Hence Xerox has incorporated software-assisted translations into the Eureka system so that technicians can input and read tips in their native languages. Introduction of electronic internal promotional platforms to build knowledge communities is not a low cost task. Hence care needs to be taken to identify the nature of the benefits which will accrue from such an investment. In discussing this issue, Davenport and Klahr (1998) have suggested that internal knowledge sharing offers the following benefits:

1   Improving the quality of technical and non-technical resolution of customer problems.
2   Ensuring greater consistency in the quality of services delivered.
3   Increasing the frequency with which frontline staff can resolve customer problems during the first time that the customer makes contact.
4   Reducing the costs associated with resolving customer problems.
5   Reducing the frequency with which technical calls have to be referred to technical staff within the organisation.
6   Reducing the need to provide field services for visiting the customer on-site.

To effectively exploit an internal system for knowledge sharing, certain issues needed to be recognised and actions taken to seek to establish networked communities. Owens and Thompson (2001) have researched the US insurance firm St Paul Companies to evolve guidance on the community development process. This company recognised the need to implement internal community formation to manage both merger activity and expansion of marketing operations into 19 countries around the world. To co-ordinate community formation the organisation created an umbrella system known as the St Paul University which provides both classroom and on-line support for employees engaged in learning. The core element of the new structure is a web site and easy-to-use intranet tools. Communities are usually based within a single work group responsible for a specific functional task. Where innovation is required involving skills from across the organisation then multidisciplinary virtual project teams are formed. Additionally the university seeks to stimulate 'communities of practice' in which people with a common interest come together voluntarily to solve an identified business problem. To assist all these communities the company has created centres of expertise constituted of identified expert employees from around the world.

Experience indicates that each community must appoint a leader to guide and facilitate activities. The community will only be successful when formation is based around a clear business purpose. Within the community participants must have the authority to modify or re-engineer work practices. There is a need to nourish trust within a community and to ensure each community has developed a sense of real identity. Where possible connectiveness between communities should be established to maximise knowledge sharing across the organisation. As time is of the essence in problem solving, communities must be granted permission to procure solutions from outside the organisation where this is perceived to be the most cost effective resolution of a problem.

Firms which have developed internal communities to engage in sharing data to assist activities such as customer communication may begin to recognise that the community is only drawing upon internal expertise. Under these circumstances there is the risk that suboptimal marketing solutions may be developed which are inadequate in terms of ensuring effective communication with customers (Brailsford 2001). Where such a trend is identified one solution is to seek ways of persuading customers to become members of the firm's internal community. One such firm which has adopted this philosophy is the American greeting card manufacturer, Hallmark. Having already established internal systems to stimulate knowledge sharing, in the year 2000 the company recruited a group of approximately 150 consumers. Half these individuals are Hallmark customers and the remainder were selected because they had never purchased the company's products. The new community, known as the Hallmark Idea Exchange, communicates via the company web site and participants commit to spending at least an hour a week on-line. The community interacts with Hallmark employees, has a bulletin board, an on-line chat room and e-mail links. The site also includes a library where community members can post articles or other materials which they feel will be of interest to others. There is also a gallery where participants can exhibit their favourite images and Hallmark designers can post pictures or product concepts with the aim of generating feedback from the community. The community has been invaluable in guiding Hallmark's thinking about both strategic issues and the effectiveness of existing advertising campaigns. By drawing upon community feedback the firm has been able to identify a whole new range of approaches for optimising future promotional activities.

10

Pricing and Distribution

CHAPTER SUMMARY

Pricing decisions can dramatically impact sales revenue. Hence marketers need in-depth knowledge about customer perceptions of prevailing prices and the influence of price changes. Customers use price as a surrogate measurement of quality. The internet has caused customers to be able to gain more knowledge about prevailing prices. This can cause price wars. To avoid on-line price competition firms must use the web as a mechanism for distributing additional knowledge that can enhance customer perceptions about product performance and quality. Distribution decisions influence the effectiveness with which firms deliver goods and services to customers. Selection of an appropriate distribution channel requires the supplier to have an in-depth understanding of market systems and the capabilities of intermediaries. E-commerce has changed the face of distribution systems. In B2B markets the increased knowledge exchange using electronic media has greatly improved the efficiency of supply chains in many sectors of industry.

INTRODUCTION

Price is an aspect of the marketing process where the degree to which marketers acquire and exploit available knowledge about customers' values, attitudes and beliefs can have a major impact upon organisational performance. A fundamental rule of pricing theory is that with the possible exception of monopoly markets customers, not suppliers, determine at what price goods will be sold in a market sector. The implications of this rule is that if a company fails to acquire adequate knowledge about the price preference of the majority of customers and, on the basis of internal operating costs and/or profit margin aspirations, sets a price that is significantly higher or much lower than that expected by customers, then the

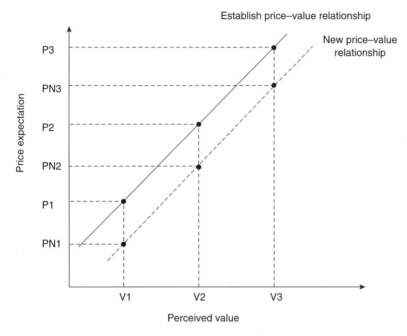

FIGURE 10.1   PRICE–VALUE RELATIONSHIPS

organisation should not be surprised to find their pricing decision may adversely impact overall sales volume.

At a conceptual level, a basic principle of economics is that for a product offering a specified bundle of benefits, as prices rise fewer and fewer customers will be interested in purchasing the goods. Conversely in a perfectly competitive market where there are no barriers to entry or departure, for a product offering a specified bundle of benefits, as prices rise more and more suppliers are will be interested in making the product available to customers. Thus as illustrated by Figure 10.1, the prevailing price within this type of market will occur at the point of intersection between what customers are willing pay for the benefits which they perceive are offered by the product or service and the price at which suppliers are willing to offer the goods or services which deliver the benefits sought by the customer. Importantly, in reaching the decision about whether to make a product available that fulfils customers' product benefit perceptions, the aim of suppliers is to manage production and other operational costs such that an adequate profit margin can be achieved upon sales.

Unfortunately there are some very critical assumptions which have been made in order for the model of the type shown in Figure 10.1 to be applicable in the real world. Firstly, it is assumed that all parties are fully informed. But in many markets the customers may have very limited access to the knowledge that is required to reach a 'fully informed' decision. Secondly, it is assumed that there are no tangible differences between goods offered by suppliers. Thirdly, it is assumed that the all suppliers (a) are physically capable of expanding supplies as prices rise and (b) desire to expand capacity. The fourth assumption in the model is that suppliers all have access to the same knowledge and have already reached similar decisions concerning other strategic issues such as advertising and distribution.

Although over the years economic theory has provided some extremely useful management paradigms, when it comes to price it is necessary to accept that 'real life' pricing is often a very much more complex affair than that illustrated in Figure 10.1. Hence a safer managerial approach is to accept that actual market price is an outcome heavily influenced by complex interactions between prevailing industrial, organisational and customer attitudes.

CUSTOMER ATTITUDES

An important customer attitude influencing real world pricing practices is that most people expect to pay a higher price for goods or services which they perceive will deliver a higher level of product benefits across areas such as performance, quality, reliability and availability of post-purchase services. The implication of this situation is shown in Figure 10.2; namely, depending upon the perceived level of benefits being offered, suppliers face a number of different pricing choices.

Organisations which are positioned on the basis of offering a high level of product benefits have three alternative pricing strategies which they might wish to consider. Firstly, *premium pricing* is based upon the use of a high price to communicate knowledge to the customer that they are being offered the highest possible level of product benefits. Secondly, firms in this sector wishing to offer a high level of benefits at an average price through aggressive or *penetration pricing* will usually find that the information communicated by the lower than expected market price may lead to a certain degree of customer suspicion about the validity of the product benefit claim. Thus a firm which wishes to build market share rapidly through penetration pricing will usually need to provide customers with knowledge sufficient to explain why the price is below that normally expected for this level of product benefit. Typically this pricing strategy can be executed only in those market sectors where the supplier is able to inform the customer that if high volumes are purchased from the outset, this will permit the supplier to drive down prices by exploiting economies of scale to reduce manufacturing costs rapidly. Thirdly, offering a low price on a superior benefit proposition through *trusted supplier value pricing* usually involves the risk that the customer, applying the adage of 'you get what you pay for', is extremely suspicious about the validity of the benefit claim.

Product value		High	Average	Low
	High	Premium pricing	Penetration pricing	Trusted supplier value pricing
	Average	Skimming	Average pricing	Sale pricing
	Low	Zero loyalty pricing	Limited loyalty pricing	Economy pricing

FIGURE 10.2   PRICE–VALUE OPTION MATRIX

This pricing strategy will only tend to be successful, therefore, if the supplier provides the customer with the knowledge that the price reduction is of a temporary nature due to short term circumstances such as a need to reduce excess inventory levels. A notable exception to this situation over customer suspicion has emerged, however, in the case of Japanese suppliers offering superior benefits at low prices in Western nation markets. It would appear in this case that customers have acquired sufficient prior knowledge of the quality of Japanese goods that they are prepared to purchase lower priced products without exhibiting any suspicion about the validity of the claims being made over the level of product benefits being offered.

A *skimming* strategy involves the supplier exploiting the knowledge that customers are willing to pay a higher than average price for goods which offer only an average level of benefits. In tangible goods markets such as cameras, marketers are aware that some people wish to purchase the latest possible technology and are price insensitive. Thus in the early stage of the product life cycle for a new product, companies skim the market by setting high prices. Subsequently they then reduce the price to an average level as the product moves into the later stages of growth on the PLC curve. *Average pricing* is used by firms which service the needs of the majority of customers seeking an average range of benefits from products purchased. *Sale pricing* involves a lower than usual price on average benefit goods. To retain customer confidence over the benefit claim, sale pricing is usually a temporary phenomenon used by firms to stimulate a short term increase in sales. If the sale price is retained for an exceptionally long period, the supplier faces the risk that customers may begin to question the validity of the benefit claim being made for such goods.

A policy of offering few product benefits at a high price through *zero loyalty pricing* is rarely one which a firm can use and concurrently expect to sustain any form of long term customer loyalty. Those organisations that use this strategy usually can survive only if new buyers with minimal product knowledge enter the market segment to replace those customers who are lost after making just a single product purchase. Similarly organisations offering few product benefits at an average price using *limited loyalty pricing* can survive only in those markets where customers who withdraw their loyalty after two or three purchases are regularly replaced by an influx of new, less knowledgeable, customers. *Economy pricing* involves offering few product benefits at highly competitive prices. This proposition usually appeals to those customers whose purchase behaviour is a reflection of limited financial means. It can be an extremely successful market position, but the low margin/unit of sale does mean the supplier has to sustain a very high level of customer transactions in order to achieve an adequate overall profit.

EXPLOITING KNOWLEDGE

The advent of market research techniques such as conjoint analysis, discrete choice analysis and multistage conjoint analysis has permitted the marketer to acquire extremely accurate data about which product benefit dimensions are critical to customers when reaching a purchase decision. Data from such research can be utilised to construct a value map where data on customers' perception over prices for different products are plotted against the perceived benefits offered by products (Rangan et al. 1992).

Products achieving an optimal mix between perceived benefits and perceived price will fall somewhere along the diagonal value equivalence line (VEL). A product which lies below the VEL can be interpreted as offering greater value than a product positioned above the line. This latter product offers the same benefits but at a perceived higher price.

Misunderstanding the Customer

The critical issue in value mapping is to ensure that the company has acquired accurate knowledge of the benefit needs of customers. Leszinski and Marn (1997) provide a case example of the Alpha Computer company which illustrates the risk of using inaccurate knowledge. This company supplies minicomputers for use as servers in network applications. The company believed that two technological attributes, processor speed and secondary access speed, were the critical benefits sought by customers. In these two areas the company outperformed the competition, yet in the market the company continued to lose share to Keycomp. This latter company supplies a product which has both a lower processor speed and secondary speed, yet is priced 10 to 15% higher.

In the face of this apparent contradiction, the Alpha marketing department undertook market research to acquire knowledge about which product benefits are actually

---

perceived as crucial by potential customers. The study revealed that processor speed and secondary speed ranked fourth and sixth respectively on customers' list of benefit requirements. Software and hardware compatibility, perceived reliability and quality of vendor support all ranked well above processor speed. This study also revealed that Keycomp was rated much more highly for compatibility, reliability, vendor support and user documentation.

Alpha's response was to rewrite its operating system and redesign its hardware plug configuration to resolve the compatibility issues. Additional service representatives were hired, toll-free access lines created for technical support and user documentation was rewritten. Following a sixth month promotional campaign to communicate knowledge of these revisions to the market, the company was able to increase market share significantly.

Understanding the Customer

An example of using knowledge about customer needs to exploit a new market position is provided by SouthWest, a US airline. At the time SouthWest Airlines was established, the industry convention was based upon (a) high fixed costs associated with operating a huge fleet of aircraft to provide national route coverage (b) delivering a reasonably high level of in-flight services and (c) a 'hub and spoke' configuration whereby airlines fly passengers to a central hub to be transferred to their ongoing destination.

Herb Kelleher of SouthWest Airlines started an operation based in Houston because he had acquired the knowledge that there were many potential customers who were willing to forgo the level of service provided by the existing airlines if in return they could purchase lower cost air travel. Hence the company was launched utilising a new business model to deliver a no frills, low price, service positioning. Specific attention was given to minimising operating costs through using non-union labour. This permitted the introduction of unconventional, far more flexible, working conditions. The company was not willing to pay the annual fees demanded of national reservation systems used by travel agents. Hence customers have to buy their tickets from the airline. Customers also carry their own bags and if they want to eat, need to bring their own food with them. Furthermore, because the firm has avoided operating out of congested airport hubs, planes can be turned round in 20 minutes. This allows the company to offer more flights per day between cities than its competitors.

To reduce operating costs further and thereby sustain low prices, in 1995, the company moved to offer ticketless travel. Passengers calling the airline receive a confirmation number instead of a ticket. Initially if passengers required a receipt this was faxed, mailed or held for collection at the airport (Berry and Yadav 1996). The company has now moved to offer customers the option of using an on-line booking system to gain access to its ticketless service. As a result of this move, despite the major carriers continually striving to match SouthWest's highly efficient operation, the airline is still able to enjoy an average seat per mile operating cost 2–4 per cent lower than the competition.

THE INFLUENCE OF KNOWLEDGE

The degree to which sellers and buyers have acquired knowledge will have a major impact on the nature of the pricing systems which are used in a market. When buyers are significantly more knowledgeable than sellers, the former can use this power to drive down prices. Where the reverse scenario prevails and sellers are much more knowledgeable than buyers, this situation tends to permit sellers to charge higher prices.

One way of illustrating the influence of knowledge over pricing conventions is to construct a buyer–seller matrix. Where both buyer and seller have a low level of knowledge about each other's attitudes, beliefs and motivations, the probable outcome is that fixed prices will prevail within the market. This scenario is found in most Western nation terrestrial consumer goods markets. The seller has limited knowledge about the purchase intentions of the buyer and the buyer has limited knowledge about the costs and profit aspirations which form the basis of the price being sought by the seller. The outcome is one of a standard fixed price being quoted to all customers. An example of this convention is provided by supermarkets where goods are displayed at a fixed price and the consumers accept these prices without question.

In those sectors where the seller is highly knowledgeable but buyers poorly informed, it is to the benefit of the seller to exploit this superior position by requesting buyers to bid for the goods on offer. The usual mechanism to achieve this aim is to offer the goods at an auction. Where the seller can attract a large number of potential buyers this further weakens the power of individual buyers. The resultant outcome is that these individuals will compete for the available goods and their bidding activities will permit the seller to maximise the potential achievable price for the product. This approach is used across a diverse number of different product categories ranging from fish landed by trawlers at a port auction to rare paintings offered by international auction houses such as Sotheby's.

The reverse scenario exists where the buyer is highly knowledgeable and can choose to purchase standard goods or services from a large number of potential suppliers. This is a very typical situation in the public sector where an organisation such as a group of hospitals or a major government department enters the market seeking items such as office materials or cleaning products. The buyer in this case is both knowledgeable about the purchase requirements and in many cases has an in-depth understanding of the operational costs of suppliers. Under these circumstances the buyer can request that sellers submit bids for the available business and this usually results in the buyer being able to minimise the actual purchase price.

In some markets both the sellers and the buyers are highly knowledgeable which means a certain degree of equality exists between all parties. An example of this scenario is provided in the defence industry where major corporations with specialist technological capability seek to fulfil the large scale purchase requirements of governments around the world. Given the relatively equal knowledge of the two parties, most price decisions are based upon extensive negotiations as the basis for reaching agreement over a price acceptable to both buyer and seller.

COST TRANSPARENCY

Sinha (2000) has presented an excellent review of the potential impact of the internet on the future level of prices that can be commanded for goods and services. He points out that it is in the seller's best interest to keep costs opaque because this permits companies to claim unique benefits for their brands and thereby command premium prices in the marketplace. Prior to the arrival of the internet, sellers were assisted in this objective because consumers in terrestrial markets encountered severe problems when seeking to acquire detailed knowledge on competitive offerings prior to reaching a purchase decision.

The advent of the internet means that consumers can use sites such as *www.pricescan.com* and on-line shopping agents such as *www.bottomdollar. com* to access knowledge rapidly on prices and features of thousands of products. They can also visit sites such as *www.epinions.com* to read about the purchasing experience of others and through sites such as *www.travelocity. com* can acquire knowledge that was once accessible only to travel agents. Similar scenarios are also emerging in business-to-business markets. For example, textile manufacturers can visit the site *www.alibaba.com* to gain free access to a directory of over 35,000 companies.

An outcome of this situation in both consumer and industrial markets is that sellers are finding their pricing strategies are becoming much more transparent to potential customers. This reduces a seller's ability to command a premium price (for example, the price wars which have broken out in the long-distance telephone market) and tends to turn branded goods into commodities. An example of this latter scenario is provided by the on-line stock-trading companies in America where it is now virtually impossible to distinguish between firms such as Ameritrade, E-Trade, National Discount Brokers and MyDiscountBroker. As a result the general public has become increasingly sceptical about the rationale for the high commissions being charged by firms such as Merrill Lynch.

One reason why the internet is so supportive of enhancing customer knowledge is that the technology permits rapid access to a diverse range of information sources. This additional knowledge helps to reduce purchase risk. For example, prospective purchasers of healthcare services can review available on-line data concerning the most appropriate source of medical treatment. Additionally the internet is able radically to enhance the efficiency of the purchaser's knowledge search. In consumer markets, as purchasers broaden their knowledge about the extensive variations in prices which exist, this begins to stimulate the attitude that suppliers can be persuaded to be more flexible on prices instead of insisting on fixed prices. Portals such as *www.priceline.com* have now come into existence which are willing to approach suppliers on behalf of the customer to determine the lowest possible price at which suppliers might be willing to offer products or services.

In order to avoid being forced into cutting prices and thereby reducing profit margins, Sinha proposes that there are a number of strategic options available to organisations. One is to seek to offer improved benefits and services superior to those available from the competition. Another approach is to bundle products together such that it is more difficult for buyers to determine the costs of any single item. Gateway, for example, is bundling internet services with its computers as a way to avoid some of the more dramatic price declines which have occurred in the PC market. A third approach is to invest in innovation that leads to the launch of new and distinctive products. AOL, for example, as well as bundling products, offers innovative services such as instant messaging, proprietary e-mail and chat rooms, parental control over children's internet access and technology to share photographs. Additionally AOL offers users of the 3Com PalmPilot the ability to read their AOL e-mails on their handheld sets.

E-pricing in Computing

The computer firm, Dell, provides an example of exploiting e-commerce technology to enhance perceived value further by providing customers with more knowledge and thereby avoid on-line buying leading to commoditisation of its products. From the first day the firm opened for business, it recognised that direct marketing requires an overwhelming commitment to maximising the effectiveness of the knowledge provision aspect of the interface which exists between the firm and the customer. The company was one of the first organisations to recognise how efficiencies offered by internet trading could contribute towards enhancing customer value (Thurm 1998). Over time Dell has evolved a web site that does much more than just take orders. Customers can access thousands of pages of information, tap into the technical guides used by Dell technicians and also use the site to track the progress of their orders from submission through to shipment. The firm has found that these types of services actually improve its selling efficiency. For example, the traditional purchaser makes five telephones calls before buying whereas users of the web site browse and then place their order during their first telephone call. Additionally Dell sales staff can interrogate the site to determine whether there is a need to follow-up a customer's search activities with a one-to-one telephone conversation.

For corporate clients the firm has now developed Premier Pages. This permits a company to specify the creation of a confidential home page to which it can direct its employees seeking information of the product specifications that the company will permit them to have when purchasing a new machine. Premium Pages also offer the capability that the client company can access databases showing what type of computers have been purchased and who within the organisation has placed the order.

Charles Schwab

An example of a firm which has exploited e-commerce to sustain a strategy of using the provision of knowledge to differentiate the firm from the competition while concurrently offering lower prices is the brokerage company Charles Schwab. In the late 1980s, this firm realised that as private citizens gained experience in investing in the stock market they had less and less need for the services available from the conventional stock broking firms. Schwab's solution was that by offering market access without providing any investment counselling support they could charge a much lower commission on trades (*Business Week* 1994). Within only a few years, however, other brokerage houses recognised that the Schwab philosophy was the way forward and redesigned their operations to reflect this market change. In response, Schwab sought to find new ways of using electronic technology to deliver increased knowledge and trading functionality to individual investors. In 1989, for example, it introduced automated telephone touchpad trading and in 1993, launched StreetSmart for Windows, a software package that allows its customers to trade via a modem. Custom Broker, a telephone, fax and paging service for active traders followed this in 1994. These entrepreneurial ideas were accompanied by the launch of OneSource, which gave investors direct access to many hundreds of no-load funds run by the country's top money managers (Wayne 1994). Following this success, Schwab entered the world of on-line trading in which the consumer, sitting comfortably at home, can use the internet to buy and sell shares at a cost over 60% lower than that which would be incurred trading through a traditional brokerage house. Currently not only is *www.e.Schwab.com* the market leader in the provision of an internet share trading service, but some observers are suggesting that this move may eventually totally revolutionise the stock broking business.

ON-LINE AUCTIONS

In the mid-1990s, Pierre Omidyar decided to exploit the internet as a way of assisting consumers to save money by providing knowledge about a broader, more diverse range of goods. His business idea was to establish an on-line auction operation. His model, launched under the trading name of eBay, was highly profitable from the start because the company does not incur the costs traditionally associated with the sale of goods such as handling inventory or distributing goods. All eBay (*www.ebay.com*) does is to take a commission on sales (*Business Week* 1999a).

The appeal of *cyberauctions* which provide customers with increased knowledge and greater power over their purchase activities is demonstrated by the fact that in 1999 it was estimated that on-line auctions accounted for the majority of goods being traded in cyberspace. The top selling auction category is computers, but it is expected that in a few years this volume of trade will be matched by other categories such as airline tickets, hotel rooms, cars and clothing.

To attract participants to a cyberauction, most sites have followed the eBay model. The visitor fills out a registration form. Access is then granted to a list of available items and knowledge is provided on the highest previous bid. Some auctions also make available data on bidding history, number of bids, bid amounts and the cybernames of the bidders. One of the early problems, which emerged in cyberauctions, is protecting sellers and buyers against fraud. One form of protection offered by eBay is that one can gain access to knowledge about a seller's or bidder's previous behaviour. The company also posts a star next to high reputation sellers and visitors who are mentioned in numerous site user complaints, are banned (Pitta 1998).

A major appeal of the internet as an auction vehicle is the size of the potential audience. Cyberauctions may eventually come to represent a major threat to the traditional auction industry. In the case of fine arts and antiques, the auction business has been dominated for over 300 years by Christie's and Sotherby's. It is estimated that these two firms control 39% of a $2 billion annual market. Hundreds of second-tier houses fight over the balance of the available market. Entrepreneurs James Corsellis and Simon Montford reasoned that if a significant number of second-tier houses could be persuaded to become involved in on-line auctions, the new entity would have sufficient critical mass to challenge Christie's and Sotheby's market domination (Plotkin 1998). The new web site, Auctions On-Line, rapidly recruited 150 art auction houses permitting the company to offer access to almost 4,000 catalogues. These catalogues contain information on over $400 million of appraised art, antiques and collectibles.

Although consumer-to-consumer cyberauctions were the first to gain popularity on the internet, they were soon followed by the creation of business-to-business sites. Many of these sites have followed the eBay model, with the site owners taking a commission on sales. Gerry Haller, the founder of FastParts (*www.century.fastparts.com*), for example, became aware that electronics firms frequently face the problem of having too many or too few spare parts, but are unwilling to trade with other firms which they perceive as business rivals. FastParts offers the opportunity for the anonymous auctioning of parts via a trusted intermediary. Over 2,500 electronics firms now use the site's thrice weekly auctions as a mechanism for improving their spare part stock levels (*The Economist* 1997b).

In the financial services sector, suppliers are also using cyberauctions to attract buyers. At the IMX Mortgage Exchange (*www.imx-exchange.com*), an on-line home-loan market, brokers post homebuyers' requests for mortgages and potential lenders bid on them. The brokers then select for their clients what they feel is the best lending proposition being offered. Another service example is provided by *www.adauction.com*. This cyberauction site started by displaying and requesting bids for unsold line advertising space. The success of this first venture has caused the company to move into offering unsold print advertising space and its eventual aim is to offer a similar service for the broadcast media (*Business Week* 1999a).

Some business-to-business sites have adopted the model of web site owners acquiring products by purchasing other firms' excess inventories, which are then offered for auction. An example of this approach is provided by QXL (*www.shopping-sites.com*) in the UK (Wilson 1999). This is a much higher risk model than the eBay philosophy because the cyber-auctioneer is taking ownership of the product and gambles that received bids will exceed product purchase costs. To a certain degree, success is influenced by the volume of active bidders using the site. Hence a major front-end cost for this type of web site is promotional expenditure to rapidly build a large, loyal customer base.

Some futurists are predicting that as consumers become familiar with bidding for products instead of accepting a supplier's listed price, on-line shopping may lead to the elimination of whole tiers of distribution and create a highly efficient, knowledge rich, price-sensitive global market (*Fortune* 1998). To date, however, such trends have yet to emerge. In part this is due to the fact that by the time the on-line customer pays the shipping and handling costs, the final delivered price may be higher than that which would have been paid by visiting a local, traditional discount retailer. Hence at the moment it would appear that although auction sites are offering the world a new type of purchase experience, for the majority of people the real benefit of the internet is in providing round-the-clock access to an incredibly diverse source of knowledge about a whole range of different goods. Additionally once cyberspace shoppers have determined their purchase preferences, they can now access a number of sites which provide comparative knowledge on prices being quoted by a number of different suppliers. Examples of this type of comparative pricing service are WebMarket (*www.webmarket.com*) and Jango (*www.jango.com*). Visitors to these sites can input brand names or model numbers to receive back a list of suppliers and published prices. Jango also offers the facility of initiating searches beyond listed suppliers to seek out products available on on-line auction sites and on-line classified advertising sites.

EXPLOITING THE NET

For those firms which wish to avoid on-line commoditisation it necessary to recognise that the internet provides new ways of exploiting knowledge as the basis for optimising cyberspace pricing strategies (Baker et al. 2001). One area of opportunity is to use the internet to acquire knowledge that can enhance the precision of the pricing decision. Virtually all products have a 'price indifference band' within which price changes have little impact on customer behaviour. Being at the top of this range can dramatsically impact profits. Determining the precise nature of these bands in the terrestrial world is both difficult and expensive. On the internet, however, companies can test customer response in real time by offering different prices to site visitors and determining the impact on purchase decisions.

The software services company Zilliant tested the on-line impact of changing prices for four products. For three of the products, sales increases following price reductions did not compensate for an overall profit reduction. For the fourth product – a high end, premium priced item – sales were more than doubled. Analysis of the sales data revealed that virtually all of the sales increase came from schools and universities which previously rarely purchased the product. Thus the price experiment revealed a new market segment which Zilliant is now exploiting by offering special prices to the education sector which are not made available to commercial sector customers.

Companies can also acquire knowledge about customer attitudes to discounting by undertaking low cost, rapid on-line tests of alternative propositions. The on-line business auction portal FairMarket found, for example, that customers buy more rapidly and accept higher prices when they are informed of a price reduction instead of being told that only limited stocks are available.

In terrestrial markets, the communication of knowledge concerning price changes can take several months because of the need to publish information and then distribute this to the sales force, distributors and end user customers. On-line pricing provides a much more adaptable mechanism through which to distribute knowledge about price changes. Changes can be made to web site price lists in a matter of minutes and instantly all subsequent site visitors become aware of the new price. Additionally if the company has a database listing the e-mail addresses of on-line customers, these individuals can be informed of the price change at the touch of a button. This instant adaptability clearly has significant implications in industrial sectors where fluctuations in demand result in excess finished goods inventories. Where this trend emerges, the companies concerned can initiate instant price reductions and once inventory imbalances have been rectified, return prices to the normal, everyday level.

The other critical aspect of on-line markets is that companies can acquire real-time data on customer behaviour. By analysing these databases, firms can identify variations in customer behaviour and utilise this information for very accurate market segmentation activities. Car manufacturers such as Ford, for example, are already using this approach to determine which groups of customers are interested in special offers such as discount financing and cash-back programmes. Major supermarket chains are assessing customer buying patterns at an individual level and then offering customised price discounts on specific products to heavy users of products.

DISTRIBUTION MANAGEMENT

Distribution of products usually involves some form of vertical system where transaction and logistics responsibilities are transferred through a number of levels (for example, fresh flowers grown by a horticulturist, sold to a local wholesaler, then sold on and transported by truck to inland wholesalers, who in turn sell and deliver the product to small florists). In terms of distribution management, Stern and El-Ansary (1988) have proposed that the following factors will need to be considered in the selection of an appropriate system:

1   The capability of intermediaries to exploit their knowledge of logistics to execute the tasks of sorting goods, aggregating products from a variety of sources and breaking down bulk shipments into saleable lot sizes.
2   The specialist knowledge that intermediaries have acquired which permits them to routinise transactions efficiently and thereby minimise costs (for example, a clothing retailer selling a variety of designer goods to consumers).
3   The exploitation of knowledge by intermediaries to assist customers to minimise search costs (for example, an office distributor having available information and samples of office furniture in its display room from a range of different suppliers).

In relation to these three factors, direct supplier–customer distribution systems tend to occur in those market systems where conventions prevail such as each end user purchases a large proportion of total output, goods are highly perishable and/or the complex nature of the goods requires a close working relationship between supplier and final customer. This scenario will be encountered, for example, in many large capital goods markets such as the aerospace and construction industries. In those markets where an indirect distribution system is perceived as being more cost effective, then the usual convention is that one or more distributors will become involved in the distribution process. These distributors will typically receive a truckload-size shipment which they break down into smaller lot sizes. These are sold to an end user outlet which will be responsible for managing both the final customer purchase transaction and any post-purchase service needs (for example, a meat wholesaler supplying branded products to small local butchers.)

A common convention in Western world economies during the twentieth century has been that of retailers perceiving scale benefits in purchasing directly from suppliers. In these cases, the outcome is usually that of 'cutting out the middleman' with the retailers acquiring the knowledge of how to establish vertically integrated procurement, warehousing, distribution and retailing systems. Effective exploitation of a diverse range of knowledge areas ahead of the competition has provided the basis for the establishment of highly successful trading operations such as Wal-Mart in the United States and Tesco in the UK.

After decades of virtually being ignored as an important aspect of marketing management processes, in the mid-1980s organisations began to realise that exploitation of knowledge within distribution channels can actually provide additional opportunities to gain advantage over the competition. A number of factors have contributed to this situation. Possibly two of the more important have been (a) the impact of knowledge concerning new or improved technology in the reduction of transportation costs and/or delivery times (for example the impact of the airfreight industry on the global over night distribution of high value goods) and (b) exponentially declining prices for IT systems across all facets of the distribution process (for example, OEMs linking their computers with the production scheduling systems of key component suppliers to create JIT manufacturing systems).

Rangan et al. (1992, 1993), in reviewing the future strategic implications of new approaches to channel management, have suggested that managers must now exploit available knowledge on the flow of goods and services in alternative channels to achieve the strategic goal of creating competitive entry barriers, enhancing product differentiation and enabling greater customer intimacy. These authors' proposal is that it is now necessary to 'unbundle' the channel functions of information provision, order generation, physical distribution and after sales service. The next step is to determine how customer needs can best be met by channel members sharing specialist knowledge to create team orientated channel partnerships in which each performs those tasks in which they excel.

E-COMMERCE DISTRIBUTION

The advent of e-commerce is causing many firms to reassess their approach to exploiting knowledge of distribution systems to acquire and sustain competitive advantage. Even prior to the arrival of the internet, Moriaty and Moran (1990) had referred to the exploitation of new electronic technologies as an opportunity for building 'hybrid marketing systems'. They perceive these technology-based systems as offering new, more customer orientated, entrepreneurial approaches to channel management.

One approach to determining an optimal strategy for selecting an optimal e-commerce distribution channel is to assume that there are two critical dimensions influencing the decision; namely, whether to retain control or delegate responsibility for transaction management and to retain control or delegate responsibility for logistics management. An example of an e-commerce market sector where the supplier tends to retain control over both distribution dimensions is on-line banking services. This is because supplier banks will usually retain absolute control over both the financial transaction and service delivery processes.

The case of the e-commerce transaction being delegated, but delivery responsibility retained, is provided by the airline industry. Many of the airlines use on-line service providers such as *www.cheapflights.co.uk* to act as retailers of their unsold seat capacity.

Possibly the most frequently encountered e-commerce distribution model is that of protecting the firm against any loss of knowledge of products and markets by retaining control over transactions and delegating physical distribution. It is the standard model that is in used among most on-line tangible goods retailers. These organisations, having successfully sold a product to a web site visitor, will use the specialist logistics know-ledge capabilities of organisations such as FedEx or UPS to manage all aspects of distribution.

In the majority of off-line, consumer goods markets, the commonest distribution model is to delegate both transaction and logistics processes (for example, major brands such as Kellogg's being marketed via super-market chains). This approach can be contrasted with the on-line world where absolute delegation of all processes is still a somewhat rarer event. The reason for this situation is that many firms, having decided that e-commerce offers an opportunity for revising distribution management practices, perceive cyberspace as a way to regain control over transactions by cutting out intermediaries and selling direct to their end user customers. This process in which traditional intermediaries may be squeezed out of channels is usually referred to as *disintermediation*.

It is necessary to recognise, however, that delegation of transaction and logistics processes may offer ways to improve market service provision by exploiting opportunities made available through *reintermediation* (Pitt et al. 1999). An example of this dual delegation of channel responsibility is provided by MP3. The advent of MP3 provided a solution for the recording companies who for many years have faced the problem of being unable to per-suade off-line retailers to stock recordings for newly signed artists or groups.

Pitt et al. (1999) have proposed that in assessing e-commerce distrib-ution strategies, there is the need to recognise that the technology has the following implications:

1 Distance ceases to be a cost influencer because on-line delivery of information is substantially the same no matter the destination of the delivery.
2 Business location becomes an irrelevance because the e-commerce cor-poration can be based anywhere in the world.
3 The technology permits continuous trading, 24 hours a day, 365 days a year.

The advent of the tremendous increase in market and customer knowledge that has become available to companies though cyberspace trading has caused many firms to examine whether restructuring of a sector supply chain can provide the basis for a new form of strategic advantage (Jallar and Capek 2001). Firms can use specialist knowledge to enhance logistics and thereby upgrade customer service. Federal Express has exploited its knowledge of IT to create a market tracking system for its clients. The firm has also exploited the knowledge contained within the organisation's elec-tronic databases to manage more effectively the daily distribution of over two million packages.

Direct contact between supplier and end user also permits a more rapid response to the distribution of needed products. Benetton, the global manufacturer of fashion goods, uses optical scanners in store to monitor buying trends. This real-time system generates buyer behaviour knowledge that can be used to implement immediate changes in the scheduling of production, distribution of goods and development of new products. The success of Benetton provides strong evidence that any firm which exploits knowledge of customer behaviour is in a much better position to utilise its on-line and terrestrial distribution systems to strengthen customer loyalty and thereby increase customer retention rates.

The internet also permits new firms to enter the supply chain offering specialist knowledge that can enhance the flow of goods or services through a market system. An example of this scenario is provided by the American car selling portal Auto-by-Tel. The firm's knowledge strategy is to minimise customer time in the product search and purchase decision process. Based upon a network of 2,700 car dealers, Auto-by-Tel matches its on-line customers with the nearest car dealer that meets their buying criteria. When an on-line customer puts in an order for a specific model, the request is sent via a server to all of the qualified dealers who are geographically close to the customer. Within 48 hours a product proposal is sent back to the customer. The service is free to the customer; revenue is generated by car dealers who pay Auto-by-Tel both a joining fee and a monthly subscription fee.

On-line or Off-line?

Many of the early dot.com entrepreneurs were firms which moved their off-line operation onto the web as a mechanism to increase the provision of knowledge to a geographically expanded market and to offer 24-hour provision of knowledge to their customers. Some have been so impressed by the power of the internet that they have subsequently closed their terrestrial or 'bricks-and-mortar' operation (McGarvey 2000). One such company is Pom Express, a Massachusetts firm that specialises in supplying products for people involved in cheerleading. Two years ago the company closed the retail operation and now conducts all distribution activities through its web site at www.pomexpress.com.

Similarly Nancy Zebrick operated a traditional travel agency in New Jersey and moved into the internet as a parallel operation in 1995. She soon found that although the profit margin per sale is lower on the net, this is more than compensated for by the increased volume that comes from operating at a national and international market level. In 1988 the firm merged with an on-line travel superstore (www.onetravel.com) and left, forever, the world of terrestrial distribution. A similar story can be found at www.egghead.com. A major leader in the retailing of software in the 1980s, this company's reaction to increasing competitive pressures in the 1990s has been to close its stores and to trade only on the internet.

Some industry observers are cautioning people who believe that stories of successful e-trading operations are adequate justification for the argument that everybody should cease terrestrial market knowledge provision and distribution activities. Certainly when one observes the large companies in sectors such as retailing and banking it is becoming clear that a dual strategy of operating both a bricks-and-mortar and an on-line operation may be a more appropriate strategy through which to satisfy the knowledge and distribution needs of differing customer groups. Many customers still want suppliers to offer personal interaction in the provision of knowledge. At the moment this requirement is usually more effectively delivered via a sales person based in a traditional terrestrial outlet.

Some small businesses are also beginning to believe that a dual strategy is more sensible for the foreseeable future. Certainly this is the view at Star Children's Wear Inc., a children's company in Washington which operates both a retail outlet and a web site (*www.shopstars.com*). Similarly in Winter Park, Florida, Wine Country Inc. has a retail outlet and also offers an on-line selling facility via its web site *www.winecountryonline.com*.

SUPPLY CHAIN TRENDS

As firms acquire understanding of the benefits of exploiting the richer sources of knowledge which are available through the use of e-technology, they soon begin to recognise that opportunities exist for enhancing the operation of their market sector's entire supply chain (Moad 1997). The advantages of exploiting the internet to manage supply chains go well beyond the savings that can be made in reducing paperwork and clerical costs. Companies such as Cisco have recognised that providing component suppliers and distributors with on-line access to the company's manufacturing and operating knowledge base means that concepts such as JIT and lean manufacturing become a much more practical reality. Such systems can be used to automate manufacturing scheduling, track inventories, implement engineering changes and manage all aspects of the procurement process.

Knowledge Sharing

Possibly one of the most financially tangible aspects of knowledge sharing is the cost savings which can be achieved through implementing extremely simple procedural changes. Merisel Inc., for example, an American distributor of software products, estimates that electronic knowledge sharing has cut the cost of processing orders by 70%. Boston Edison has found that the electronic integration of its supply chain has not just enhanced operational efficiency but even more importantly it has resulted in the firm attracting much more competitive bids from suppliers.

Not all originators of supply chain restructuring have been major OEMs. In some cases other supply chain members have been the initiators. In the US computer industry,

213

Sun Data Corporation, Georgia, is a reseller of new and refurbished PCs and mid-range computer systems. The company business model is that of generating sales from end user customers and then sourcing product requirements from a diverse range of computer manufacturers. Sun Data has decided to contract the web selling and distribution responsibilities to Federal Express. This latter operation's Virtual One IT system exploits the company's accumulated specialist knowledge of logistics management to undertake on behalf of the customer all of the tasks associated with warehousing, order fulfilment and distribution. By delegation of these tasks, Sun Data perceives that it is then more able to concentrate on its primary role of providing knowledge to its customers about the availability of alternative solutions for optimising IT hardware purchase decisions.

Global Operations

In a world where global companies have operations in numerous countries there is an ever increasing pressure on managers to optimise all aspects of their supply chain operations. Thus as never before, knowledge which can be exploited to reduce both inventory levels and order-to-deliver cycles is perceived as being incredibly valuable (Siekman 2000). One firm which has moved to exploit the growing demand for knowsledge about supply chain operations management is the US corporation, UPS. This company realised some years ago that new opportunities were emerging in logistics. It has created a new venture, UPS Logistics Delivering Solutions, which specialises in solving company- and sector-specific supply chain problems. As well as locating specialist staff around the world, where a client operation needs new knowledge it has sometimes resolved this dilemma by acquiring other firms. This approach, for example, was used to create a system to establish a lorry fleet dedicated to the distribution of perishable food products.

One UPS Logistics specialism has been the creation of a service parts supply operation for firms such as Compaq Computers. Operating from a dedicated parts management complex in Louisville, Kentucky, UPS Logistics manages parts warehouses and undertakes the distribution of spare parts to its clients' own technicians or to the clients' end user customers. The company also can manage the entire order placement–product delivery cycle for clients. For the on-line Nike.com operation, Louisville maintains inventories of Nike shoes and clothing, manages the receipt of orders, organises product delivery and handles product returns. For BasketBall Marketing, UPS Logistics receives the company's product shipments from suppliers, mainly Asian, and manages all aspects of the delivery of goods to sporting goods retailers.

More recently the company has entered the equipment repair business. For Sony and Toshiba the company collects faulty laptops from customers, flies them to Louisville, undertakes the repairs and then returns the item. The company provides the same service for Lexmark printers. For this latter client, if the repair is relatively simple UPS undertakes the work. Only those printers where a very serious operating fault is identified are shipped back to Lexmark. Ultimately Lexmark is hoping that UPS will acquire the knowledge to be able to undertake all of Lexmark's product repair activities.

Outsourcing

Solectron Corporation of California is a contract electronics manufacturer which exploits the growing trend for computer and telecommunications equipment companies such as Cisco, Hewlett-Packard, Nortel and Sun Microsystems to enhance the operation of their supply chain by 'outsourcing' a proportion of their product assembly activities. The company has long recognised that ongoing expansion in the outsourcing market can be made feasible only by continually seeking new knowledge that can support manufacturing capability diversification. A significant proportion of this knowledge pool expansion has come from embarking on an aggressive company acquisitions programme.

Solectron's principal source of revenue remains the manufacture of printed circuit board assemblies. The company philosophy is that new opportunities will most probably emerge from multinational OEMs outsourcing the design, manufacture and distribution of bottom end, low cost items in their product range. Hence the primary focus on knowledge expansion through corporate acquisition has been to buy companies, often from Solectron's own OEM customers, which provide the opportunity to improve the firm's knowledge base about designing and manufacturing electronic goods. Solectron is committed to the idea that the firm's OEM customer base has superior expertise in identifying and developing demand for goods in end user markets. The company, therefore, has reached the strategic decision of avoiding any involvement in downstream activities associated with supplying end user markets.

Retaining Control

One market where clearly time really is of the essence is the supply of maternity clothes. Given the rapidly changing proportions of women during pregnancy, there is little point in responding to customers by suggesting they should wait while out-of-stock clothes are back ordered. Thus in marketing maternity clothing, having the knowledge required to manage all aspects of JIT stock management is a critical capability.

One firm in this sector which has invested in developing a deep and diverse knowledge base is the Philadelphia firm Mother Works. The company decided that self-ownership of the majority of the supply chain is the only route to survival in this market.

The company owns over 700 retail outlets and uses its point-of-sale cash registers to generate knowledge of customer purchase trends. These data are used by the firm to operate a centralised warehouse system. Near to this warehouse, Mother Works has a fabric-cutting room and a textile warehouse. These latter operations supply pre-cut fabrics to local, independently owned sewing companies. In addition to these sewing operations based around Philadelphia, over the years the company has sought to optimise product costs. Thus it has also forged links with clothing manufacturers in over 20 other countries around the world. The primary focus of activity of the firm's clothing suppliers in the United States is on the manufacture of the firm's more expensive, lower volume fashion goods for which demand is relatively volatile and in undertaking rapid assembly of short runs of product lines which have sold faster at retail level than was originally forecast.

A core knowledge capability is the operation of the company's central warehouse. For flat-packed items such as sweaters and blouses, the company computer generates internal orders directing the move of product from the bulk storage area to where the shipping bins for individual stores are located. Order pickers are allocated to each shipping bin and their activities are directed by a computer-controlled traffic light system which monitors that specific store replenishment requirements are being met. Elsewhere in Philadelphia the company has another automated warehouse operation dedicated to order picking of non-foldable garments such as dresses and suits which are shipped to the retail outlets on hangers.

The company's extensive accumulated knowledge of managing stock levels and minimising distribution delays means that a move into on-line trading was extremely simple. Having created its web site at *www.Motherswork.com*, the only critical issue in linking the site into the company's existing stock management system was the need to service the received orders for single items from individual consumers instead of handling the multiproduct, multi-item needs of the Mother Works' retail stores.

Managing Services and Customer Relationships

CHAPTER SUMMARY

The provision of services is an increasingly dominant component of developed nation economies. Service markets exhibit certain specific characteristics. To meet customer needs, the service marketer must have the knowledge of how to fulfil customer expectations. A technique, the service gap model, can be used to generate the knowledge required to close service quality gaps and thereby optimise customer purchase experiences. Recently CRM has been recognised as critical in service markets. Emphasis is being placed upon acquiring knowledge sufficient always to meet customer needs. E-commerce permits data acquisition that can be analysed and exploited using data warehousing and data mining techniques. Employees are crucial in the delivery of services. Hence service firms need to ensure their staff can access the knowledge they require to optimise the execution of their assigned tasks.

INTRODUCTION

A characteristic of twentieth-century Western nation economies has been the increasing importance of service industries as both a contributor to gross national product (GNP) and a source of employment. In the 1980s, as many service markets became more competitive, organisations recognised the need to modernise their marketing philosophies. The popular solution was to employ transactionalist orientated managers from fmcg companies such as Procter & Gamble, General Foods and Nestlé. These individuals persuaded their new employers to adopt a highly conventional approach towards the management of the marketing process. This resulted in a major expansion of expenditure on various forms of mass marketing activity.

In some cases, these purist, conventional fmcg approaches were extremely successful (for example, the global expansion of fast food chains

217

such as Burger King, Pizza Hut and Kentucky Fried Chicken). Other areas of the service sector, however, were not similarly rewarded. The UK banks in the late 1980s, for example, having expended millions on television advertising found that (a) the number of consumers opening current accounts remained virtually unchanged and (b) many of their new customers were individuals who, being dissatisfied with their current supplier, switched loyalties but continued to complain about the costs and/or quality of services being delivered by their new bank.

This mixture of success and failure within the service sector prompted both academics and practitioners to revisit marketing theory. As a result, it has become widely accepted that the marketing of services probably demands a whole new range of marketing conventions and operating principles (Cowell 1984). Initially many of the writings on this topic focused on purist service marketing in sectors such as financial services and retailing. More recently, however, there has been a growing recognition that in many manufacturing sectors, firms can gain competitive advantage, not by following the convention of marketing their capabilities to deliver a tangible core product, but through exploiting internal knowledge to augment their product offering with a portfolio of unconventional value-added services.

Quinn et al. (1990), for example, have described how many of the firms at the top end of the pharmaceutical industry have relied upon exploiting their internal knowledge to develop unconventional added-value services to survive in the face of competitive threats from price orientated, generic drug producers. Firms such as Glaxo (*www.glaxowellcombe.com*) and Merck (*www.merck.com*) have added value to their product line through service activities such as R & D, constructing legal and patent defences, rapidly progressing new drugs through the clinical clearances demanded by regulatory bodies, supporting clinicians in their use of new treatments and offering advisory support on optimising the provision of healthcare by their customers such as large hospitals and health authorities.

Baxter UK

The renal division of Baxter UK markets disposable bags used for peritoneal kidney dialysis in the home (Vandermerwe 2000). Although market share in 1997 was 80% peritoneal dialysis (PD) was losing sales to hemodialysis (HD) which removes toxic waste from blood. On a bag-to-bag basis HD is cheaper, which forced Baxter into cutting prices. What the company then needed to do was to find a way increasing revenue to compensate for the erosion in profit margin. Its solution was to examine how exploitation of knowledge could create new services which would be perceived by the customer as adding value to the product proposition.

Renal patients with serious kidney problems usually begin their treatment at home using PD and then move on to HD which requires four hours in hospital three days a week. Timing of the move to HD depends upon how quickly the disease is diagnosed and treated. Baxter's objective was to obtain increased depth and length of spending by getting more people onto PD earlier and for longer. To increase patient awareness, the company created a web site, *www.Kidneywise.com*, established mobile diagnostic centres to speed up diagnosis and referral and expanded general practitioner outreach activities. The outcome was patients staying on PD treatment for longer which led to an increase in sales for the company's core product, the disposable bag.

From research the company discovered that patients who move onto HD choose hospital treatment rather than home treatment if they have not had sufficient time to think about how they will manage their changed lives. Baxter therefore decided to use a knowledge-based marketing proposition to offer HD treatment at home. Educators were placed in pre-dialysis clinics to take patients through the treatment options and to provide information on benefits to which they are entitled. Their web site offers more information. Once the patient has entered the treatment phase, Baxter trains patients to care for themselves and provides guidance on lifestyle changes. Patients can get help to set up equipment and can obtain 24-hour emergency clinical and technical help via the telephone or the internet. Home care includes management of supplies, waste disposal and delivery of drugs. Nurses monitor progress and telemedicine devices capture patient information which is disseminated via the internet to those supervising care and to the Baxter R & D team.

THE CHARACTERISTICS OF SERVICE GOODS

One of the primary reasons writers posited the view that service marketers must break with traditional, branded goods conventions is that service markets exhibit some very specific characteristics. One of these, *intangibility* the item cannot be touched, smelled, seen or tasted, is encompassed by Kotler's (1997) definition, namely: 'a service is any act or performance that one party can offer to another that is essentially intangible and does not result in the ownership of anything. Its production may or may not be tied to a physical product'.

It is necessary to recognise, however, that the degree of intangibility will vary across product sectors. At one extreme, service is a minor component of the product proposition (for example, a new car which comes with a three-year free repair and service guarantee). At the other extreme, service may be the dominant or sole product component (for example, an on-line purchased, car insurance policy). The implication of intangibility does mean that a service, unlike physical products, cannot be seen, tasted, felt, heard or smelled before purchase. Thus one of the tasks of service marketers is to develop mechanisms which, by providing customers with additional knowledge, can reduce customers' uncertainty about intangibility. Typical solutions across the sector include exploiting variables such as:

219

1 **Place**, which is the knowledge provided by physical setting around which the provision of services are delivered (for example, the atmosphere in a dentist's surgery).
2 **People**, who provide knowledge by working at the customer/organisation interface (for example, the shop assistant).
3 **Equipment**, which can be used to assist in the knowledge provision process (for example, the user information displayed by a bank ATM).

Another characteristic of services is *inseparability*, which describes the fact that many services are simultaneously produced and consumed. The implication of this situation is that for many service outcomes to occur, both the provider and the customer must be able to interact with each other. A further characteristic of services is their *variability*, which is caused by both differing customer needs, and the capabilities of employees within the provider organisation. Unlike manufactured goods, which can be produced and inventoried for later use, another characteristic of many services is that they are highly *perishable*. For example, an inability to sell every seat on a specific airline flight on a specific day means that a proportion of total revenue on this occasion has been lost forever. Sasser (1976) has proposed that by exploiting knowledge about customer needs and behaviour it is possible to develop a number of marketing strategies for effectively matching supply and demand. These include:

- **Differential pricing** to move demand away from peak to off-peak periods.
- **Alternative service provision** to meet the varying needs of customers during peak periods.
- **Service modification** to ensure that during peak periods the needs of major purchasers receive priority.
- **Demand management systems**, which permit the service provider to rapidly (a), identify current available capacity and (b) propose alternative solutions.
- **Temporary capacity expansion** whereby the provider can increase the ability to respond to customer needs during peak periods.
- **Service sharing** where a number of organisations work together and are willing to cross refer customers.
- **Customer participation** in which customers are encouraged to become self-providers.

CUSTOMER EXPECTATIONS

Prior to interaction with the service provider, the customer has already formed expectations about the ensuing service experience. Once formed these expectations constitute standards against which actual performance is compared. Discrepancy creates a mental state of disconfirmation. *Positive disconfirmation* results when performance exceeds expectations. *Negative disconfirmation* results when performance is worse than expectations and customers express indifference when performance meets expectations.

Zeithmal et al. (1993) posit that expectations are formed as an outcome of the knowledge acquired by the customer. They propose there are various sources which influence the knowledge acquisition process. *Explicit service promises* are the personal and non-personal statements about service provision made by the supplier. Statements are personal when they are communicated by an employee. Non-personal statements are delivered by indirect media such as advertising and brochures. The implication for the supplier is to ensure that knowledge acquired from the service promise is both accurate and realistic. This means ensuring employees are not making promises that cannot be met and that claims made in promotional campaigns will be substantiated by the subsequent service experience.

Implicit service promises are service-related cues other than explicit promises that lead to an inference about what the service should and will be like. For example, a service provider quoting a higher price will be assumed to be likely to deliver a higher level of service. Knowledge provided by word of mouth communication occurs when individuals and organisations other than the supplier provide information about the nature of available services. This source of knowledge (for example, friends or relatives; an article in a travel magazine) is typically seen as very important by customers because they perceive such information sources as being unbiased in their opinions.

The other source of knowledge shaping customer expectations is the customer's previous exposure to the service. This knowledge can come from prior contact with one supplier. As customers acquire knowledge from exposure to a number of suppliers (for example, by visiting a number of different web sites) accumulated knowledge can also cause customers to form generic expectations about a service sector. For example, generic expectations about air lines will be formed as a result of flying on a number of different airlines.

Given the diverse sources of knowledge which influence expectations this means that the service provider will need to monitor all of these contact sources to understand the impact they are having on existing and potential customers. The implication of this conclusion is that the firm's market research should not just focus on the actual service experience but should be extended to encompass all of the factors that contribute to the process of expectation formation (Webb 2000).

SERVICE GAP THEORY

The fundamental objective of service provision is to minimise the gap between customers' desires and actual experience (that is, the gap between what they hope will happen and what actually occurs). To permit service marketers to understand and manage service gaps requires access to feasible techniques for the measurement and analysis of customer expectations and perceptions. This need has been met through the activities of Parasuraman, Zeithmal and Berry (1985, 1988, 1994) who implemented a carefully sequenced research project aimed at delivering an effective model for assessing the effectiveness and quality of the service provision process.

The first stage of their research was to identify some common variables, which could be used to categorise how customers assess service quality. By the use of focus groups they identified the following five variables:

1 **Reliability**, which is the ability to perform the promised service dependably and accurately.
2 **Tangibles**, which are the images, created by the appearance of physical facilities, equipment, personnel and communication materials.
3 **Responsiveness**, which is the willingness to help customers and provide prompt service.
4 **Assurance**, which is the process by which the knowledge, ability and courtesy of employees engenders customer trust and confidence in the service provider.
5 **Empathy**, which is created by the caring, individualised attention that employees offer the customer.

Having identified these generic variables, Parasuraman et al. then went on to create the SERVQUAL model, which defined the following types of gap, which could exist between expectations and perceptions:

> **Gap 1**, which exists between the customer's expectations and the organisation's perceptions of customer need.
> **Gap 2**, which exists between the organisation's perceptions and the definition of appropriate standards for the quality of service to be delivered.
> **Gap 3**, which exists between the specified standards of service and the actual performance of the service provision process undertaken by the organisation's employees.
> **Gap 4**, which is the gap between actual service delivered, and the nature of the service promise made in any communications with the customer.
> **Gap 5**, which represents the overall gap between customer expectations and perceptions, created by the combined influence of gaps 1 through to 4.

Effective closure of service gaps will involve the service provider in an extensive period of knowledge acquisition and application to identify the cause of each problem and then to initiate appropriate action. In the case of gap 1, where the customer and supplier have different views about expectations, market research will be required. This research will focus upon issues such as what service features are important to customers, what the customers think about the company and what customers think the company should do in the event of a service delivery failure.

Only once an organisation understands what customers expect is it in a position to close gap 2 by translating this knowledge into specifying service quality standards against which actual performance of tasks and processes can be measured. To achieve this objective in many cases all of the interactions during the service encounter between the customer and supplier will need to be analysed. Knowledge generated by analysis of the service encounter permits the definition of standards of behaviour and actions which are important to the customer. Reliability standards, to ensure no mistakes occur in service provision, and responsiveness standards, to define the speed with which a customer can expect response to an enquiry to occur, can be set. Having set such standards it is then critical that they are monitored and reviewed regularly.

Inadequate execution of service processes relative to the standards specified will lead to the emergence of gap 3. Delivery of the service process is usually dependent upon both frontline employees and those supporting them in the back office operations. As a result the success of most service provision is crucially vested in the organisation's workforce. Thus having hired the right people, the organisation must provide the necessary training to ensure that all employees have the necessary knowledge of both the technical competencies and interactive skills which are required to undertake their assigned tasks. Examples of technical skills are the ability to operate the computer-based passenger management system at an airline check-in desk or processing a client claim in an insurance company. Interactive competencies include abilities such as listening, problem solving and communication.

To be efficient and effective in their jobs, employees require internal support systems which can provide access to any additional knowledge needed to execute their service delivery task. Increasingly firms are relying upon the use of sophisticated computer systems to maximise the speed with which employees can access the knowledge they require. Most call centres, for example, have computer systems which permit their frontline staff to access customer files when accepting an order or seeking to resolve a customer complaint.

A critical aspect of service quality is to ensure that employees have sufficient knowledge of company operations to avoid making a service promise that cannot be met. For this aim to be achieved requires that frontline employees understand every aspect of the firm's order-to-delivery process cycle, service guarantees and accounting policies. Concurrently very effective horizontal communications systems must be in place in order that process delivery staff are provided with knowledge about the activities being undertaken by frontline employees and the commitments they are making to customers.

CALL CENTRES

In order to deliver services across a geographically dispersed customer base, firms, especially those in service sectors, have turned to the use of call centres. The modern call centre combines the services of a human agent and a database to distribute knowledge to customers. The call centre may have the role of servicing inbound enquiries (for example, acceptance of an order from the customer) and/or outbound enquiries (for example, contacting a customer to confirm a shipment has been made) (Adria and Chowdrey 2002).

The objective of the call centre is to provide a single entry point to the organisation to manage all aspects of the knowledge distribution process. For example, a call centre in New Jersey owned by Chase Manhattan Bank and Mellon Bank provides a stock transfer service to over 2,000 publicly held companies. The centre helps clients determine account balances, carry out stock transactions, collect proceeds from stock sales and distribute dividends.

As the primary point of contact with customers, the call centre operators have a significant responsibility in terms of influencing customer satisfaction. Their ability to impart knowledge that can fulfil customer requirements is a critical component in how customers judge the competence of the supplier organisation. Volvo Action Parts Service, for example, supports Volvo's truck, buses, boats and construction equipment operations. The call centre staff assist customers' order parts and also provide technical and repair services to Volvo customers. In order to ensure staff have sufficient knowledge to assist the customer, agents are divided into three groups. One group handles parts ordering, another the provision of technical support and a third group dispatches emergency field support.

Although call centres are not the only way that corporate knowledge is shared with customers, they are increasingly becoming the central component of such activities. Although the staff have access to database templates to assist them in their knowledge provision role, these staff also need the skill to appreciate when they lack the competencies required to satisfy customer needs. In these latter circumstances they need the ability to seamlessly link the customer with another individual in the organisation who can take responsibility for filling the knowledge gap which has emerged during the interaction with the customer. To achieve this intraorganisational linkage the call centre staff need to be able to communicate both vertically and horizontally. *Vertical communication* occurs when the call centre operator needs to put the customer in contact with an expert inside the organisation. *Horizontal communication* occurs when the call centre operator transfers the enquiry to a colleague within the call centre who has more expertise in the matter being discussed with the customer.

Knowledge sharing between call centre staff and with others within the organisation is usually heavily reliant upon IT as an integrating technology. Many firms have created intranets to assist the creation and dissemination of knowledge. These systems often permit the creation of electronic forms that can be circulated and filed in the integrated databases that exist inside the organisation. The adoption of such IT support systems allows the organisation to customise the service response. In the insurance industry, for example, it is now standard practice that call centre staff are immediately linked with the client-specific record relevant to the enquiry being made by the customer.

A current evolution of call centre technology is to link together a firm's internet operation with human support services. In these systems, the customer initially uses the company's web site to acquire information and to communicate with the organisation. If, however, the customer encounters problems, then by clicking an agent connection button the customer can be immediately put in contact with a human agent. This latter individual is provided with information about both the web pages being accessed by the customer and also any other information which may already exist on the firm's database about the customer's previous purchase history. In this way the call centre employee is in a much more informed position in terms of rendering assistance to the customer.

CUSTOMER RELATIONSHIP MANAGEMENT

Berry (1982) in America was one of the earliest writers to propose that in service markets, the orientation should be towards seeking to build long term relationships with customers. Meanwhile in Europe the Industrial Marketing and Purchasing (IMP) Group was formulating similar concepts concerning the management of buyer–seller relationships in industrial markets. Impetus for firms to consider moving from transactional to relationship marketing was provided by Reichfeld and Sasser (1990). These researchers demonstrated dramatic increases in profits from small increases in customer retention rates.

Effective customer relationship management is critically dependent upon having accurate and up-to-date knowledge about customers. Analysing and classifying customers is not a new marketing concept. In the 1990s, however, advances in computer technology made it feasible to undertake rapid and detailed analysis of customer data. In other words, firms now had the capability to convert customer information into knowledge that could be used to create and sustain relationships with customers.

Towards the end of the 1990s the advent of the internet afforded companies with an opportunity to build closer relationships than had previously been possible in an off-line world (Winer 2001). Although CRM is being adopted across virtually every sector of industry, some of the earliest exploiters of IT-based CRM were service firms such as financial institutions, airlines and on-line retailers. By combining the abilities to respond directly to customer requests and to provide customers with highly interactive, customised experiences, companies have an even greater ability to use their real-time knowledge to further sustain market relationships.

These on-line capabilities complement personal interactions provided through sales personnel, customer service representatives and call centres. At the same time, companies can choose to exploit the low cost of the web to reduce service costs and offer lower quality services by only permitting the customer to contact the firm via an electronic medium. The flexibility of web-based interactions thus permits firms to choose to whom they wish to offer services, the nature of the services to be offered and to use increased knowledge about their customers to customise service quality in relation to market expectations.

The first step in gaining a deeper knowledge of customer behaviour is the construction of a customer database. For web-based businesses constructing a database is a relatively straightforward task because the customer transaction and contact information is accumulated as a natural part of the interaction with on-line customers. For off-line firms which have previously not recognised the value of acquiring knowledge about customer behaviour, work will be necessary to extract data from internal sources such as accounting records and customer service contacts. It may also be necessary to undertake market research to close identified gaps in the firm's knowledge of customers. At a minimum the firm should create a database containing the following information:

- A complete record of customers' purchase histories.
- The contact points which exist between customer and company (including, if relevant, contact between the customer and the firm's intermediaries).
- Descriptive information about customers that can provide the basis for segmentation of customer groups.

DATA WAREHOUSING

As firms have moved into CRM they have frequently faced problems in extracting knowledge from their existing databases. To overcome this obstacle organisations are creating data warehouses (Ryals and Payne 2001). A *data warehouse* is an integrated store of data, collected from a variety or sources both inside and outside the organisation. Data sources might include information from call centres, the sales force, market surveys, competitor information and geo-demographic data.

Data warehouses are different from operational systems in terms of their databases. Query processing of operational systems is difficult because of a lack of integration, efficiency and access. Trying to interrogate a database within an operational system for customer information may slow the performance of transaction processing activities. Additionally the structure may complicate the interrogation process and, given the rapidly changing nature of operational databases as transactions are being processed, this will mean that the answers will be constantly changing. In a data warehouse the database is refreshed or updated at intervals, which means it is a non-volatile system where interrogation is a more feasible process. This is why most organisations use data warehouses and smaller data marts to collect, clean and store information about customers.

Data warehouses comprise large databases which collect all the information available about an entire business unit. *Data marts* are mini data warehouses. They deal with subsets of data because in some cases the data warehouse is too large and contains too much information to carry out data analysis effectively.

Utilising a data warehouse to extract knowledge about customer behaviour involves *data exploitation*. This process takes two main forms, namely reporting and data visualisation. *Reporting* is simply output in alphanumeric form and is used for quality control, profitability analysis, management reporting and marketing activity analysis. *Visualisation* uses software tools to present data in a visual form such as charts and tables. These visual materials can be rapidly manipulated which permits their application in activities such as market segmentation, trend analysis and customer profiling.

To extract even more knowledge about customers, the organisation can undertake *data mining*. This is a process which involves selecting, exploring and modelling large amounts of data to attempt to identify new patterns, correlations or irregularities in the data sets using a range of statistical analysis tools. Techniques which are applied include *cluster analysis* (to identify groups of similar behaviours), *conjoint analysis* (to identify preferences) and *regression analysis* (to explore patterns between variables). Artificial intelligence algorithms can also be used to uncover even more complex relationships between and within combinations of variables.

The ease with which firms can create data warehouses is strongly influenced by the number of interactions which they have with customers. A durable good manufacture might use warranty cards to construct a database. Unfortunately this source of information is based upon low customer interaction. In contrast service companies such as banks and on-line retailers are in a better position because they enjoy much higher customer interaction rates. This is the reason that service sector companies have been able more rapidly to exploit the benefits offered by initiating CRM programmes.

CUSTOMER TARGETING

Having analysed data on customer behaviour a firm is in a much stronger position to consider which customers should be targeted with the firm's marketing programmes. If segmentation-type analysis has been undertaken, customers in the most desired segments (for example, highest purchasing rates, greatest brand loyalty) can be selected to be the focus of customer retention campaigns. Other segments can be chosen depending upon prevailing circumstances. For example, if customers in the heaviest purchase segment already buy at a rate which implies purchase saturation has been achieved, then a second tier of customers who purchase less frequently might be selected for targeting.

Using large numbers of customers to create segments does presume that subsequent marketing efforts will be directed towards the average customer in the group. The advent of data warehousing and data mining is now permitting firms to understand the behaviours of individual customers. This permits the firm to analyse the past and future profitability of individual customers which in turn permits the marketer to implement highly targeted, customised marketing campaigns.

Mass marketing techniques such as television or print advertising are effective for generating wide scale awareness but are poorly suited for CRM activities because of their impersonal nature. More effective approaches for targeting selected customers include a portfolio of direct marketing methods such as telemarketing, direct mail and one-to-one selling. The advent of the internet has permitted the use of e-mails to communicate with customers. E-mail marketing has become extremely popular because the delivery cost per 1,000 customers is significantly lower than using direct mail. Unfortunately the rapid adoption of e-mail marketing by firms around the world has caused many customers to become angry because every day their e-mail system has become filled with unsolicited communications. To overcome this problem the more customer orientated firms have now moved to permission-based schemes whereby the customer must first opt-in by agreeing to receive messages from a company.

RELATIONSHIP PROGRAMMES

Any contact that the customer has with a firm represents a service encounter that can be used to deepen the relationship between buyer and seller. *Reactive service* is where the customer has a problem (for example, questions about a delivery, wishing to return the product) and contacts the company seeking a solution. Most companies have recognised that a key aspect of CRM is to provide a seamless service in relation to resolving problems because a dissatisfied customer may opt to switch to another supplier. Hence these organisations have built systems whereby the employee handling the contact has immediate access to customer information which places them in a position to respond immediately to the customer's needs.

Having created these databases some firms have now moved into the provision of *proactive services*. In this situation the database is used to identify a potential need which a customer may have. Contact is made to determine whether the customer is interested in the additional service proposition. Thus, for example, a bank might develop a profile of high income customers and make contact offering such individuals the additional service of having a named individual within the bank appointed to provide a personalised response service to take care of their future banking needs.

Another way of rewarding repeat customers is to enrol them in a loyalty programme. Most large retailers in countries such as the US and the UK now offer some form of loyalty scheme to their regular customers. In many sectors, however, questions exist about whether they increase customer loyalty or cause higher spending by the customer. Unfortunately their widespread availability now means that for many large consumer service firms, such programmes have become a competitive necessity. Nevertheless, as evidenced by some sectors such as the airline industry, loyalty programmes can be extremely effective. In this sector products such as frequent flyer miles that can be redeemed for free flights or service upgrades increase customer switching costs, thereby creating barriers to entry by competitors.

Furthermore as firms accumulate knowledge about individual customers this permits them to begin to offer customised services designed to further deepen the customer relationship. Thus an airline can analyse travel patterns of frequent flyers and then target them with a promotional offer aimed at generating further purchases by such customers.

Firms can also act to create communities of customers by persuading these customers of the benefits of entering into information exchanges between themselves and the company. The goal of this approach is to create a closer, more personalised relationship in which customers and company employees perceive themselves as members of a supportive family group. The advent of the internet and the creation of chat rooms has greatly accelerated the move by firms to create on-line communities. The process, for example, is extremely popular with software companies. These organisations have created web sites for users and developers. Site visitors are able to exchange information about their product usage experiences and contribute solutions to problems being encountered by others.

A Cautionary Tale

An implicit assumption in many CRM programmes is that loyal customers generate the highest level of profit for the company. Having identified their loyal customers, this assumption often causes firms to concentrate their marketing campaigns on this group with the aim of sustaining on-going loyalty. Recent research by Reinartz and Kumar (2002), however, suggests that this assumption, which is caused by firms having insufficient knowledge of customer behaviour, may not always be valid.

The researchers analysed the customer databases of four major firms which permitted them to examine behaviour, revenue and profitability of more than 16,000 customers over a four year period. Using profitability as the variable by which to classify customers the researchers concluded there are four categories by which relationships should be managed.

One category, which they call *strangers*, consists of those customers who exhibit no loyalty and because of their low level of purchasing they bring in no profits. The recommendation is to identify these individuals as early as possible and then expend no funds attempting to build a relationship. Another category is comprised of the *butterflies*. Again these individuals tend to be transient customers shopping around for the best deal. Nevertheless their volume of purchase is such that they are highly profitable. The advice in this instance is to follow-up the purchase with a short intensive promotional blitz. Then if there is no response do not expend any further marketing funds seeking to convert them into loyal customers.

Loyal customers are divided into *true friends* and *barnacles*. True friends are profitable customers who tend to purchase regularly, but not intensively, over time. A common error is that firms direct too much marketing effort towards this group such as frequent direct mailings or numerous contacts by the sales force. In many cases this is overkill and profitability can be increased by reducing the level of marketing activity.

Barnacles are the most problematic customers. They are loyal but their level of purchase relative to marketing funds expended means that no profit is generated from sales. What is required with this category is to determine whether the problem is a 'small wallet' (the customer has insufficient money to make them worth pursuing) or the firm is achieving a small share of the customer's wallet. The former group, once identified, should be removed from receiving any further marketing attention. The latter do have the potential to be converted into true believers if the firm can persuade them to increase their volume of purchase. Hence efforts should be expended on marketing campaigns designed either to increase purchase frequency or to persuade the customers to expand the breadth of their purchase portfolio. In the event that such efforts prove unsuccessful then the customers should be treated in the same way as the small wallet barnacle group.

DEFINING THE ROLE OF EMPLOYEES

Given that knowledge errors at either the buyer–seller interface and/or during the execution of the internal processes associated with service delivery can both impact customer satisfaction, there has been widespread debate on how best to define the role of employees within service sector organisations. In two classic articles, Levitt (1972, 1976) eloquently argued for the adoption of a manufacturing orientation in the management of services. He believed that this approach was required because it allowed for (a) simplification of tasks, (b) clear division of labour, (c) substitution of equipment and systems for employees and (d) minimal decision-making being required of the employees.

Many fast food chains demonstrate the validity of Levitt's proposals. To minimise the need to access and exploit new knowledge, operatives are taught how to greet the customer and ask for their order in a scripted way designed to suggest the purchase of additional items. To further minimise the need for additional knowledge, clearly defined procedures are laid down for assembling the order, placing them on the tray, positioning the tray on the counter and collecting the money. Meanwhile in the 'back room', other operatives are executing tasks, developed through the application of time and motion studies, designed rapidly and efficiently to produce food of uniform quality. The net result is that this production line approach permits the employees with only a limited level of knowledge to contribute to the operation an efficient, low cost, high volume food service business which concurrently also delivers customer satisfaction.

The concept of the industralisation of service operations has not been without its critics. Such individuals argue that the approach is dehumanising. Additionally it also results in an inability to respond to heterogeneous customer needs because employees are forced to respond to all situations by only using that knowledge which is contained within the rigid guidelines laid down in the organisation's operating policy manual. Zemke and Schaaf (1989) would argue that service excellence is more likely to be achieved by 'empowerment', which involves encouraging and rewarding employees to draw upon tacit or explicit knowledge to exhibit initiative and imagination. Similar views are expressed by Jan Carlzon (1987) the chief executive attributed with the successful turnaround of Scandinavian Airlines. His perspective on the exploitation of knowledge is contained in his statement that:

> to free someone from the rigorous control by instructions, policies and orders, and to give that person freedom to take responsibility for his ideas, decisions and actions, is to release hidden resources that would otherwise remain inaccessible to both the individuals and the organisation.

Bowen and Lawler (1992) have presented a somewhat more balanced view of the industrialisation versus employee empowerment service delivery debate. They point to the contrasting example of two very successful American firms in the international package delivery business, Federal Express and United Parcel Service (UPS). The Federal Express company motto of 'people, service and profits' is the foundation stone for an organisation built around self-managed teams and empowered employees using all available knowledge to be able to offer a flexible and creative service to customers with varying needs. In contrast UPS, with a philosophy of 'best service at low rates', uses controls, rules, a detailed union contract and rigidly defined operational guidelines to guarantee customers will receive a reliable, low cost service.

Bowen and Lawler posit that appropriateness of a service philosophy is a contingency issue; namely an industralisation or empowerment orientation will be dependent upon the market in which the firm operates, definition of corporate strategy and the influence of overall corporate culture on the selection of appropriate internal organisational processes. By building upon their views it is possible in Table 11.1 to define factors that may have influence over determining which are likely to be the most appropriate service products and delivery processes for achieving the goal of customer satisfaction.

TABLE 11.1   FACTORS INFLUENCING THE SERVICE STYLE DECISION

Factor	Industrial	Empowered
Customer orientation	Transactional	Relationship
Service product need	Standard solutions	New, innovative solutions
Business environment	Predictable, stable	Changing, unstable
Service delivery technology	Simple	Complex
Firm's closeness to customer	Low	High
Firm's service solution orientation	Established, well known	Applying new approaches
Average skills of workforce	Adequate for executing standard tasks	Capable of executing complex tasks
Managerial orientation	Directive	Delegators

Applying the factors of influence in Table 11.1 permits the suggestion that there are probably four alternative management styles which can be utilised by service organisations. These are:

1 **Conservative-transactional service organisations**, which operate in stable markets where the customer desires to obtain standard solutions without forming a close relationship with the provider. Required services can usually be delivered by a relatively unskilled workforce with minimal knowledge requirements and who do not have to resort to the use of complex technologies to access additional sources of knowledge (for example, a car wash business).

2 **Conservative-relationship service organisations**, which operate in changing markets where the customer seeks to form a close relationship with the provider as a way of obtaining service solutions modified to suit their specific needs. Customisation may demand employees use complex technologies to access additional knowledge and/or involve creative inputs from highly skilled knowledge workers (for example, a distributor of IBM-specification PCs which offers customised computer installation, maintenance and IT training services).

3 **Entrepreneurial-transactional service organisations**, which operate in rapidly changing markets where the customer, although facing unique problems demanding a completely new solution, does not wish to form a strong close relationship with any one, single provider. Solutions may demand application of complex technologies to access additional knowledge and/or involve creative inputs from highly skilled, specialist knowledge workers (for example, many of the major consulting firms which develop and then market concepts such as process re-engineering, which require carefully researched new approaches in order to be suitable in a client-specific situation).

4 **Entrepreneurial-relationship service organisations**, which operate in rapidly changing markets where the customer, seeking to resolve a unique

problem demanding a completely new solution, does so by forming a strong close relationships with a preferred service provider. Solutions will demand application of complex technologies to access additional knowledge and/or involve creative inputs from highly skilled, specialist knowledge workers engaging in a collaborative partnership with the client's own knowledge workers (for example, computer software designers developing new risk management systems for international financial institutions involved in global currency and/or share trading).

It is proposed that there are two empowerment dimensions associated with these four alternative styles. One dimension is the degree to which employees are empowered to use knowledge to revise the nature of the service delivery process. The other dimension is the degree to which employees are empowered to exploit knowledge in the formulation of totally new forms of service. In the case of the conservative-transactional firm, employees are permitted little freedom to modify either the form of service or the service delivery process. Customers of conservative-relationship firms are usually interested in the service providers optimising the service delivery process by being prepared to exploit knowledge to customise some aspects of what essentially is a standardised service. For example, a delivery service willing to modify the routing of its transportation fleet to ensure successful delivery of urgently needed spare parts to a remote location. Thus to achieve this goal, the service provider employees should be permitted to seek out and exploit sources of knowledge that can assist in the resolution of any problems which might be encountered.

Entrepreneurial-transactional firms have clients who face a major problem, resolution of which will probably require a new, radical approach. This can only be achieved if the provider is willing to delegate authority to its employees who are charged with using knowledge to develop an appropriately innovative solution. As most contracts of this type contain fixed penalties for failure, the provider will, however, demand that staff adhere to clearly defined guidelines concerning all aspects of the project management process. This can be contrasted with the situations often confronting the entrepreneurial-relationship service firm. Here the client and the provider both fully realise that collaborative 'blue sky' thinking by each other's employees is probably the only route to evolving a feasible solution. Hence the provider will seek to instil an attitude of employee empowerment in relation to the use of knowledge to assist both the generation, and delivery, of the most effective service solution which can be developed in the time available.

NEW ORGANISATIONAL FORMS

In an excellent review of the myths surrounding the management of services, Zeithmal and Bitner (1996) have proposed that, contrary to popular belief, it is feasible simultaneously to deliver lower cost outputs while maximising personalisation and customisation of customer services. Achievement of these joint goals, however, demands the creative use of available knowledge, leading edge technologies and acceptance of new organisational configurations.

Quinn and Parquette (1990) argue it is merely strategic dogma that causes conflicts to exist between low cost and high flexibility in service sector scenarios. In their view the secret lies in (a) designing knowledge systems as microunits located close to the customer (for example, the insurance advisor using a laptop-based project costing system to execute an on-site review of a manufacturing firm's needs for coverage appropriate to current trading circumstances) and (b) using technology to permit inexperienced people to access the knowledge required to perform very sophisticated tasks (for example, front-line staff in a travel agency using on-line reservations systems to create complex, customised holiday packages). In the process of achieving these goals, the organisation will probably recognise that new organisational forms are now demanded in order to optimise employees' use of knowledge to optimise productivity.

Computer-based information systems appear to mean that there is virtually no limit to the span of control between supervisor and operatives. This means that service organisations can safely consider moving to create 'infinitely flat' organisations in which authority is delegated to the lowest possible level and all employees are empowered to use available knowledge to make the best possible decision to satisfy changing customer needs. Federal Express, for example, has over 42,000 employees in more than 300 cities worldwide, but has a maximum of only five organisational layers between operatives and senior management. Optimisation of service provision activities is achieved by permitting all employees to have access to the organisation's DADS and COSMOS computerised MIS.

As large international organisations such as accounting and consultancy firms offering complex client-specific services act to sustain localised customer contact by opening offices around the world, the problems of updating staff knowledge about the latest technological advances, and thereby sustaining leading edge service quality, becomes an ever increasing problem. Fortunately the advent of technologies such as Lotus Notes and video conferencing has permitted these organisations to reorientate themselves into networked structures which use electronic media to ensure the dispersed nodes of the service operation can continually access knowledge held at other office locations. Quinn and Parquette (1990) have, for example, described the structure of a leading consulting firm which used the latest available technology to link together its 40,000 staff in over 200 different countries. One of the major benefits of this system is that an individual facing a difficult client problem can now use the organisation's electronic bulletin board to discover if anybody elsewhere in the world may have already evolved an effective solution.

Process Implementation

12

CHAPTER SUMMARY

Firms must optimise new and existing knowledge exploitation if they wish to remain successful. The advent of IT and web-based technologies has greatly improved knowledge acquisition and distribution processes. Culture can be a barrier. Typical culture problems are lack of trust and an unwillingness to accept new knowledge. Some firms decide they need to access additional sources of knowledge and therefore enter into strategic alliances with other organisations. Again trust is a critical issue in determining the success of alliances. There are different forms of alliances ranging from very informal through to highly formalised. There may be equality in the alliance or one partner may be more dominant. If effective the alliance will permit all parties faster access to new knowledge that can contribute towards significantly enhancing market performance.

INTRODUCTION

Seeking to manage knowledge within the marketing operation to enhance organisational performance usually evolves as a three phase process (Foote et al. 2001). In the first phase the organisation recognises that knowledge exists within one employee group which, if shared with others, can contribute towards improving current marketing operations. For example, the sales force may be aware of the factors which influence customers' service quality expectations. By sharing this knowledge with other departments actions can be taken to reduce the occurrence of incidents which cause customer dissatisfaction.

The next phase of knowledge exploitation is where knowledge is used to expand the marketing operation by entering new markets or acquiring new customers. In this situation lessons about the causes of current success are codified and examined to determine how this knowledge can be used to exploit new sources of opportunity. Thus, for example, a consultancy business can review management of existing client projects as the basis for defining how acquired competencies can provide the basis for pursuing new clients.

The third phase is to recognise that knowledge management can represent an entirely new value proposition for customers. A business might, for instance, decide to offer previously internal knowledge as part of the product proposition. The World Bank, for example, used primarily to provide financial resources to developing countries. During these activities a vast pool of knowledge was accumulated about economic development. This is now made available to governments in developing nations to assist them more effectively to manage their economic development programmes.

Progressing the organisation from using knowledge to upgrade current operations to the point where knowledge is the source of new value propositions is not a simple process. Armbrecht et al. (2001) have examined a wide range of different initiatives and from this have synthesised the *six imperatives*. These are as follows:

1 Instil across the entire organisation the message that the exploitation of knowledge is fundamental to the achievement of all goals and strategies.
2 Seek out mechanisms that enhance access to tacit knowledge which resides in the minds of the employees and work teams. Techniques can include IT collaboration tools, training, seminars and creation of communities or practice. The aim is to 'know what we know' and 'use what we know'.
3 Develop search and retrieval tools to acquire internal and external information. The advent of the internet and related technologies has greatly simplified this process because repositories of information can be rapidly searched and knowledge retrieved almost instantaneously.
4 Promote the importance of bringing creative thinking into the problem resolution process. Place emphasis on providing employees with a proportion of work time that can be allocated to the pursuit of new directions and the development of new ideas.
5 Ensure that new tacit and explicit learning is captured in order that it can be reused. Techniques that can be used include training of other employees, mentoring, formal documentation and evaluation of both successful and unsuccessful projects.
6 Create a culture which is supportive of the idea of maximising the degree to which employees seek and share knowledge. Promote the philosophy of active collaboration between employees and identify mechanisms for rewarding those who are clearly committed to the exploitation of knowledge in the fulfilment of their assigned job roles.

236

KNOWLEDGE INTO ACTION

Heineken USA, in seeking to become a more competitive force in the US beer industry, took the decision in 2001 to integrate technological knowledge, consumer research and business analysis to evolve an approach that 'turns knowledge into action' (Chase 2001). The organisation perceives knowledge management as a three step process, namely:

1 Create, collect, manage and disseminate information.
2 Turn information into actionable knowledge.
3 Transfer that knowledge to key decision makers, resulting in increased sales.

Fundamental in the process has been a move to improve the way information is collected by the creation of enhanced data management systems. In order that non-technical people can use this information the company has made available enterprise-wide decision support tools. To optimise these activities, various new information channels have been accessed to acquire more data. Knowledge is created by combining fact-based analysis with customer and employee information and experiences. To implement this strategy the company took advantage of web-enabled technology and enterprise data warehousing software to simplify and integrate its internal and external information structures.

Making the knowledge management vision happen is seen as a four phase project which will take five years to complete. The four phases are starting, consolidating, embedding and supporting. Various activities were associated with phase one. These included gaining senior management commitment to the programme, acquiring an appropriate technology infrastructure, activating B2B and B2Bemployee portals, automating the annual planning system, merging data services and providing actionable knowledge to groups such as the sales department, marketing and senior management. In order to implement these actions two new departments were created: content management and business analysis.

During phase two, Heineken will focus on broadening the scope of its knowledge management activities. This will involve encouraging both internal and external stakeholders to participate in the process of capturing and exploiting knowledge. To support this phase new software applications and tools will be introduced that can facilitate knowledge sharing and learning.

In phase three the aim is to gain a better understanding of how customer behaviour and key market drivers influence business performance. To achieve this aim respondent-level consumer research will be transferred to the enterprise data warehouse. Business intelligence tools will be introduced to expand the quantity and level of market analysis undertaken by the company. Simulation tools will also be introduced that will permit brand teams and sales personnel to develop additional strategic planning capabilities. Systems will also be evolved more effectively to capture trade account-specific data as a path through which to upgrade channel management activities. Once these activities are complete, the final phase will be to align knowledge management practices more formally with the firm's overall corporate strategy and core values.

Heineken will use a number of metrics to measure the success of the project. One metric will be the speed with which information is made more accessible. Another metric is ensuring greater retention of expertise and more effective frontline decision-making capabilities that facilitate collaboration between employees, customers and business partners. The overarching metric is that the investment in knowledge management is reflected in increased beer sales and higher profitability.

KNOWLEDGE MANAGEMENT ARCHITECTURE

For the organisation to remain competitive requires that processes exist to create, locate, capture and share knowledge to solve problems and exploit opportunities. This is not a simple goal because in most organisations knowledge is fragmented, difficult to locate and rarely shared (Zack 1999). There is also the issue that knowledge often exists mainly in a tacit form which is subconsciously understood by the individual but is difficult to articulate. Under these circumstances sharing tends to occur only as a result of informal processes such as conversation and storytelling.

To become widely shared and exploited within the organisation knowledge usually has to be made available in an explicit form. Hence to maximise the availability of explicit knowledge across the organisation will require actions that explicate tacit knowledge such that it can be efficiently and meaningfully shared. A failure to explicate critical knowledge can cause the organisation to miss an opportunity to evolve new forms of competitive advantage.

Once the organisation has made the decision to maximise the availability of explicit knowledge, four primary resources will need to be established, namely:

1 Repositories of explicit knowledge.
2 Refineries for accumulating, managing and distributing knowledge.
3 Definition of management knowledge roles.
4 Creation of IT systems to support the storage and distribution of knowledge.

Within the repositories, the basic structural component is the knowledge unit. This is a formally defined collection of knowledge that can be labelled, indexed, stored and retrieved. The format, size and content of knowledge units can be expected to vary dramatically. What is critical, however, is that the repository structure has systems for linking and cross-referencing the knowledge which has been stored.

The knowledge refinery process involves both the creation and distribution of knowledge contained within repositories. Before adding new knowledge to a repository it will require cleansing, labelling, indexing, sorting, abstracting, standardising, integrating and categorisation. Linkages between potential users and the repository will need to be constructed to support knowledge distribution across the organisation.

As knowledge has become recognised as a critical corporate asset, some organisations have established the role of a chief knowledge officer to manage the knowledge distribution process. These individuals are responsible for championing knowledge management, educating the organisation, mapping knowledge and ensuring all knowledge is integrated into the architecture of the organisation. Other organisations have opted to cluster knowledge into expertise centres. Each centre is allocated the responsibility for managing a particular body of knowledge. As the number of centres increases it is often the case that an individual is assigned the role of ensuring all centres are fulfilling their responsibilities for offering a knowledge provision service across the organisation.

Capturing knowledge and storing it in a searchable form which permits multiple usage has been greatly assisted by using IT. For example, the internet and groupware can permit a firm to build a multimedia repository of rich, explicit knowledge. It is necessary to recognise, however, that knowledge communication systems must be reflective of the communicative skills of the users. Where communicators share similar knowledge then total reliance can be placed on completely electronically mediated systems such as groupware. However, where communicators share only a moderate level of common understanding, more interactive communication channels such as e-mails or discussion databases may be more appropriate. In those situations where communicators have very limited common knowledge and knowledge is primarily in a tacit form, then sharing is possibly best achieved through meetings, face-to-face conversations or video conferencing.

KNOWLEDGE PROCESSING

Zack (1999) has proposed that knowledge processing can be categorised into two main classes: integrative and interactive. *Integrative applications* exhibit a sequential flow of explicit knowledge in and out of a repository. Producers and users interact with the repository rather than with each other. Thus the repository becomes the primary vehicle for knowledge exchange.

Some integrative applications may contain very stable knowledge which once created requires very few updates. An example of this type of repository could be an on-line database created by the HRM department which specifies the procedures for implementing a grievance procedure against a superior. Other integrative applications although still exhibiting a sequential flow may permit users to add their personal experience to the system thereby building a repository of collective knowledge. For example, a group of sales engineers may use a best-practice database to share their experiences of solving common technical problems that they have encountered while servicing the company's products in the field.

The integrative database requires knowledge creators, finders and collectors. Capturing orally conveyed knowledge also demands the use of interviewers and transcribers. Knowledge refining will involve analysts, classifiers and editors. Somebody must be assigned the overall responsibility for managing the database and take responsibility for knowledge distribution.

Interactive applications usually focus upon supporting interaction between people with tacit knowledge. Thus the repository is a by-product of interaction and collaboration rather than the primary focus of the application. Content is dynamic and emergent. A common form of an interactive repository is an electronic discussion space where people can search for help or advertise their expertise. As participants interact they contribute towards the accumulation of experiences. If somebody then accepts an editorial role by applying appropriate structuring and indexing of content a repository emerges which can be searched by others seeking to reapply the accumulated knowledge.

The Buckman Knowledge Forum

Buckman Laboratories is a $300 million international speciality company which seeks to build market share not from selling products but by solving customers' chemical treatment problems (Zack 1999). Selling and applying Buckman products requires practical field experience in solving customer problems. This knowledge is tacit, residing with the field staff across the world. Field-based knowledge is complex, having to handle many interacting variables and may be specific to a geographic area, customer plant or a specific machine.

To ensure this knowledge is captured and shared the company has created the Buckman Knowledge Network, K'Netix. The system is founded on several key principles. One is the importance of direct exchange of information among employees. Another is the universal, unconstrained ability to gain access to and to contribute to the firm's knowledge. The company has already placed much of its explicit knowledge about customers, products and technologies into on-line repositories. By the creation of the Tech Forum the company is able to capture and distribute the applied knowledge and experiences of all employees. The forum uses a standard structure, comments are threaded in conversational sequence and indexed by topic, author and date. The content typically comprises questions, responses and field observations.

The company has established a knowledge transfer department within which subject experts take the lead in guiding discussions and providing quality assurance on the advice given by others. The experts working with the knowledge transfer department

---

periodically review the Tech Forum to identify threads. The threads are extracted, edited, summarised and assigned key words. Individuals such as product development managers can then use the forum to offer on-line technical advice to field staff as well as to gain insights into the latest problems confronting customers.

MANAGING CULTURE

De Long and Fahey's (2000) research suggests that knowledge management and the culture of the organisation are inextricably linked. *Organisational culture* consists of the tacit preferences or values that are embedded into the organisation. The values which exist are difficult to articulate but are reflected in the behaviour of the employees. Norms which are derived from values are beliefs held by the majority of the workforce. The other aspect of culture is the accepted practices within the organisation. These are reflected in wide understanding of repetitive behaviours such as completing reports, following documented work procedures.

Culture heavily influences perceptions about what is considered important or valid knowledge. For example, an accounting firm may give priority to financial management knowledge whereas a manufacturing firm may consider engineering knowledge is the most critical asset within the organisation. Hence in the latter case a management initiative to create and share knowledge about improving cost controls may face the barrier that the prevailing culture could mean that employees do not perceive the accumulation of financial knowledge as very important in terms of fulfilling their job role.

Within organisations one often encounters variation in culture between groups and/or departments. This variation reflects the existence of *subcultures*. For example, manufacturing values may focus on efficiency and productivity. In contrast marketing and sales may have values which are orientated towards maximising customer satisfaction. Such a difference in subculture can create conflict because the two departments will probably place different values on knowledge concerning optimising manufacturing processes versus knowledge about the effectiveness of the organisation in serving the downstream needs of customers. To overcome such conflict the two departments would need to develop a shared understanding about why both areas of knowledge should be given priority in seeking to achieve convergence between optimising manufacturing operations and ensuring satisfaction of customer needs.

Culture can influence how knowledge is distributed between individuals and the organisation of which they are a member. It is not unusual that the prevailing culture encourages people to seek to retain control of the knowledge to which they have access. This orientation would be an obstacle where management is seeking to improve knowledge distribution by the creation of common databases. This is because the prevailing culture would mean employees would tend to keep knowledge to themselves and not wish to contribute information to the databases being constructed. Two factors which commonly cause this situation to exist are lack of trust and variation in status between units within the organisation.

In those cases where there is a low level of trust between employees or departments the level of knowledge sharing will be greatly impeded. Thus if the marketing department has a practice of publicising errors made by the sales force then this latter group is likely to restrict the information which it will share with marketing staff. Similarly, the same situation will exist if certain individuals or departments are perceived to be more highly valued by management than others.

The degree to which prevailing culture supports social interaction will also influence the level of knowledge sharing within the organisation. Collaboration and knowledge sharing can be expected to be much higher in an organisation which actively promotes social interaction between employees than one which does not. The impact of social interaction should be assessed in relation to both vertical and horizontal interactions. In the case of *vertical interaction*, the scale of social interaction between subordinates and their superiors will influence in the degree to which sub-ordinates are willing to raise sensitive issues during knowledge exchange. In low trust cultures superiors will be perceived as non-approachable and knowledge sharing will be extremely limited.

In the case of *horizontal interaction* between employees culture will influence the degree to which interaction is perceived as necessary for individuals to fulfil their assigned work roles. The nature of this inter-action may be highly formalised using activities such as meetings to bring individuals together or it may be based around unstructured interactions between employees. In theory the advent of the internet and other elec-tronic technologies has assisted the degree to which employees interact horizontally. In practice, however, if the prevailing culture is orientated towards low levels of interaction, then these new technologies will not be utilised by staff.

Another aspect of horizontal interaction is the degree to which the pre-vailing culture is supportive of collaboration. In those organisations where the management of customer needs is perceived as a marketing or sales responsibility, minimal collaboration between departments can be expected to occur. Whereas in those organisations committed to serving the customer, high levels of departmental collaboration will occur with employees shar-ing knowledge with the aim of ensuring customer needs are fully satisfied.

Ultimately a firm's culture is heavily shaped by the way new know-ledge about the external environment is created, accepted and distributed across the organisation. Firms which adopt new external knowledge and rapidly utilise this source to change strategic direction or redefine internal resource allocation can be expected to outperform their competitors. De

Long and Fahey (2000) suggest there are a number of characteristics that are exhibited by firms which are effective exploiters of new external knowledge.

One characteristic is the assumption that new external knowledge can provide the starting point for stimulating innovation. Successful firms place emphasis on reviewing new knowledge, determining the relevance to the organisation and then specifying actions to exploit this source of opportunity. Another characteristic is that innovation rarely occurs unless the prevailing culture is supportive of using new knowledge to stimulate wide ranging debate by employees about the strategic or operational implications of the opportunities offered by the newly acquired knowledge.

Wide ranging debate between employees will only be productive if the culture also permits employees to challenge existing assumptions and beliefs which have shaped the firm's previous activities. Questioning fundamental beliefs and current work practices is often a challenge for managers. The organisation must have a culture which permits the use of new knowledge to question the validity of existing strategic and operational assumptions. Without such a culture new ideas will be rejected and the organisation will be unable to implement the changes needed to respond to newly emerging market opportunities.

STRATEGIC ALLIANCES

Traditionally large firms which have been successful in one country have sought to expand sales further by entering overseas markets. During the twentieth century this trend has seen the creation of multinational corporations (MNCs) across sectors such as electronics, cars, banking and insurance. Since the 1980s, the increasing importance of firms being able to participate in the global economy and concurrently respond to the fast pace of technological change has raised questions about the relative efficiency and effectiveness of individual firms' abilities to facilitate the flow of cross-border organisational knowledge between their operations located in various parts of the world. One way some firms have sought to overcome this problem is through the formation of co-operative relationships (or strategic alliances) as a knowledge exchange mechanism which can provide the basis for acquiring or sustaining competitive strategic advantage in world markets.

Companies entering into global alliances are attempting to divide the activities of a value chain on a worldwide basis with one or more partners (Chonko 1999). There are a number of potential benefits which can accrue from the alliance. One of the partners in the alliance may already be located in a marketplace, thereby providing another partner with the opportunity of entering into that market by exploiting an existing distribution management system. Both partners will be able to exchange knowledge that has already been learned, resulting in the need for less primary data collection and more rapid understanding of new business opportunities. An alliance may permit one partner to offset its areas of operational weakness by taking advantage of another partner's strengths. As not all companies have equal capability in the area of technological competence the alliance may offer opportunities to develop technological synergies between the participants.

Early theories concerning strategic alliances used a transaction cost rationale to explain the interaction between firms. The emphasis in transaction cost theory is upon seeking to minimise costs. Thus, for example, a television manufacturer facing high production costs might decide to shift manufacturing operations off-shore by entering into a strategic alliance with a manufacturer based in another country where labour costs are lower. Das and Teng (2000) have suggested, however, that because in many alliances participants are seeking to achieve value maximisation through the pooling of resources, then it would be more appropriate to consider strategic alliances by adopting a resource-based theory approach. One of their reasons for adopting this view is that there are two distinct motives for entering an alliance, namely to acquire another's resources and to retain and develop one's own resources.

In terms of acquiring resources, alliances are often superior to mergers or purchasing another firm because in alliance one avoids becoming the owner of resources which are undesirable or redundant to needs. This is due to the fact that in the case of alliances, the participants can concentrate completely on the exchange of resources which are of value to each of the partners. In relation to retaining resources one of the partners may have under-utilised resources such as manufacturing capacity or R & D personnel which can be allocated to the alliance. In this way the firm temporarily relinquishes resources which then remain available for future internal deployment. Alternatively allocation of staff to the alliance may permit these employees to acquire knowledge and skills which can be of benefit during the firm's implementation of new projects in the future.

In terms of resources utilised in an alliance, Miller and Shamsie (1996) propose these can be classified into two broad categories. *Property-based resources* are legal properties owned by firms which include financial capital, physical resources and human resources. The firm enjoys clear property rights to these resources and their use is under the control of the firm because they can be controlled by mechanisms such as contracts and patents. *Knowledge-based resources* consist of the intangible know-how and skills which exist within the organisation. Copying this type of resource is difficult because they are vague and ambiguous. Nevertheless the firm is rarely in a position to create legal forms of protection to prevent such resources being transferred by actions such as the departure of staff to a competitor.

The Avon–Mattel Alliance

In 1997 Avon and Mattel began a series of joint marketing initiatives (Chonko 1999). Among the joint initiatives was the involvement of Avon in the selling of new Barbie dolls in the United States and the international marketing of a line of Barbie Registered Trademark cosmetics. Avon was also provided with two exclusive Barbie Registered Trademark dolls that would only be made available through the Avon direct sales force. The alliance can be characterised as a product opportunity for Avon and a promotional alliance for Mattell. Both companies are gaining the benefit of a larger scale of operation through the pooling of resources. Mattell brings well known brands to the alliance and Avon provides access to a global distribution network.

Chonko proposes that the two companies exhibit certain characteristics which are critical to a successful global alliance. Firstly, both firms have already formulated a global vision for their operations which can be articulated to their partner within the relationship. Secondly, both firms have managers who are experienced in international operations which means that obstacles created by a lack of joint understanding of issues can be avoided. Thirdly, both firms have developed strong international business networks which means they have already developed effective relationships with other members of the value chain around the world such as suppliers and distributors. Fourthly, both parties can bring a unique capability to the relationship. In the case of Avon this a high performance sales force and with Mattell it is a capability to manage branded product lines.

Global Airfreight by Alliance

One of the fastest growing areas of business in the transportation industry is the provision of airfreight services (Morton 2002). The problem facing major airlines, however, is that they only fly a limited number of routes but customers expect a 'one stop shop' global coverage service. The solution is for airlines to form alliances. One such alliance is Sky Team which has six members: AeroMexico, Air France, Alitalia, Czech Airlines, Delta and Korean Air.

To achieve success the members have accepted a common policy in relation to the knowledge issues of:

1 Ensuring that all parties offer exactly the same product line.
2 Merging the sales structure such that a common form of customer–supplier interface is encountered by the customer at all points around the globe.
3 Integrating warehousing and ground operations to ensure smooth connectivity as freight is transferred from one airline to another.

Another airfreight alliance is WOW whose members include Lufthansa, Japan Airlines, SAS and Singapore Airlines. As creator of the alliance Lufthansa has sought to use its extensive knowledge to develop products which differentiate it from the competition. By sharing this knowledge with the partners this ensures that customers can access the differentiated product across the world. One such example is the development of service package solutions tailored to the needs of specific industry sectors. Cool, Ltd is a service package for temperature sensitive shipments such as medications and pharmaceutical products. This package has achieved widespread adoption as the standard distribution solution for multinational drugs and biotechnology companies.

ALLIANCE STRUCTURES

Equity joint ventures are created when partners wish to closely integrate their efforts. This structure offers the best opportunity for accessing each other's tacit knowledge because of the close working relationship which emerges between employees. This type of joint venture can significantly facilitate interfirm transfer of technologies. Under these circumstances some firms will be wary of the structure because of the risk of giving away their knowledge-based resources to their partners. This may cause them to prefer the structure if knowledge-based resources are not their primary resource type in the alliance. They tend to prefer contributing property-based resources because these are legally protected as property rights.

In minor equity alliances one or more partner takes an equity position in others. The complicated nature of equity investments will usually mean this type of structure will only be considered if the alliance is expected to last over a long timeframe. The investing firm normally intends to contribute knowledge-based resources to the alliance and its partners will provide property-based resources. The assumption is that by holding an equity stake, the knowledge resource provider will be protected from partners attempting to act opportunistically by misusing the knowledge to which they have been granted access.

As equity joint ventures facilitate the process of transferring knowledge-based resources, they can be a disadvantage if the partners both have substantial knowledge-based resources in the alliance. The concern is that partners may find tacit knowledge is being appropriated by the other partner. In that sense equity joint ventures' loss of critical tacit knowledge may be too high a price to pay for learning about other partners' know-how. In this situation the alliance will usually be of a contractual nature. Once created the partners may perceive they have entered into a learning race with both parties believing that they can win. Once one party perceives it has reached this position then it is common for it to decide the contract should be terminated.

Where both partners intend to contribute property-based resources to an alliance then it is usual that a *unilateral contract-based alliance* will be established. The types of property resources which might be exchanged include capital, distribution channels, patents and copyrights. Hence unilateral contracts are often used in alliances associated with licensing or subcontracting. Neither firm will be very interested in attempting to acquire the other's tacit knowledge.

In those cases where the partners' objective is one of mutual learning involving the transfer of knowledge over a defined timeframe then some form of *bilateral contract-based alliance* will be established. Unlike unilateral contracts, bilateral contracts require partners to put in resources and work together on a continuing basis. Examples of bilateral contracts include joint production, joint marketing and joint promotional activities. Managers must recognise, however, that the closeness of the relationship does mean that it will difficult to prevent some transfer of critical tacit knowledge between the participant organisations.

LEARNING WITHIN AN ALLIANCE

Although there is a tendency in literature to focus on how partners learn specific skills from each other, Tsang (1999) proposes that in practice the learning process is much broader. He suggests that another dimension of learning is in acquiring the capability to optimise the performance of the specific alliance and the generic capability to perform more effectively in any future alliances. Case evidence tends to suggest that the experience of firms within an alliance is reflected over time by the participants becoming more effective managers of the relationship in terms of developing partner rapport and understanding the life cycle of a project.

If an alliance takes a firm to an industry or country other than its own, the firm will also learn how to operate in a new environment. For example, when entering a new country the firm will have to learn how to deal with government bodies, regulations, building connections within the supply chain and adjusting products to suit local tastes. In this situation, the firm's partner will be a source of knowledge that can assist the rapidity of the learning process.

If both partners have the same objective of learning in relation to the alliance experience, the resultant pattern is known as *symmetrical learning*. Where different learning objectives exist, the pattern is *asymmetrical learning*. This latter pattern is typical in those cases where a firm from a developed nation uses an alliance with a local firm to enter a developing country. There is usually a large gap in the technical competence of the two partners. The objective of the firm from the developed nation is to learn how to operate in a developing country. This contrasts with the in-country partner who is usually seeking to learn about new technologies.

There are certain risks with asymmetrical learning. From the viewpoint of the firm from the developed nation there is the risk of unintended knowledge flows to the local firm which may permit the latter to become a competitor in the future. A number of Western nation firms, for example, have encountered the problem in China that over time their local partner begins to exploit acquired technological knowledge to produce products that are in direct competition with their foreign partner's product line. From the viewpoint of the developing nation partner, there is the risk that its foreign partner will exaggerate the value of the knowledge which it is making available. As a result it may pay too high a price to acquire the technology which is on offer. Another risk for the developing nation partner is that the firm lacks the absorptive capacity to be able learn effectively from the alliance. This is not an unusual scenario when the developing nation firm enters into an alliance which is outside the firm's core business activities.

In the case of symmetrical learning the process may involve either non-mutual or interparty learning. With *non-mutual learning* although the partners have the same learning objective for the alliance, they do not learn from each other. This could occur, for example, in a joint venture between two partners seeking to enter an overseas market. Neither partner possesses technological skills of interest to the other. They have come together because they wish to share the risk and costs associated with involvement in international marketing activities. Such alliances are often formed for reasons other than seeking to learn. As a result learning will tend to be experiential with partners adopting a somewhat passive attitude towards any learning opportunities.

In contrast with *interpartner learning* each partner is seeking to learn from the other. Usually desired knowledge is in a tacit form which means to acquire it will necessitate close observation and interaction with employees from the parent organisation. This type of learning can be subdivided into competitive and non-competitive learning. In the case of *competitive learning* the partners are competitors in relation to products and target customers (for example, the alliance between IBM and Apple). Under these circumstances a race to learn can emerge. The company which is able most rapidly to internalise the knowledge of the other partner will tend to dominate the relationship and over time will gain a competitive advantage over its partner. Not surprisingly the level of trust in competitive learning situations can remain very low and this will act as a barrier to the effective transfer of knowledge between the participants.

On the other hand, in *non-competitive learning* the partners are not usually in direct competition and have no intention of becoming direct competitors in the foreseeable future. In this situation there will be no race to acquire knowledge and the probable outcome is that both parties gain significantly from the relationship. This is because the perceived absence of competition permits a high degree of trust to develop between the partners. Both parties will perceive there are strong benefits from collaboration and knowledge transfer will probably be much higher than that which occurs in a competitive learning situation.

Interorganisational learning can be achieved by the transfer of existing knowledge from one firm to another and by the creation of completely new knowledge as a result of interaction between participants within an alliance. Both transfer and knowledge creation requires all partners to simultaneously exhibit transparency and receptivity (Larsson et al. 1998). Transparency is the willingness of a firm to be prepared openly to disclose knowledge. Receptivity is the ability of a firm to absorb knowledge which has been disclosed.

Transparency is somewhat more difficult than merely a willingness to make knowledge available. In many cases critical knowledge may be in a tacit form, thereby creating difficulties when attempting to make the knowledge available to the other partner. Transparency may also be restricted by social constructs such as different languages, customs and traditions. Such variables can create communications barriers between partners from different countries which then limits the ability of firms to learn from each other.

The level of receptivity within a firm can be influenced by a number of factors (Hamal 1991). Due to capacity problems, the organisation may not have the ability to make employees available to participate in the learning process. A problem can occur if the disclosed knowledge is quite unrelated to the previous knowledge of the organisation. In this situation the disclosed knowledge will make little sense to the recipient firm because the latter does not share the experience of the context in which the knowledge was originally created. Receptivity will also be limited by the intent of the firm to learn. If the organisation lacks the motivation to receive knowledge due to disinterest, neglect of employees or greater priority given to other issues, then very little learning can be expected to occur.

EVOLVING THE ALLIANCE

The Union Steamship Company of New Zealand (USSCo) and Win. Holyman & Sons Ltd were both shipping firms which grew out of the early opportunities associated with the gold rush years of the late nineteenth century (Boyce and Lepper 2002). Both prospered by the provision of services to the communities of Tasmania, Australia, and by operating services across the Tasman Sea between Australia and New Zealand.

By the early twentieth century the level of competition between shipping lines in the area had become intense. To overcome this problem USSCo sought to forge a joint venture relationship with Holyman. To ensure creation of a successful agreement, USSCo needed in-depth knowledge of the Holyman operations. This they achieved by identifying individuals who had strong influence over Holyman. One such example was a local shipping agent, Ellerker. Other sources included members of the firms' mutual business networks such as bankers. From this analysis USSCo was in a position to determine that the joint venture would be with a firm with a successful track record, sound credit rating and effectively managed. The joint venture which emerged operated from 1910 through to 1976.

A critical factor in the success of the alliance is that over time both parties developed a deep sense of trust in each other and could be confidant that knowledge exchange was always open and honest. To ensure transparency in communications, the firms created performance standards defined by contracts and supported by sets of procedures that ensured compliance with these standards. These systems were a critical foundation stone in building trust and co-operation between the partners.

To curb opportunistic behaviour both parties agreed to the creation of a post-contractual review process. This system was utilised to provide knowledge about whether any contractual breaches had occurred and to identify the nature of financial compensation to be paid to the disadvantaged partner. A critical component of this system was an open bookkeeping process whereby everybody had access to each others' monthly earnings and disbursements. This was underpinned by half yearly audits of the partners' accounts.

Just as critical as trust and co-operation was the provision of soft information. This was achieved by branch managers across the two companies openly exchanging information about their respective trading activities. Managers were also encouraged to share ideas about ways of improving procedures and identifying new business opportunities. The head offices of both companies recognised that failure to delegate decisions could interfere with effective relationships developing at the branch management level. Hence both companies agreed on a common system whereby branch managers delegated authority to make business deals with each other without having to wait for prior approval from head office.

A common culture is seen as critical to the success of the alliance. One aspect of culture was the empowerment of branch managers. Secondly, all employees were conditioned to expect that others would behave according to commonly observed norms. Thirdly, the level of financial commitment by the partners to the joint venture was a signal of shared objectives based upon mutual trust and confidence.

The other key factor was the volume of knowledge exchange between the two companies. On average a formal exchange between USSCo in Dunedin, New Zealand, and Holyman in Sydney, Australia, occurred every second day. On average each communication consisted of 232 words covering a diversity of issues from HRM matters through to detailed financial analysis. The cost effectiveness of this system is reflected in the fact that all forms of communication interfaces such as letters and cables cost the venture less than 0.5% of all operating expenses.

BARRIERS TO ALLIANCE SUCCESS

Although global strategic alliances can offer many benefits to participants, it is necessary to recognise that bringing firms together from different parts of the world does mean that a number of potential barriers exist which can frustrate effective knowledge exchange (Parkhe 1991). One of the most obvious potential barriers is that employees' values and behaviours are influenced by the society of which they are members. Societal culture can, for example, result in differences in the partners' approaches to problem solving and conflict resolution. In some cultures problems are actively solved and managers must take deliberate actions to influence their environment. In other cultures life is seen as a series of preordained situations that are fatalistically accepted. Similarly in some cultures conflict is seen as healthy, natural and an inevitable part of relationships inside the organisation. This contrasts with other cultures where vigorous conflict and open confrontation are deemed distasteful. Embarrassment and loss of face to either party must be avoided at all costs by talking indirectly and ambiguously until common ground can be found. Thus given the cultural differences which exist around the world, if an international alliance is to be successful at knowledge exchange employees from the partner organisations must develop a high degree of understanding of intercultural differences and be prepared to modify their behaviour to suit the cultural environment in which they are operating.

In addition to the influence of societal culture, the behaviour of employees will be influenced by the corporate culture of the organisation of which they are a part. Where there are differences in corporate cultures exhibited by partners, this can create problems within the alliance. For example, one partner may have a culture that is investor orientated, which places emphasis on quarterly earnings reports and overall financial performance. This would create friction in an alliance where the other partner is marketing orientated and feels the issues of priority should be achievement of market share and the management of distribution channels. To overcome these differences there would need to be a meshing of the two cultures with employees from each partner making an effort to learn the ideologies and values of their counterparts. This can usually be achieved by high levels of socialisation which can permit the employees concerned with alliance operations to find common areas of agreement that can lead to the development of an intermediate corporate culture acceptable to all within the operation.

Strategy determines the goals, objectives and breadth of actions available to an organisation. It is possible that partners may have different strategies which could cause conflicts in relation to issues of speed of response and future marketing plans. In order to overcome such strategic incompatibility, the partners will need to build flexibility into the partnership structure which permits them to adjust their attitude towards responding to changes in their internal and external environments. One of the most effective ways of developing such flexibility is by initiating the alliance on a small scale basis related to the resolution of a specific short term problem. Knowledge transfer during this first project can then provide the foundation for the partners to learn how to modify their respective strategic orientations and adopt a more compatible attitude in the execution of longer term, larger scale alliance activities.

Due to factors such as societal culture, corporate culture and strategic orientation, partner firms may utilise very different management practices. Among the differences that may exist are style of management (participatory or authoritarian), decision making (centralised versus decentralised) and the degree of reliance upon the use of formal planning and control systems. These dimensions of interfirm diversity can be so major that they can force the dissolution of the alliance. Probably the most effective way of avoiding the problem is for the partners to reach agreement on the nature of the management practices to be adopted within the alliance operation and to grant employees within the alliance full autonomy over ongoing decisions concerning management processes and organisational structure.

Problems with Systems

Led by United Airlines, Star Alliance is a consortium of major airlines seeking to deliver a truly global service to customers (McDonald 2000). However, in the early years of the alliance members encountered real problems over the fact that their computer systems were incompatible. For example, a United Airlines employee when dealing with a Brazilian Airlines frequent flyer customer had no way of knowing the number of air miles the customer had. Even more critical was the fact that problems occurred when the partner airlines needed to access each others' reservations systems.

Although systems standards do exist within the airline industry, these have not been sufficient to ensure compatibility between the systems across the airlines which are Star Alliance members. To resolve this problem has required investment in a new computer solution through the creation of new 'middleware' software. The task of middleware software is to permit each alliance member to continue to retain its legacy system and thereby permit employees to operate in an on-line environment with which they have a full understanding.

One of the leading suppliers of such systems is Eland Technologies based in Ireland. This company develops servers which sit in between the airlines in an alliance wishing to exchange knowledge. The server examines each message to determine which host should provide a response, creates a host-specific version of the input message and forwards the translated message using the native host's transport protocol. Similarly having received the host's response the system translate this into a generic message that can be sent to the client who initiated the original request for knowledge.

PROBLEMS THAT CAN EMERGE

Hutt et al. (2000) adopted a case study approach to determining the nature of problems which can occur during the formation of a new alliance. Their study was based upon examining a joint marketing alliance between two Fortune 500 firms. Although not identified, Firm Alpha is a telecommunications company and Firm Omega is a financial services firm.

Having reached agreement to launch an alliance, the first operational problem was that of knowledge exchange through the integration of the partners' databases. Each firm's customer list was a significant corporate asset and neither party was willing to give the other partner open access. It took several months of negotiation to reach agreement on the terms of the knowledge sharing. During this period vital opportunities to build market share were lost forever.

Other issues also emerged in the first year of trading. These included which company name customer service representatives would use when answering service calls from joint customers and which company logo would be at the top of the partners' letterhead. Again the negotiations to resolve such matters were very lengthy and further impaired revenue generation in year 1.

Conflict also emerged between personnel at all levels across the two organisations. To overcome this obstacle, programmed team-building exercises involving core team members were introduced. This move was not perceived as very effective by some employees. It was not until the companies introduced the concept of 'working vacation' meetings involving interfirm social activities that any degree of mutual trust between employees began to emerge. Even this initiative, however, did little to assist the fact that Alpha operated a culture of strong managerial control over employees whereas Omega favoured an approach of employee empowerment.

By year 2 what probably saved the relationship was that lower level employees along with junior and middle managers were beginning to develop new friendships with their respective contacts within the other organisation. Through self-initiated open discussions with each other they were able to resolve their differences over key issues such as communication, competition and the integrity of team members. These individuals also discovered that their counterparts faced exactly the same day-to-day problems and frustrations of working in large, rapidly growing organisations.

The case studies also reveal, however, that senior managers from the two organisations made much less effort to develop close ties with their counterparts in the partner company. In the Alpha–Omega alliance participation of senior staff was unbalanced. Omega assigned greater strategic importance to the alliance and top-level executives were more closely involved in day-to-day operations. Alpha's senior team were preoccupied by other strategic priorities and as a result were much less aware of the interfirm trust problems that hampered rapid development of an effective market alliance.

References

Aaragon, I. (1997), Finding middle ground, *PC Week*, 15 September, pp. 91–92.

Adler, C. (1999), Going online, don't sacrifice marketing for technology, *Fortune*, 25 October, pp. 358–359.

Adria, M. and Chowdrey, D. (2002), Making room for the call center, *Information Systems Management*, Winter, pp. 71–80.

Alsop, S. (1999), The five new rules of web technology, *Fortune*, 21 June, pp. 185–186.

American Marketing Association (1985), *Defining Philosophy*, AMA, Chicago.

Anderson, J.C. and Narus, J.A. (1991), Partnering as a focused market strategy, *California Management Review*, Spring, pp. 95–113.

Anderson, R. (1994), *Essentials of Personal Selling: The New Professionalism*, Prentice Hall, Englewood Cliffs, NJ.

Argyris, C. and Schon, D.A. (1978), *Organisational Learning: A Theory of Action Perspective*, Addison-Wesley, Reading, Mass.

Armbrecht, F.M.R., Ross, C. and Chapelow, C.C. (2001), Knowledge management in R & D, *Research Technology Management*, Jul.–Aug., Vol. 44, No. 4, pp. 28–49.

Arthur Andersen (1999), Study finds European business at crossroads of e-commerce, www.ac.ac.com/showcase/ecommerce/ecom_estudy98.html

Baker, S and Baker, K. (1998), Mind over matter, *Journal of Business Strategy*, Vol. 19, No. 4, pp. 22–27.

Baker, S. and Baker, K. (2000), Going up! Vertical marketing on the web, *Journal of Business Strategy*, Vol. 21, No. 3, pp. 30–37.

Baker, W., Marn, M. and Zawada, C. (2001), Price smarter on the net, *Harvard Business Review*, February, pp. 122–127.

Bartholomew, D. (2000), Service to order, *Industry Week*, 3 April, pp. 19–20.

Beasley, A. (1996), Time compression in the supply chain, *Industrial Management & Data Systems*, Vol. 96, No. 2, pp. 12–17.

Beck, R. (1998), World wide web means world wide lawsuits, *Direct Marketing*, July, pp. 60–63.

Bell, D. (1973), *The Coming of Post Industrial Society*, Basic Books, New York.

Benady, A. (2001), Brand new you, *Real Business*, May, pp. 50–57.

Benjamin, R. and Wigand, R. (1995), Electronic markets and virtual value chains on the information superhighway, *Sloan Management Review*, Winter, pp. 62–72.

Berry, L.L. (1982), Relationship marketing, in L.L. Berry, G.L. Shostack and G.D. Upah, eds, *Emerging Perspectives on Service Marketing*, American Marketing Association, Chicago, pp. 25–28.

Berry, L.L. and Yadav, M.S. (1996), Capture and communicate value in the pricing of services, *Sloan Management Review*, Vol. 37, No. 4, pp. 41–52.

Berthon, P. (1996), Marketing communication and the world wide web, *Business Horizons*, Vol. 39, No. 5, pp. 24–33.

Bicknell, D. (2000), E-commerce outpaces strategy, *Computer Weekly*, 24 February, pp. 20–21.

Biggiero, L. (1999), Markets, hierarchies, networks, districts, *Human Systems Management*, Vol. 18, No. 2, pp. 71–87.

Bird, J. (1999), Time to get real and get out there with the big boys, E-business supplement, *Sunday Times*, 14 November, pp. 8–9.

Birkinshaw, J. (1999), Acquiring intellect: managing the integration of knowledge-intensive acquisitions, *Business Horizons*, May–June, pp. 33–41.

Bloch, M., Pigneur, Y. and Segev, A. (1996), On the road to electronic commerce – a business value, framework, gaining competitive advantage and some research issues, http://www.stern.nyu.edu/-mbloch/docs/roadtoec/ec.htm.

Bone, P.F. (1991), Identifying mature segments, *The Journal of Services Marketing*, Vol. 5, pp. 47–60.

Booth, E. (1999), Will the web replace the phone?, *Marketing*, 4 February, pp. 25–27.

Boston Consulting Group (1999), Online retailing to reach $36 billion, www.bcg.com/features/shop/main_shop.html.

Bowen, D.E. and Lawler, E.E. (1992), The empowerment of service workers: what, why, how and when, *Sloan Management Review*, Spring, pp. 31–39.

Bowonder, B. and Miyake, T. (1992), A model of corporate innovation management: some recent high tech innovations in Japan, *R&D Management*, Vol. 22, No. 3, pp. 319–336.

Boyce, G. and Lepper, L. (2002), Assessing information quality theories, *Business History*, Vol. 44, No. 4, pp. 85–112.

Bradbury, D. (1999), 10 steps to e-business, *Computer Weekly*, 28 October, pp. 42–43.

Brailsford, T.W. (2001), Building a knowledge community at Hallmark Cards, *Research Technology Management*, Vol. 44, No. 5, pp. 18–29.

Brand, A. (1998), Knowledge management and innovation at 3M, *Journal of Knowledge Management*, Vol. 2, No. 1, pp. 17–22.

Brickau, R. (1994), Responding to the Single Market: a comparative study of UK and German food firms, Unpublished PhD dissertation, University of Plymouth, Plymouth.

Brooker, K. (1999), E-rivals seem to have Home Depot awfully nervous, *Fortune*, 8 August, pp. 28–29.

Brown, S.P. and Stayman, D.M. (1992), Antecedents and consequences of attitudes towards the ad: a meta analysis, *Journal of Consumer Research*, Vol. 19, pp. 143–158.

Burns, P. (1994), Keynote address, Proceedings 17th ISBA Sheffield Conference, ISBA, Leeds.

Business Week (1994), The Schwab revolution, 19 December, p. 89.

Business Week (1999a), Going, going, gone, 12 April, pp. 30–31.

Business Week (1999b), The information gold mine, 26 July, pp. 10–12.

Business Week (2000), First America, then the world, 26 February, pp. 159–162.

Business Week (2001a), Sharing the wealth, 19 March, pp. 36–38.

Business Week (2001b), Collecting consumer knowledge on-line, 3 April, pp. 22–23.

Buzan, T. (1993), *The Mindmap Book*, BBC Publications, London.

Cahill, D.J. (1997), Target marketing and segmentation: valid and useful tools for marketing, *Management Decision*, Vol. 35, No. 1, pp. 10–14.

Cannon, T. (1996), *Welcome to the Revolution: Managing Paradox in the 21st Century*, Pitman, London.

Carlzon, J. (1987), *Moments of Truth*, Ballinger, New York.

Carson, D.J., Cromie, S., Mcgowan, P. and Hill, J. (1995), *Marketing and Entrepreneurship in SMEs*, Prentice Hall, London.

Cartellieri, C., Parsons, A.J., Rao, V. and Zeisser, M.P. (1997), The real impact of internet advertising, *The McKinsey Quarterly*, Summer, No. 3, pp. 44–63.

Castogiovanni, G.J. (1996), Pre-startup planning and the survival of new small business, *Journal of Management*, Vol. 22, No. 6, pp. 801–823.

Chait, L.P. (1999), Creating a successful knowledge management system, *Journal of Business Strategy*, Mar.–Apr., pp. 36–43.

Chase, C. (2001), Turning knowledge into action at Heineken USA, *Knowledge Management Review*, Vol. 5, No. 2, pp. 22–25.

Chaston, I. (1996), Critical events and process gaps in the D.T.I. SME structured networking model, *International Small Business Journal*, Vol. 14, No. 3, pp. 71–84.

Chaston, I. (1999a), *Entrepreneurial Marketing*, Macmillan Business, London.

Chaston, I. (1999b), *New Marketing Strategies*, Sage, London.

Chaston, I. (2000a), *E-Marketing Strategy*, McGraw-Hill, Maidenhead.

Chaston, I. (2000b), Relationship marketing and the orientation customers require of suppliers: assessing the influence on service satisfaction in the UK SME manufacturing sector, *Services Industries Journal*, Vol. 20, No. 3, pp. 36–47.

Chaston, I. and Mangles, T. (1997), Core capabilities as predictors of growth potential in small manufacturing firms, *Journal of Small Business Management*, Vol. 35, No. 1, pp. 47–57.

Chaston, I., Badger B. and Sadler-Smith, E. (1999), Organisational learning systems in relation to innovation management in small UK manufacturing firms, *Journal of New Product Management and Innovation*, Vol. 1, No. 1, pp. 32–43.

Chen, A. (2000), Buying online: may we have your fingerprint?, *PC Week*, 28 February, pp. 55–56.

Chonko, L.B. (1999), Case study: alliance formation with direct selling companies, *Journal of Personal Selling & Sales Management*, Vol. 19, No. 1, pp. 51–63.

Christensen, C.M. (1997), *The Innovator's Dilemma: When New Technologies Cause Great Firms to Fail*, Harvard Press, Boston, Mass.

Christensen, C.M. and Tedlow, R.S. (2000), Patterns of disruption in retailing, *Harvard Business Review*, Jan.–Feb., pp. 42–46.

Churbuck, D. (1995), Where's the money, *Forbes*, 30 January, pp. 100–105.

Clark, K. and Fujimoto, T. (1991), *Product Development Performance: Strategy, Organisation and Management in the World Autoindustry*, Harvard Business School Press, Boston, Mass.

Cooper, R.G. (1975), Why new industrial products fail, *Industrial Marketing Management*, Vol. 4, pp. 315–326.

Cooper, R.G. (1986), *Winning at New Products*, Wesley, Reading, Mass.

Cooper, R.G. (1988), The new product process: a decision guide for managers, *Journal of Marketing Management*, Vol. 3, No. 3, pp. 285–255.

Cooper, R.G. (1990), Stage-gate systems: a new tool for managing new products, *Business Horizons*, Vol. 33, No. 3, pp. 44–54.

Cooper, R.G. (1994), Third-generation new product processes, *Journal of Product Innovation Management*, Vol. 11, pp. 3–14.

Cooper, R.G. and Kleinschmidt, E.J. (1990), *New Products: The Key Factors of Success*, American Marketing Association, Chicago.

Coopers & Lybrand (1994), *Made in the UK: The Middle Market Survey*, Coopers & Lybrand, London.

Coover, H.W. (2000), Discovery of Superglue shows power of pursuing the unexplained, *Research Technology Management*, Sept.–Oct., pp. 36–39.

Cort, S.G. (1999), Industry corner: industrial distribution: how goods will go to market in the electronic market place, *Business Economics*, Vol. 34, No. 1, pp. 53–56.

Cowell, D. (1984), *The Marketing of Services*, Heinemann, London.

Crawford, C.M. (1994), *New Products Management*, 4th edn, Irwin, Burr Ridge, Ill.

Cross, R. and Smith, J. (1995), Internet marketing that works for customers, *Direct Marketing*, Vol. 58, No. 4, pp. 22–25.

Crowley, A.E. and Hower, W.D. (1994), An integrative framework for understanding two-sided persuasion, *Journal of Consumer Research*, March, pp. 44–55.

Cyert, R.M. and March, J.G. (1963), *A Behavioural Theory of the Firm*, Prentice Hall, Englewood Cliffs, NJ.

Danneels, E. (1996), Market segmentation: normative model versus reality, *European Journal of Marketing*, Vol. 30, No. 6, pp. 36–52.

Das, T.K. and Teng, B. (2000), A resource-based theory of strategic alliances, *Journal of Management*, Vol. 26, No. 1, pp. 31–62.

Davenport, T.H. and Klahr, P. (1998), Managing customer support knowledge, *California Management Review*, Vol. 40, No. 3, pp. 195–208.

Day, G.S. (1994), The capabilities of market-driven organisations, *Journal of Marketing*, Vol. 58, No. 4, pp. 37–53.

De Guess, A.P. (1988), Planning as learning, *Harvard Business Review*, Mar.–Apr., pp. 70–74.

De Long, D.W. and Beers, M.C. (1998), Successful knowledge management projects, *Sloan Management Review*, Winter, Vol. 39, No. 2, pp. 43–48.

De Long, D.W. and Fahey, L. (2000), Diagnosing cultural barriers to knowledge management, *The Academy of Management Executive*, Vol. 14, No. 4, pp. 113–126.

DePrince, A.E. and Ford, W.F. (1999), A primer on internet economics, *Business Economics*, October, pp. 42–51.

DiBella, A.J., Nevis, E.C. and Gould, J.M. (1996), Understanding organizational learning capability, *Journal of Management Studies*, Vol. 33, No. 3, pp. 361–379.

Dinar, J. (2001), Herbsway: the making of a niche-market, http://www.healthwell exchange.com/manzone/11_00/herbsway.cfm.

Doyle, P. (1998), *Marketing Management and Strategy*, Prentice Hall, Hertfordshire.

Dysart, J. (2001), Integrate online and offline promotions to attract audiences to your web site, *Association Management*, July, pp. 49–58.

Dzinkowski, R. (1999), Mining intellectual capital, *Strategic Finance*, October, pp. 42–42.

Easterby-Smith, M. (1997), Disciplines of organisational learning: contributions and critiques, *Human Relations*, Vol. 50, No. 9, pp. 1085–1113.

Eckman, M. (1996), Are you ready to do business on the internet?, *Journal of Accountancy*, Vol. 181, No. 1, pp. 10–11.

The Economist (1997a), In search of the perfect market, 10 May, pp. 3–5.

The Economist (1997b), Going, going .... on-line auctions, 31 May, pp. 61–62.

The Economist (1999), Digital rights and wrongs, 17 July, pp. 75–76.

The Economist (2000a), Reuters, 12 February, pp. 67–71.

The Economist (2000b), A thinker's guide, 1 April, pp. 64–68.

The Economist (2000c), All yours, 1 April, pp. 57–61.

The Economist (2001), A long march: mass customisation, 14 July, pp. 1–6.

Eddy, P. (1999), The selfish giants, *Sunday Times Magazine*, 14 March, pp. 43–48.

Electronics World (2000), Cycles in chip production, September, pp. 3–5.

Evans, P. and Wurster, T.S. (1999), Getting real about virtual commerce, *Harvard Business Review*, Nov–Dec, pp. 85–93.

Feedman, D.H. (1997), Sonic boom, *Inc. Magazine*, Goldhirsh Group, Boston, pp. 36.

Fingleton, J. (1997), Competition between intermediated and direct trade, *Oxford Economic Papers*, Vol. 49, No. 4, pp. 543–557.

Foote, N.W., Matson, E. and Rudd, N. (2001), Managing the knowledge manager, *The McKinsey Quarterly*, No. 3, pp. 120–129.

Forsyth, J., Gupta, S., Haldar, S., Kaul, K. and Kettle, K. (1997), A segmentation you can act on, *The McKinsey Quarterly Review*, Summer, pp. 7–11.

Fortune (1998). Web commerce shopping, 16 November, pp. 244–245.

Fortune (1999), Net stock rules: masters of the parallel universe, 7 June, pp. 66–73.

Foxall, G. and Goldsmith, R. (1994), *Consumer Psychology for Marketing*, Routledge, London.

Fultz, P. (1999), One-to-one marketing, *Direct Marketing*, August, pp. 63–68.

Garda, R.A. and Marn, M.V. (1993), Price wars, *The McKinsey Quarterly*, Summer, No. 3, pp. 87–101.

Garvin, D.A. (1987), Competing on the 8 dimensions of quality, *Harvard Business Review*, Nov.-Dec., pp. 101–109.

Geroski, P.A. (1999), Early warning of new rivals, *Sloan Management Review*, Vol. 40, No. 3, pp. 107–118.

Ghosh, I.F. (1998), Making sense of the internet, *Harvard Business Review*, Mar.-Apr., pp. 127–135.

Giacobbe, M.N. (1994), Market segmentation and competitive analysis for super-market retailing, *International Journal of Retail and Distribution Management*, Vol. 22, No. 1, pp. 38–49.

Gibb, S. and Simkin, L. (1997), A program for implementing market segmentation, *Journal of Business & Industrial Marketing*, Vol. 12, No. 1, pp. 51–66.

Gielgud, R.E. (1998), *How to Succeed in Internet Business by Employing Real-World Strategies*, Actium Publishing, New York

Gillies, C., Rigby, D. and Reichfeld, F. (2002), The story behind successful customer relations management, *European Business Journal*, Vol. 14, No. 2, pp. 73–79.

Glazer, R. (1999), Winning in smart markets, *Sloan Management Review*, Vol. 40, No. 4, pp. 59–73.

Glyn, M.A. (1996), Innovation genius: a framework for relating individual and organisational intelligence, *Academy of Management Review*, Vol. 21, pp. 1072–1085.

Goddard, J. (1997), The architecture of core competence, *Business Strategy Review*, Vol. 8, No. 1, pp. 43–53.

Goldfinger, C. (2002), Internet banking issues paper, http//www.fininter.net/ retailbanking/InternetBankingIssues/paper

Gore, C. and Gore, E. (1999), Knowledge management: the way forward, *Total Quality Management*, July, pp. 554–561.

Goss, E. (2001), The internet's contribution to US productivity growth, *Business Economist*, Vol. 36, No. 4, pp. 32–44.

Green, P.E., Wind, Y. and Jain, A.K. (2000), Benefit bundle analysis, *Journal of Advertising Research*, Vol. 40, No. 6, pp. 32–38.

Grocer (1996), Niche marketing is the way to grow, 1 June, pp. 34–35.

Gronroos, C. (1994), From marketing mix to relationship marketing, *Journal of Academic Marketing Science*, Vol. 23, No. 4, pp. 252–254.

Grossman, L.M. (1993), Federal Express, UPS face off over computers, *Wall Street Journal*, 17 September, pp. B1.

Gummesson, E. (1987), The new marketing – developing long-term interactive relationships, *Long Range Planning*, Vol. 20, No. 4, pp. 10–20.

Gupta, K. and Govindarajan, V. (2000), Knowledge management's social dimensions: lessons from Nucor Steel, *Sloan Management Review*, Vol. 42, No. 1, pp. 71–83.

Haley, R.J. (1963), Benefit segmentation: a decision orientated research tool, *Journal of Marketing*, July, pp. 30–35.

Hamal, G. (1991), Competition for competence and interpartner learning within international strategic alliances, *Strategic Management Journal*, Vol. 12, pp. 83–103.

Hamal, G. and Prahalad, C.K. (1993), Strategy as stretch and leverage, *Harvard Business Review*, Mar.–Apr., pp. 75–84.

Hamal, G. and Prahalad, C.K. (1994), *Competing for the Future: Breakthrough Strategies for Seizing Control of Your Industry and Creating the Markets of Tomorrow*, Harvard Business School Press, Boston, Mass.

Hamal, G. and Sampler, J. (1998), The e-corporation, *Fortune*, 7 December, pp. 80–81.

Hammer, M. and Champy, J. (1993), *Re-engineering the Corporation: A Manifesto for Business Revolution*, HarperCollins, New York.

Harari, O. (1997), Closing around the customer, *Management Review*, Vol. 86, No. 11, pp. 29–34.

Harpin, S. (2000), *Kick-Start-Com: The Definitive European Internet Start-Up Guide*, Macmillan, London.

Hartley, J.R. (1992), *Concurrent Engineering*, Productivity Press, Cambridge, Mass.

Heldey, B. (1977), Strategy and the business portfolio, *Long Range Planning*, February, pp. 1–14.

Herbert, I. (2000), Knowledge is a noun, learning is a verb, *Management Accounting*, Vol. 78, No. 2, pp. 68–73.

Hitt, M.A. and Ireland, R.D. (1985), Corporate distinctive competence, strategy, industry and performance, *Strategic Management Journal*, Vol. 6, pp. 273–293.

Hornell, E. (1992), *Improving Productivity for Competitive Advantage: Lessons from the Best in the World*, Pitman, London.

Houston, M.J., Childers, T.L. and Hoeckler, S.E. (1987), Effects of brand awareness on choice for a common, repeat purchase product, *Journal of Marketing Research*, Vol. 14, pp. 404–420.

Hu, J., Huang, K., Kuse, K., Su, G. and Wang, K. (1998), Customer information quality and knowledge management, *Journal of Knowledge Management*, Vol. 1, No. 3, pp. 225–236.

Hunt, S.D. and Morgan, R.M. (1995), The comparative advantage theory of competition, *Journal of Marketing*, Vol. 59, No. 2, pp. 1–15.

Hunt, S.D. and Morgan, R.M. (1996), The resource-advantage theory of competition: dynamics, path dependencies and evolutionary dimensions, *Journal of Marketing*, Vol. 60, No. 4, pp. 107–115.

Hutt, M.D., Stafford, E.R., Walker, B.A. and Reingren, P.H. (2000), Case study defining the social network of a strategic alliance, *Sloan Management Review*, Vol. 41, No. 2, pp. 51–72.

Inmon, B. and Kelley, C. (1994), The 12 rules of data warehouse for a client/server world, *Data Management Review*, Vol. 4, No. 5, pp. 6–16.

International Journal of Retail and Distribution Management (1993), Kentucky Fried Chicken's recipe for globalisation, Vol. 21, pp. 3–5.

Internet Indicators (1999), The internet economy indicators, http://www. internetindicators.com/features.html, 22 June, pp. 1–5.

Jackson, B.B. (1985), *Winning and Keeping Industrial Customers: The Dynamics of Customer Relationships*, D.C. Heath, Lexington, Mass.

Jallar, F. and Capek, M.J. (2001), Disintermediation in question: new economy, new networks, new middlemen, *Business Horizons*, Vol. 44, No. 2, pp. 55–64.

James, D. (1999), Merr-e Christmas!, *Marketing News*, 8 November, pp. 1–3.

Jap, S.D. and Mohr, J.J. (2002), Leveraging internet technologies in B2B relationships, *California Management Review*, Vol. 44, No. 4, pp. 15–24.

Jarillo, J.C. (1993), *Strategic Networks: Creating the Borderless Organization*, Butterworth-Heinemann, Oxford.

Jassawalla, A.R. and Sashittal, H.C. (2001), The role of senior management and team leaders in building collaborative new product teams, *Engineering Management Journal*, Vol. 13, No. 2, pp. 33–39.

Jaworski, B. and Kohli, A.K. (1966), Market orientation: review, refinement and roadmap, *Journal of Market Focused Management*, Vol. 1, No. 2, pp. 119–135.

Jaworski, B. and Kohli, A.K. (1993), Market orientation: antecedents and consequences, *Journal of Marketing*, Vol. 57, Jan., pp. 53–70.

Jaworski, B., Kohli, A.K. and Sahay, A. (2000), Market-driven versus driving markets, *Journal of the Academy of Marketing Science*, Vol. 28, No. 1, pp. 45–54.

Jenkins, M. and McDonald, M. (1997), Market segmentation: organisational archetypes and research agendas, *European Journal of Marketing*, Vol. 31, No. 1, pp. 17–28.

Kalin, S. (1998), Conflict resolution, *CIO Web Business*, February, pp. 28–36.

Kelly, E.P. and Rowland, H.C. (2000), Ethical and online privacy issues in electronic commerce, *Business Horizons*, Vol. 43, No. 3, pp. 3–16.

Kemp, T. (2001), E-retailer's personal touch, *InternetWeek*, 12 February, pp. 50–51.

Kleindl, B. (1999), Competitive dynamics and opportunities for SMEs in the virtual market place, *Proceedings of the AMA Entrepreneurship SIG*, University of Illinois at Chicago, Chicago, pp. 21–27.

Knill, B. (1998), Managing flow in the supply chain, *Transportation & Distribution*, April, pp. 2–5.

Kobayashi, K. (1986), *Computers and Communication: A Vision of C&C, Translation*, M.I.T., M.I.T. Press, Cambridge, Mass.

Kotler, P. (1994), *Marketing Management: Analysis, Planning and Control*, 8th edn, Prentice Hall, New York.

Kotler, P. (1997), *Marketing Management: Analysis, Planning, Implementation and Control*, 9th edn, Prentice Hall, Upper Saddle River, NJ.

Kotler, P. (1999), *Marketing Management: The Millennium Edition*, Prentice Hall, Upper Saddle River, NJ.

Lahti, R.K. and Beyerlein, M.M. (2000), Knowledge transfer and management consulting: a look at the 'firm', *Business Horizons*, Vol. 43, No. 1, pp. 65-74.

Larsson, R, Bengtsson, L., Henriksen, K. and Sparks, J. (1998), The interorganisational learning dilemma, *Organization Science*, Vol. 9, No. 3, pp. 285-306.

Lawson, B. and Sampson, D. (2001), Developing innovation capability in organisations, *International Journal of Innovation Management*, Vol. 5, No. 3, pp. 377-398.

Leibs, S. (2000), World of difference, *Industry Week*, 7 February, pp. 23-25.

Leong, E.K.F., Huang, X. and Stanner, P.J. (1998), Comparing the effectiveness of the web site with traditional media, *Journal of Advertising Research*, Vol. 38, No. 5, pp. 44-53.

Leszinski, R. and Marn, M.V. (1997), Setting value, not price, *The McKinsey Quarterly*, Winter, pp. 98-116.

Levitt, T. (1972), Production-line approach to service, *Harvard Business Review*, Sept.-Oct., pp. 41-52.

Levitt, T. (1976), Industrialisation of services, *Harvard Business Review*, Sept.-Oct., pp. 63-74.

Li, T. and Calantone, R.J. (1998), The impact of market knowledge competence on new product advantage: conceptualization and empirical examination, *Journal of Marketing*, Vol. 62, pp. 13-29.

Lindsay, V. (1990), *Export Manufacturing – Framework for Success*, New Zealand Trade Development Board, Wellington.

Linneman, R.E. and Stanton, J.L. (1992), Mining for niches, *Business Horizons*, May-June, pp. 43-52.

Litan, R.E. and Rivlin, A.M. (2001), Prospecting the economic impact of the internet, *American Economic Review*, Vol. 91, No. 2, pp. 313-317.

Lord, R. (1999), The web audience, *Campaign*, 28 May, pp. 10-14.

Loutfy, R. and Belkhir, L. (2001), Managing innovation at Xerox, *Research Technology Management*, Jul.-Aug., pp. 15-24.

Mahoney, J.T. and Pandian, J.R. (1992), The resource-based view within the conversation of strategic management, *Strategic Management Journal*, Vol. 13, pp. 363-380.

Management Today (2000), Top of the dot.coms, March, pp. 12-13.

Marketing (1997), Relaunching organics, 17 April, p. 4.

Marsh, H. (1999), Children's choice, *Marketing*, 15 July, pp. 27-29.

Mathews, J.A. (2001), Competitive interfirm dynamics with an industrial market system, *Industry and Innovation*, Vol. 8, No. 1, pp. 79-107.

McCoy, M. (2002), Soaps and detergents, http://pubs.acs.org/cen/coverstory/8003/8003soaps.html.

McCright, J.S. (2001), Exchange turning to P2P platforms, *eWeek*, 26 March, pp. 29-30.

McCune, J. (1997), Employee appraisals, the electronic way, *Management Review*, October, pp. 44-47.

McDonald, M. (2000), A journey to middleware, *Air Transport World*, August, pp. 57–58.

McGarvey, R. (2000), Connect the dots, *Entrepreneur*, March, pp. 78–82.

McGovern, J.M. (1998), Logistics on the internet, *Transportation & Distribution*, Vol. 39, No. 7, pp. 68–72.

The McKinsey Quarterly (1998), Best practice and beyond: knowledge strategies, Winter, pp. 19–26.

McLuhan, R. (2000), A lesson in online brand promotion, *Marketing*, 23 March, pp. 31–32.

McWilliam, G. (2000), Building stronger brands through online communities, *Sloan Management Review*, Vol. 41, No. 3, pp. 43–57.

Miles, R. and Snow, C.C. (1986), Organisation: new concepts for new forms, *California Management Review*, No. 28, pp. 53–72.

Miller, D. and Shamsie, J. (1996), The resource-based view of the firm in two environments, *Academy of Management Journal*, Vol. 39, pp. 519–543.

Mintzberg, H. (1989), Strategy formation: schools of thought, in J. Fredickson, ed., *Perspectives on Strategic Management*, Ballinger, San Francisco.

Mintzberg, H. (1994), *The Rise and Fall of Strategic Planning*, Prentice Hall, Englewood Cliffs, NJ.

Mintzberg, H. and Waters, J.A. (1982), Tracking study in an entrepreneurial firm, *Academy of Management Journal*, Vol. 25, No. 3, pp. 465–499.

Moad, J. (1997), Forging flexible links, *PC Week*, 15 September, pp. 74–79.

Morgan, R.E., Katsikeas, C.S. and Appuh-Adu, K. (1998), Market orientation and organisational learning capabilities, *Journal of Marketing Management*, Vol. 14, pp. 353–381.

Moriaty, R.W. and Moran, U. (1990), Managing hybrid marketing systems, *Harvard Business Review*, Nov.–Dec., pp. 146–155.

Morton, R. (2002), Fourth annual air cargo report, *Transportation & Distribution*, Vol. 43, No. 9, pp. 18–25.

Moschis, G.P., Euhun, L. and Mathur, A. (1997), Targeting the mature market: opportunities and challenges, *Journal of Consumer Marketing*, Vol. 14, No. 4, pp. 282–294.

Munch, A. and Hunt, S.D. (1984), Consumer involvement: definition issues and research directions, in T. Kinnear, ed., *Advances in Consumer Research*, Vol. 11, Association for Consumer Research, Provo, Utah.

Murphy, J. and Lanfranconi, C. (2001), PixStream Inc., *Ivy Business Journal*, Vol. 65, No. 4, pp. 49–57.

Myers, S.C. and Rajan, R.G. (1998), The paradox of liquidity, *Quarterly Journal of Economics*, Vol. 113, No. 3, pp. 733–762.

Nakache, P. (1998), Secrets of the new brand builders, *Fortune*, 22 June, pp. 167–172.

Nakata, C. and Sivakumar, K. (1996), National culture and new product development: an integrative review, *Journal of Marketing*, Vol. 60, No. 1, pp. 61–73.

Nobeoka, K., Dyer, J.H. and Madhok, A. (2002), The influence of customer scope on supplier learning, *Journal of International Business Studies*, Vol. 33, No. 4, pp. 717–727.

Nonaka, I. (1994), A dynamic theory of organisational knowledge creation, *Organization Science*, Vol. 5, pp. 14–37.

Norman, R. and Ramirez, R. (1993), From value chain to value constellation, *Harvard Business Review*, Jul.–Aug., pp. 65–77.

Noto, A. (2000), Vertical vs. broadline e-retailers: which will survive? *Cnetnews.com*, 2 March.

Nystrom, H. (1990), *Technological and Market Innovation: Strategy for Product and Company Development*, Wiley & Sons, Chichester.

Oates, B., Shafeldt, L. and Vaught, B. (1996), A psychographic study of elderly and retail store attributes, *Journal of Consumer Marketing*, Vol. 13, No. 6, pp. 14–28.

OECD (2000), E-commerce: impacts and policy challenges, *OECD Economic Outlook*, June, OECD, Paris.

Owens, D. and Thompson, E. (2001), Fusing knowledge and learning at the St Paul companies, *Knowledge Management Review*, Vol. 4, No. 3, pp. 6–12.

Owens, D., Brown, S.P. and Stayman, D.M. (1992), Antecedents and consequences of attitude towards the ad: a meta analysis, *Journal of Consumer Research*, Vol. 19, pp. 143–158.

Parasuraman, A., Zeithmal, V.A. and Berry, L.L. (1985), A conceptual model of service quality and its implications for future research, *Journal of Marketing*, Vol. 49, Fall, pp. 34–45.

Parasuraman, A., Zeithmal, V.A. and Berry, L.L. (1988), SERVQUAL: a multiple item scale for measuring consumer perceptions of service quality, *Journal of Retailing*, Vol. 64, No. 1, pp. 12–23.

Parasuraman, A., Zeithmal, V.A. and Berry, L.L. (1994), Reassessment of expectations as a comparison standard in measuring service quality, *Journal of Marketing*, Vol. 58, pp. 111–24.

Parkhe, A. (1991), Interfirm diversity, organisational learning and longevity in global strategic alliances, *Journal of International Business Studies*, Vol. 22, No. 4, pp. 579–601.

Parzinger, M.J. and Frolick, M.N. (2001), Creating competitive advantage through data warehousing, *The Executive's Journal*, Summer, pp. 10–15.

PC Week (1997), New alliance to reflect customs of Arab culture, 8 September, p. 88.

Pechman, S. (1994), Custom clusters: finding your true customer segments, *Bank Marketing*, July, pp. 33–38.

Pepper, D., Rogers, M. and Dorf, B. (1999), Is your company ready for one-to-one marketing, *Harvard Business Review*, Jan.–Feb., pp. 151–162.

Peters, T. (1992), *Liberation Management*, A.F. Knopf, New York.

Pine, J.B. (1993), *Mass Customization: The New Frontier in Business Competition*, Harvard Business School Press, Boston, Mass.

Piore, M. and Sabel, C. (1984), *The Second Industrial Divide*, Basic Books, New York.

Pitt, L., Berthon, P. and Berthon, J. (1999), Changing channels: the impact of the internet on distribution strategy, *Business Horizons*, Vol. 42, No. 2, pp. 19–34.

Pitta, J. (1998), Competitive shopping, *Forbes*, 9 February, pp. 92–94.

Plotkin, H. (1998), Art net, *Forbes*, 6 April, pp. 29–32.

Polanyi, M. (1996), *The Tacit Dimension*, Routledge, London.

Porter, M.E. (1980), *Competitive Strategy: Techniques for Analysing Industries and Competition*, The Free Press, New York.

Porter, M.E. (1985), *Competitive Advantage: Creating and Sustaining Superior Performance*, The Free Press, San Francisco.

Porter, M.E. (1998), *On Competition*, Harvard Business School Press, Boston, Mass.

Porter, M.E. and Miller, V.E. (1985), How information technology gives you competitive advantage, *Harvard Business Review*, Jul.–Aug., pp. 149–160.

PR Newswire (2000), Offer web-based employee benefits and HR administrative services, California, 14 June, 12.00 a.m.

Prahalad, C.K. and Hamal, G. (1990), The core competence of the corporation, *Harvard Business Review*, May–June, pp. 79–91.

Puente, M. (2000), Art discovers the internet, *USA Today*, 10 January, pp. 5–6.

Quinn, J.B. (2000), Outsourcing innovation: the engine of growth, *Sloan Management Review*, Vol. 41, No. 4, pp. 13–28.

Quinn, J.B. and Parquette, P.C. (1990), Technology in services: creating organisational revolutions, *Sloan Management Review*, Winter, pp. 67–78.

Quinn, J.B., Anderson, P. and Finkelstein, S. (1996), Leveraging intellect, *Academy of Management Executive*, August, pp. 7–27.

Quinn, J.B., Doorley, T.L. and Parquette, P.C. (1990), Technology in services: rethinking strategic focus, *Sloan Management Review*, Winter, pp. 79–87.

Rangan, V.K., Moriaty, R.T. and Swartz, G. (1992), Segmenting customers in mature industrial markets, *Journal of Marketing*, Vol. 56, October, pp. 72–82.

Rangan, V.K., Moriaty, R.T. and Swartz, G. (1993), Transaction cost theory: inferences from field research on downstream vertical integration, *Organization Science*, Vol. 4, No. 3, pp. 454–477.

Rapp, S. (1990), From mass marketing to direct mass marketing, *Direct Marketing*, May, pp. 63–65.

Rapp, S. and Collins, T.L. (1994), *Beyond Maxi-Marketing*, McGraw-Hill, New York.

Reed, M. (1999), Going beyond the banner ad, *Marketing*, 29 April, pp. 25–27.

Reichfeld, F.F. and Sasser, W.E. (1990), Zero defections: quality comes to services, *Harvard Business Review*, Sept.–Oct., pp. 301–307.

Reinartz, W. and Kumar, V. (2002), The mismanagement of customer loyalty, *Harvard Business Review*, Jul.–Aug., pp. 86–95.

Richman, T. (1989), Growth strategies: cart tricks, *Inc. Magazine*, Goldhirsh Group, Boston, pp. 138.

Rob, P. and Coronel, C. (2000), *Database Systems: Design, Implementation & Management*, 4th edn, Thomson Learning, Cambridge, Mass.

Robertson, T.S. and Barich, H. (1992), A successful approach to segmenting industrial markets, *Journal of Marketing*, December, pp. 5–11.

Romano, C. (1995), The new gold rush?, *Management Review*, November, pp. 119–124.

Ryals, L. and Payne, A. (2001), Customer relationship management in services, *Journal of Strategic Marketing*, Vol. 9, pp. 3–27.

Rycroft, R.W. and Kash, D.E. (2000), Steering complex innovation, *Research Technology Management*, Vol. 43, No. 3, pp. 18–23.

Sasser, W.E. (1976), Match supply and demand in service industries, *Harvard Business Review*, Nov.–Dec., pp. 133–140.

Schoeffler, S., Buzzell, R.D. and Heany, D.F. (1974), Impact of strategic planning on profit performance, *Harvard Business Review*, Mar.–Apr., pp. 137–145.

Schonberger, R.J. (1990), *Building a Chain of Customers: Linking Business Functions to Create the World Class Company*, Hutchinson, London.

Schuette, D. (2000), Turning e-business barriers into strengths, *Information Systems Management*, Vol. 17, No. 4, pp. 20–26.

Schwartz, J. (2000), Schwab reaps benefits of early net investments, *InternetWeek*, 12 June, pp. 61–62.

Schwarz, B. (2000), E-business: new distribution models coming to a site near you, *Transportation & Distribution*, Vol. 41, No. 2, pp. 3–4.

Sellers, P. (1999), Inside the first e-christmas, *Fortune*, 1 February, pp. 52–55.

Senge, P. (1990), *The Fifth Discipline: The Art and Practice of the Learning Organisation*, Doubleday, New York.

Seybold, P.B. and Marshak, R.T. (1998), *Customer.com: How to Create a Profitable Business Strategy for the Internet and Beyond*, Random House, New York.

Shapiro, C. and Varian, H.R. (1999), *Information Rules*, Harvard Business School Press, Boston, Mass.

Sharman, G. (2002), How the internet is accelerating supply chains, *Supply Chain Management Review*, Mar.–Apr., pp. 19–26

Siekman, P. (2000), New victories in the supply-chain revolution: still looking for ways to tighten shipping, inventory and even manufacturing costs at your company? *Fortune*, 30 October, pp. 208–218.

Sinkula, J.M. (1994), Market information: processing and organisational learning, *Journal of Marketing*, Vol. 58, January, pp. 125–134.

Sinkula, J.M., Baker, W.E. and Noordewier, T. (1997), A framework for market-based organisational learning: linking values, knowledge and behaviour, *Journal of the Academy of Marketing Science*, Vol. 25, No. 2, pp. 305–318.

Sinha, I. (2000), Cost transparency: the net's real threat to processes and brands, *Harvard Business Review*, Mar.–Apr., pp. 43–52.

Slater, S.F. and Narver, J.C. (1994), Does competitive environment moderate the market orientation-performance relationship, *Journal of Marketing*, Vol. 58, January, pp. 46–55.

Slater, S.F. and Narver, J.C. (1995), Marketing orientation and the learning organisation, *Journal of Marketing*, Vol. 59, July, pp. 63–74.

Slywotzky, A.J. (1996), *Value Migration: How to Think Several Moves Ahead of the Competition*, Harvard Business School Press, Boston, Mass.

Smith, C.G. (1995), How newcomers can undermine incumbents' marketing strengths, *Business Horizons*, Sept.–Oct., pp. 16–24.

Smith, D.S. (1999a), Web makes a world of difference, *Sunday Times Enterprise Network*, 21 November, pp. 1–7.

Smith, D.S. (1999b), Boating partners face stern test, *Sunday Times Enterprise Network*, 10 January, pp. 19–20.

Smith, W. (1956), Product differentiation and market segmentation as alternative marketing strategies, *Journal of Marketing Research*, July, pp. 3–8.

Sonoda, T. (2002), Honda: global manufacturing and competitiveness, *Competitiveness Review*, Vol. 12, No. 1, pp. 7–13.

Sorce, P., Tyler, P.R. and Loomis, L.M. (1989), Lifestyles in older Americans, *The Journal of Consumer Marketing*, Vol. 6, pp. 53–63.

Sowalski, R. (2001), The five CRM essentials for insurance, *National Underwriter*, 9 July, pp. 24–27.

Stackpole, B. (1999), A foothold on the web: industry-specific net markets, *PC Week*, 10 May, pp. 78–80.

Starkey, K. and McKinley, A. (1996), Product development in Ford of Europe, in K. Starkey, ed., *How Organisations Learn*, Thomson Business Press, London, pp. 214–229.

Stauffer, D. (1999), Sales strategies for the internet age, *Harvard Business Review*, Jul.–Aug., pp. 3–5.

Stern, L.W. and El-Ansary, A.I. (1988), *Marketing Channels*, 3rd edn, Prentice Hall, Englewood Cliffs, NJ.

Stewart, T.A. (1998), The leading edge, cold fish, hot data, new profits, *Fortune*, 3 August, pp. 3–7.

Stewart, T.A. (1999), Telling tales at BP Amaco: knowledge management at work, *Fortune*, 7 June, pp. 220–221.

Storey, J. (ed.) (1994), *New Wave Manufacturing Strategies: Organisational and Human Resource Management Dimensions*, Paul Chapman Publishing, London.

Straub, D. and Klein, R. (2001), E-competitive transformation, *Business Horizons*, Vol. 44, No. 3, pp. 3–14.

Sugar, A. (1999), Show us the money, *Computer Weekly*, 4 March, pp. 34–35.

Sviokla, J.J. (1996), Knowledge workers and radically new technology, *Sloan Management Review*, Summer, pp. 25–41.

Synder, B. (1994), The great escape, *PC Week*, 4 April, pp. 13–15.

Tedlow, R.S. (1990), *New and Improved: The Story of Mass Marketing in America*, Heinemann, Oxford.

Teng, A. (2000), Detergent market update, http://www.happi.com/jan204.htm.

Thorson, E. and Friestadt, M. (1989), The effectiveness of emotion on episodic memory for TV commercials, in L. Percy and A.G. Woodside, eds, *Advertising and Consumer Psychology*, Lexington Books, Lexington, Mass.

Thurm, S. (1998), Leading the PC pack, *Wall Street Journal*, 7 December, pp. 4.

Toffler, A. (1990), *Powershift: Knowledge, Wealth and Violence at the Edge of the 21st Century*, Bantam Books, New York.

Tsang, E.W. (1999), A preliminary typology of learning in international strategic alliances, *Journal of World Business*, Vol. 34, No. 3, pp. 211–230.

Vaas, L. (2000), Customer privacy lockdown, *eWeek*, 16 October, pp. 73–76.

Vandermerwe, S. (2000), How increasing value to customers improves business results, *Sloan Management Review*, Vol. 24, No. 1, pp. 27–37.

Ville, S. and Fleming, G. (2000), The nature and structure of trade-financial networks: evidence from the New Zealand pastoral sector, *Business History*, Vol. 42, No. 1, pp. 41–63.

Violino, B. (2000), UPS sketches a broad e-commerce agenda, *InternetWeek*, 8 May, pp. 1–4.

von Krogh, G. and Cusumano, M.A. (2001), Three strategies for managing growth, *Sloan Management Review*, Vol. 42, No. 2, pp. 53–62.

Vowler, J. (1999), Trouble free, seamless service, *Computer Weekly*, 14 October, pp. 28–33.

Wagner, M. (2000), Hilton's online strategy, *InternetWeek*, 12 December, pp. 89–90.

Wah, L. (1999), Behind the buzz, *Management Review*, April, pp. 17–21.

Wasson, C.R. (1978), *Dynamic Competitive Strategy and Product Life Cycles*, Austin Press, Austin, Tex.

Wayne, L. (1994), The next giant in mutual funds?, *New York Times*, 20 March, Section 3, pp. 8–9.

Webb, D. (2000), Understanding customer role and its importance in the formation of service quality expectations, *The Service Industries Journal*, Vol. 20, No. 1, pp. 1–21.

Webster, F.E. (1992), The changing role of marketing in the corporation, *Journal of Marketing*, Vol. 56, October, pp. 1–17.

Weinberg, N. (2000), Not.coms, *Forbes*, 17 April, pp. 424–425.

Weinstein, L. (2000), Using technology to reach the next generation, *Bank Marketing*, December, pp. 14–16.

Whittington, R. (1993), *What Is Strategy and Does it Matter?*, Thompson Business Press, London.

Wiersema, F. (1996), *Customer Intimacy: Pick Your Partners, Shape Your Culture, Win Together*, HarperCollins, London.

Wilson, G. (1973), *The Psychology of Conservatism*, Academic Press, London.

Wilson, S. (1999), Going once, going twice, *Intelligent Business*, December, pp. 84–89.

Winer, R.S. (2001), A framework for customer relationship management, *California Management Review*, Vol. 43, No. 4, pp. 89–105.

Wong, V., Saunders, J. and Doyle, P. (1988), The quality of British marketing, *Marketing Management*, Vol. 4, pp. 32–46.

Woodruff, R.B. (1977), Customer value: the next source of competitive advantage, *Journal of the Academy of Marketing Science*, Vol. 25, No. 2, pp. 139–153.

Young, K.M., El Sawy, O.A, Malhotra, A. and Gosain, S. (1997), The relentless pursuit of 'Free Perfect Now': IT enabled value innovation at Marshall Industries, 1997 SIM International Papers Award Competition, http://www.simnet.ord/public/programs/capital/97papers/paper1.html.

Zack, M.H. (1999), Managing codified knowledge, *Sloan Management Review*, Vol. 40, No. 4, pp. 45–56.

Zeithmal, V.A. and Bitner, M.J. (1996), *Services Marketing*, McGraw-Hill, New York.

Zeithmal, V.A., Parasuraman, A. and Berry, L.L. (1993), The nature and determinants of customer expectations of service, *Marketing Science Institute Research Program Series*, May, Report No. 11, pp. 91–113.

Zemke, R. and Schaaf, I.R. (1989), *The Service Edge: 101 Companies that Profit from Customer Care*, New American Library, New York.

Index

Page numbers in *italics* refer to boxes and tables.